P9-CRN-381

Best of the Best

COOKBOOK RECIPES

the
BEST RECIPES
from the
25 BEST COOKBOOKS
of the year

FOOD & WINE

FOOD & WINE BEST OF THE BEST VOL. 14

EDITOR **Kate Heddings**
DESIGNER **Michelle Leong**
FEATURES EDITOR **Michael Endelman**
SENIOR EDITOR **Susan Choung**
ASSOCIATE FOOD EDITORS **Justin Chapple, Maggie Mariolis**
ASSOCIATE WINE EDITOR **Megan Krigbaum**
COPY EDITOR **Lisa Leventer**
DEPUTY PHOTO EDITOR **Anthony LaSala**
PRODUCTION MANAGER **Matt Carson**

FOOD & WINE MAGAZINE

S.V.P./EDITOR IN CHIEF **Dana Cowin**
CREATIVE DIRECTOR **Stephen Scoble**
MANAGING EDITOR **Mary Ellen Ward**
EXECUTIVE EDITOR **Pamela Kaufman**
EXECUTIVE FOOD EDITOR **Tina Ujlaki**
EXECUTIVE WINE EDITOR **Ray Isle**
EXECUTIVE DIGITAL EDITOR **Rebecca Bauer**
DEPUTY EDITOR **Christine Quinlan**
ART DIRECTOR **Courtney Waddell Eckersley**

AMERICAN EXPRESS PUBLISHING CORPORATION

PRESIDENT/C.E.O. **Ed Kelly**
CHIEF MARKETING OFFICER & PRESIDENT, DIGITAL MEDIA **Mark V. Stanich**
S.V.P./CHIEF FINANCIAL OFFICER **Paul B. Francis**
V.P./GENERAL MANAGERS **Frank Bland, Keith Strohmeier**

V.P., BOOKS & PRODUCTS/PUBLISHER **Marshall Corey**
DIRECTOR, BOOK PROGRAMS **Bruce Spanier**
SENIOR MARKETING MANAGER, BRANDED BOOKS **Eric Lucie**
ASSISTANT MARKETING MANAGER **Stacy Mallis**
DIRECTOR OF FULFILLMENT & PREMIUM VALUE **Phil Black**
MANAGER OF CUSTOMER EXPERIENCE & PRODUCT DEVELOPMENT **Charles Graver**
DIRECTOR OF FINANCE **Thomas Noonan**
ASSOCIATE BUSINESS MANAGER **Uma Mahabir**
OPERATIONS DIRECTOR (PREPRESS) **Rosalie Abatemarco Samat**
OPERATIONS DIRECTOR (MANUFACTURING) **Anthony White**

FRONT AND BACK COVERS AND PAGE 10

PHOTOGRAPHER **Tina Rupp**
FOOD STYLIST **Alison Attenborough**
STYLE EDITOR **Jessica Romm**

INSIDE FLAP

PORTRAITS PHOTOGRAPHER **Andrew French**

Copyright © 2011 American Express Publishing Corporation

All rights reserved. No part of this book may be reproduced or transmitted in any form or by any means, electronic or mechanical, including photocopying, recording or by any information storage and retrieval system, without prior permission in writing from the publisher.

ISBN 10: 1-60320-203-X
ISBN 13: 978-1-60320-203-9
ISSN 1524-2862

Published by American Express Publishing Corporation
1120 Avenue of the Americas, New York, New York 10036

Manufactured in the United States of America

Best of the Best

COOKBOOK RECIPES

the
BEST RECIPES
from the
25 BEST COOKBOOKS
of the year

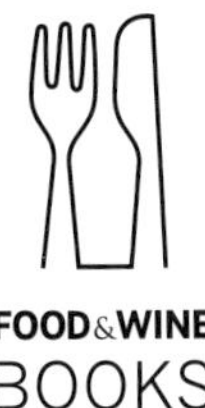

FOOD & WINE BOOKS

American Express Publishing Corporation, New York

CONTENTS

Recipe titles in **bold** are brand-new dishes appearing exclusively in *Best of the Best Cookbook Recipes*.

CONTENTS

BAKED
EXPLORATIONS

CHEWY
GOOEY
CRISPY
CRUNCHY
MELT-IN-YOUR-MOUTH COOKIES BY
ALICE
MEDRICH

SUSTAINABLY
DELICIOUS
MICHEL NISCHAN

JAMIE'S
AMERICA
EASY TWISTS ON GREAT AMERICAN CLASSICS, AND MORE
JAMIE OLIVER

James Peterson
meat
A Kitchen Education

AVEC ERIC
ERIC RIPERT

Ethan Stowell's
New Italian Kitchen

Recipe titles in **bold** are brand-new dishes appearing exclusively in *Best of the Best Cookbook Recipes*.

RECIPES

meat

vegetables

brunch

desserts

Braised chicken with endives, shallots and jerusalem artichoke puree, page 117

FOREWORD

At *Food & Wine* we're on a quest to find the best of everything related to eating and drinking, and that includes cookbooks. We tested over 150 of them to find the 25 that made the cut for this edition of *Best of the Best Cookbook Recipes*. All the winners meet three criteria: They have a strong point of view, entice readers into the kitchen and deliver clearly written recipes that result in wonderful food. We are proud of our picks, like *Around My French Table* (Dorie Greenspan's culinary memoir of her life in France) and Kim Boyce's *Good to the Grain* (which champions flours made from whole grains like spelt and teff). We love how eclectic the collection is, ranging from Ming Tsai's pork kimchee with noodles to Michel Nischan's all-American corn chowder.

Because the best food and wine belong together, we're introducing something new this year: a concise wine glossary, defining the major grapes and recommending categories of wine and specific bottles to accompany many of the recipes. (As always, the recipes themselves appear as they do in the original books.)

We are thrilled to have found so many outstanding cookbook recipes. And we're especially pleased with the never-before-published recipes that many of the authors share here; we think you'll find they're some of the best of the best of the best!

Dana Cowin
Editor in Chief
FOOD & WINE Magazine

Kate Heddings
Editor
FOOD & WINE Cookbooks

PHCTOGRAPH BY PAUL ELLEDGE

FIESTA AT RICK'S →01

Rick Bayless with Deann Groen Bayless

In his five previous cookbooks, Chicago chef Rick Bayless has taught readers how to make authentic Oaxacan specialties, quick-and-easy tacos and countless varieties of salsa. *Fiesta at Rick's* is his take on Mexican party food, and it's all designed for a big, hungry crowd. There are creative tapas-style snacks (Tuna in Jalapeño Escabeche), Mexican-ized backyard grill recipes (smoky-sweet Chipotle-Glazed Baby Back Ribs) and fun, shareable plates (Wild Mushroom Queso Fundido, an earthy, spicy dish of molten cheese that Bayless calls "the stuff of memories"). As always, Bayless offers tips for cooks without access to a Mexican grocery, like how to make *crema* from scratch for his Roasted Vegetable Enchiladas with Creamy Tomatillo Sauce and Melted Cheese. *Published by W. W. Norton & Company, $35*

This dish has the intense flavor of wild mushrooms, the gooeyness of melted cheese and the communal fun of fondue. It's best eaten warm right out of the pot.

WILD MUSHROOM QUESO FUNDIDO

SERVES 4
AS A SOFT TACO FILLING

¾ ounce (about ½ cup) dried porcini (or other wild mushrooms)
2 tablespoons olive or vegetable oil
Hot green chile(s) to taste (roughly 1 large jalapeño or 2 serranos), stemmed, seeded (if you wish) and finely chopped
1 medium white onion, cut into ¼-inch pieces
1 large ripe tomato, cored, seeded (if you wish) and cut into ¼-inch pieces
3 tablespoons beer, preferably a full-flavored beer like Mexico's Bohemia
8 ounces Mexican melting cheese (such as Chihuahua, *quesadilla* or *asadero*) or Monterey Jack, mild cheddar or brick, shredded (you'll have about 2 cups)

If you love the flavor of wild mushrooms—I mean true *wild mushrooms, not just "exotic" cultivated mushrooms like shiitakes or colorful oysters—this* queso fundido *is a wonderful way to experience it. A little dried mushroom, briefly rehydrated, infuses the whole dish with flavor, while the beer adds a lovely hint of malty sweetness and a creamy texture.*

If making the dish with fresh mushrooms (wild or cultivated) appeals to you more, you'll need about 5 ounces. Trim the stems and chop them into small pieces (you'll have about 2 loosely packed cups), then cook them in 3 tablespoons of oil over medium-high for about 3 minutes with a sprinkling of salt. Add the other fresh vegetables and continue on with Step 2.

A soft taco of Wild Mushroom Queso Fundido with a spoonful of roasted tomatillo salsa is the stuff of memories.

1. REHYDRATE THE MUSHROOMS Scoop the mushrooms into a small bowl, cover with boiling water and let stand for 20 minutes, stirring for even rehydration. Drain off the liquid (it's great added to mushroom soups), pressing on the mushrooms to remove all the water. Chop into ¼-inch pieces.

2. PREPARE THE FLAVORINGS Heat the oil in a large (10-inch) skillet over medium-high. Add the chile(s), onion, tomato and mushrooms and cook, stirring nearly constantly, until the onion begins to soften and brown, 7 or 8 minutes. Add the beer and stir until the liquid has evaporated and the mixture is once again dry looking.

3. FINISH THE QUESO FUNDIDO With the skillet of beery vegetables over medium-low, sprinkle in the cheese. Stir slowly and constantly until just melted—too long over the heat and the cheese will become tough, oily and stringy. Immediately scoop into a warm serving dish (a small fondue dish with a tea light below is ideal) and serve with warm tortillas for making soft tacos or chips to dip.

WORKING AHEAD The dish can be prepared through Step 2; cover and refrigerate. Just before serving, heat the vegetables to sizzling and continue with Step 3.

Enchiladas suizas (Swiss-style enchiladas), so named because of the creamy, béchamel-like sauce, are usually filled with shredded chicken. Bayless uses a mix of roasted vegetables for his version.

ROASTED VEGETABLE ENCHILADAS
with creamy tomatillo sauce & melted cheese

SERVES 4 TO 6

- 1 pound (6 to 8) tomatillos, husked and rinsed
- 1 medium white onion, sliced about ¼ inch thick
- 3 garlic cloves, peeled
- Fresh hot green chiles to taste (2 or 3 serranos, 1 or 2 jalapeños), stemmed
- 1½ tablespoons vegetable oil, plus extra for roasting the vegetables and brushing or spraying the tortillas
- 2 cups vegetable or chicken broth, plus a little extra if needed
- ½ cup Mexican *crema*, crème fraîche or heavy (whipping) cream
- 8 cups cubed vegetables (about ½-inch cubes are good)—delicious choices are chayote, carrots, white or red onions, small turnips, kohlrabi, mushrooms and peeled butternut squash
- Salt
- 12 corn tortillas
- ⅔ cup shredded Mexican melting cheese (like Chihuahua, *quesadilla* or *asadero*) or Monterey Jack, brick or mild cheddar
- A few sliced rounds of white onion, separated into rings, for garnish
- Fresh cilantro sprigs, for garnish

EDITOR'S WINE CHOICE
Fruity, soft Chenin Blanc (see page 265)

Practically everyone who visits Mexico City sits at one time or another at the coffee shop counter toward the rear of the old Sanborns in downtown Mexico City, the place where creamy enchiladas suizas *were invented. And the perceptive ones know that within the four walls of that blue-and-white-tiled sixteenth-century-palace-turned-twentieth-century-retailer a good number of important historical events have transpired over the last five centuries. But none outshines, in my opinion, the development of the* enchiladas suizas, *a dish I think straddles the transition between old-fashioned regional cooking and that of the modern world stage. The original sauce was made with tomatoes, but it's evolved into tomatillos in most cooks' versions, offering a tangy counterpoint to the richness. And here I'm nudging the dish into yet another stage of evolution: richly textured roasted vegetables replacing shredded chicken, rolled into warm corn tortillas, doused with that luscious tomatillo sauce, nestled under a little melted cheese. Clearly a dish that's ready for prime time.*

A note about vegetables: feel free to use broccoli, asparagus, zucchini and other green vegetables, too. Just roast them on a separate baking sheet, since they'll be done 5 to 10 minutes quicker than those suggested in the recipe.

1. MAKE THE SAUCE Roast the tomatillos, sliced onion, peeled garlic and chiles on a rimmed baking sheet 4 inches below a hot broiler until the tomatillos are soft and blotchy black on one side, 4 or 5 minutes. Turn everything over and roast the other side. Remove and reduce the oven temperature to 400°F.

Scrape the tomatillo mixture into a blender or food processor. Process to a smooth puree. Heat the 1½ tablespoons of oil in a medium-large (4- or 5-quart) pot over medium-high. When the oil is hot enough to make a drop of the puree sizzle, add the puree all at once. Stir nearly constantly for several minutes until darker and thicker. Add the broth and the *crema*, reduce the heat to medium-low, partially cover and simmer for about 30 minutes.

continued on page 18

STAUB

vegetable enchiladas continued

2. ROAST THE VEGETABLES Spread the cubed vegetables on a rimmed baking sheet. Drizzle or spritz with oil, sprinkle with salt and stir to coat evenly. Roast, stirring regularly, until the carrots are crunchy-tender, about 25 minutes.

3. FINISH THE SAUCE, HEAT THE TORTILLAS If the sauce has thickened beyond the consistency of a light cream soup, stir in a little more broth (or water). Taste and season with salt, usually about 1 teaspoon. Lightly brush or spray both sides of each tortilla with oil. Slide into a plastic bag and microwave on high (100 percent) for 1 minute to warm and soften.

4. FINISH THE ENCHILADAS Smear a few tablespoons of the sauce over the bottom of four to six 9-inch individual ovenproof baking/serving dishes or smear about 1 cup of the sauce over the bottom of a 13-by-9-inch baking dish. Working quickly so the tortillas stay hot and pliable, roll a portion of the roasted vegetables into each tortilla, then line them all up in the baking dish(es). Douse evenly with the remaining sauce, then sprinkle with the cheese. Bake until the enchiladas are heated through (the cheese will have begun to brown), about 10 minutes. Garnish with onion rings and cilantro sprigs. These are best served piping hot from the oven.

WORKING AHEAD The sauce can be made a day or two ahead; refrigerate covered. After the tortillas have been heated in the oven, you need to work quickly and steadily toward serving in order to preserve their beautiful texture. Once out of the oven, the finished dish softens to near mush over a period of 15 to 20 minutes.

This is a Mexican take on a Spanish tapa that can be put together on short notice. Seek out high-quality, olive oil–packed tuna for the dish.

TUNA IN JALAPEÑO ESCABECHE

MAKES 3 SCANT CUPS, SERVING 6 AS A SOFT TACO FILLING, BRUSCHETTA OR TOSTADA TOPPING, OR TAPA

One 12-ounce can pickled jalapeños
¼ cup good-quality olive oil
1 large white onion, cut into ¼-inch slices
Two 6-ounce cans tuna (you can use tuna in a pouch here, if you like)
¼ cup (loosely packed) roughly chopped flat-leaf parsley (optional)

EDITOR'S WINE CHOICE
Lively, tart Sauvignon Blanc (see page 266)

Though I'm not one of the world's greatest fans of canned tuna, I really like the way spicy-tangy pickled jalapeños—together with caramelized onions and fresh-tasting flat-leaf parsley—take that tuna in a deliciously Mexican direction. Not to mention that the ingredients are probably already in your pantry and that you can make it in about 10 minutes. The casual dish you turn out here is particularly good piled on tostadas (or chips) or on grilled or toasted bread, bruschetta style. It's great picnic food.

A brand of pickled jalapeños like Embasa typically includes a lot of vegetables—perfect for this recipe.

Remove the jalapeños and vegetables (typically carrots and onions) that have been packed with them; reserve the liquid. Cut the stems off 2 to 3 of the jalapeños, cut them in half and scrape the seeds out. Thinly slice them (you need about ¼ cup), then thinly slice some of the vegetables (you need about ¼ cup of these also).

In a large skillet, heat the olive oil over medium. When hot, add the onion and cook until richly golden, about 10 minutes. Remove from the heat and stir in ¼ cup of the jalapeño pickling juice. Let cool. In a medium-size bowl, stir together the onions, tuna, sliced jalapeños and vegetables, and parsley (if you're using it). Cover and refrigerate if not using right away.

WORKING AHEAD The dish can be made a day ahead, leaving out the parsley; cover and refrigerate. Bring to room temperature, stir in the parsley and check seasonings shortly before serving.

Made from canned chipotles and honey, this glaze is very easy to pull together. The result is sweet, spicy, smoky and sticky—everything you want in a rib sauce.

CHIPOTLE-GLAZED BABY BACK RIBS

SERVES 8

FOR THE DRY RUB

- 4 garlic cloves, peeled and roughly chopped
- 1/3 cup ground ancho chile
- 4 teaspoons brown sugar
- 1 teaspoon dried oregano, preferably Mexican
- 1/2 teaspoon ground cumin
- 4 teaspoons ground black pepper
- 5 teaspoons salt

FOR THE RIBS AND GLAZE

- 4 large slabs (about 6 1/2 pounds) baby back ribs
- One 7.5-ounce can chipotles *en adobo*
- 3/4 cup honey

EDITOR'S WINE CHOICE
Rustic, peppery Malbec
(see page 268)

This is a rather unconventional approach to rib cooking: First, baby back ribs—not the larger spareribs—are showered with a dry rub that's not too far from the one I learned in my parents' barbecue restaurant in Oklahoma City; overnight the rub cures the flesh lightly, ensuring a juicy outcome. Then they're slowly baked until they're juicy-done. And, when all the hungry have assembled, the ribs are grill-singed and slathered with a sticky chipotle chile glaze—smoky, sweet, porky and anything but fainthearted. Richard James, our long-time chef de cuisine *in Frontera Grill, developed this take on ribs—reliable, manageable, crowd pleasing—for the Saturday nights when ribs are the special and we serve 400 guests. Which pretty much describes a typical Frontera Saturday night.*

1. SEASON THE RIBS Combine all the dry rub ingredients in a food processor and run until thoroughly blended. Sprinkle the mixture on both sides of each slab of ribs, rub it in to ensure even coverage, then cover and refrigerate overnight. You'll probably have a little dry rub left; in a tightly closed jar in the refrigerator it will last several months.

2. FIRST RIB COOKING Heat the oven to 300°F. Lay the ribs in a single layer on two rimmed baking sheets and bake for about 1 1/4 hours, until the meat is tender when tested with a fork. (This cooking may be done early in the day you're serving. Cover and refrigerate the cooked ribs until an hour before serving.)

3. SECOND RIB COOKING Turn on a gas grill to medium or light a charcoal grill and let the coals burn until medium-hot and covered with white ash.

continued on page 22

baby back ribs continued

In a food processor, blend the can of chipotles with the honey. Scrape into a small bowl and carry to the grill, along with a basting brush.

Lay the ribs on the grill, convex-side down. When hot and well browned, about 3 minutes, flip them over and brush liberally with the chipotle glaze. Cover the grill and cook about 7 minutes for the glaze to set and begin to brown a little. There will likely be leftover glaze, which can be covered and refrigerated for a week or two.

Cut the ribs apart (that's my preference) and serve right away.

WORKING AHEAD The ribs are best when baked the same day you eat them and grilled within a few minutes of serving. They will hold well in a very low oven for a half hour or so before serving.

BEST OF THE BEST EXCLUSIVE

The cherry-chipotle glaze on this ham is delightful, but what makes this a standout is the unusual salsa, which combines dried cherries, onion, jicama and cilantro. Any leftover ham and salsa would be terrific in a taco the next day.

CHERRY-CHIPOTLE-GLAZED HAM

with cherry-jicama salsa

SERVES 12

- One 8- to 9-pound fully cooked spiral-cut ham
- One 12-ounce jar cherry preserves
- 2 canned chipotle chiles in adobo, plus 1 tablespoon adobo sauce
- 3 cups finely diced peeled jicama (about 1½ pounds)
- 1½ cups chopped dried sweet cherries
- 1 red onion, finely diced
- ¼ cup apple cider vinegar
- ½ cup chopped cilantro
- Kosher salt and freshly ground pepper

EDITOR'S WINE CHOICE
Juicy, spicy Grenache
(see page 268)

1. Preheat the oven to 250°F and position a rack in the bottom third. Put the ham cut side down in a large oven-safe cooking bag set in a 9-by-13-inch baking dish. Gather the bag over the ham, press out the air and fasten with the enclosed tie. Trim any excess bag and make six ½-inch slits around the top of the bag. Bake the ham for 1½ hours, until an instant-read thermometer inserted in the thickest part of the meat registers 100°F.

2. Meanwhile, in a food processor, puree the cherry preserves with the chipotles and adobo until smooth.

3. Carefully cut off and discard the bag, leaving the ham in the roasting pan. Spoon off all but ¼ cup of the juices. Brush the ham all over with all but ½ cup of the cherry-chipotle glaze. Bake the ham for 40 minutes longer, until the top is caramelized and an instant-read thermometer inserted in the thickest part of the meat registers 130°F.

4. Meanwhile, in a large bowl, combine the reserved ½ cup of cherry-chipotle glaze with the jicama, dried cherries, onion, vinegar and cilantro. Season the salsa with salt and pepper and refrigerate.

5. Transfer the ham to a platter, tent with foil and let rest for 15 minutes. Serve the ham with the cherry-jicama salsa.

MAKE AHEAD The cherry-jicama salsa can be refrigerated overnight. Add the cilantro just before serving.

RICK BAYLESS ONLINE

rickbayless.com

Chef Rick Bayless

@Rick_Bayless

Oatmeal sandwich bread, page 26

GOOD TO THE GRAIN

→ 02

Kim Boyce with Amy Scattergood

Are you curious about baking with teff or spelt? Anyone looking for healthier alternatives to refined flours will find an essential guide in this new book by Kim Boyce, a former pastry chef at L.A.'s Campanile. Her recipes manage to retain the character of whole-grain flours—the grassy notes of amaranth, the malty taste of rye—while mixing them with traditional pastry flours to achieve the right texture. For her Ginger Peach Muffins—muffins being the "cornerstone of everyday baking"—Boyce uses three kinds of flour (including standard all-purpose white flour) to get "the light structure of a great muffin as well as complex flavor." The real accomplishment is that her chewy Soft Rye Pretzels and fragrant Oatmeal Sandwich Bread don't feel like inferior, good-for-you versions of the foods we love, but entirely new items that easily stand on their own. *Published by Stewart, Tabori & Chang, $29.95*

The molasses adds a touch of sweetness and a dark mahogany color to this oversize loaf of bread, which has a substantial crust and crumbly interior.

OATMEAL SANDWICH BREAD

MAKES 1 LARGE LOAF

Butter for the bowl and the pan

- 1 package active dry yeast
- 3 tablespoons unsulphured (not blackstrap) molasses
- 2½ cups whole-wheat flour
- 2 cups bread flour
- 1 cup rolled oats
- 2 ounces (½ stick) unsalted butter, melted and cooled slightly
- 1 tablespoon kosher salt

This is a moist, slightly sweet loaf, and it's fantastic for toast and sandwiches. The dough uses a method known as autolyse, in which all the ingredients except the salt are mixed together and then allowed to rest before kneading. This rest gives the flour time to absorb the water, yielding a wetter dough and a moister bread with a better, more irregular crumb. I make this dough in a mixer, as I find you don't need to use as much flour this way. If you prefer to make the bread by hand, knead the dough for about fifteen minutes, adding flour as needed.

1. Lightly butter a large bowl and a bread loaf pan about 9 by 5 by 3 inches. The dough can also be formed into a *boule* (round loaf) and baked on a baking sheet.

2. Add 2 cups of warm water, yeast, and molasses to the bowl of a standing mixer. Stir, allowing the yeast to bloom for about 5 minutes, until it begins to bubble. (If it doesn't, it may be inactive; throw it out and start over with a new package.)

3. To autolyse, measure the flours, oats, and butter into the bowl with the yeast mixture and stir together with a wooden spoon. Cover with a towel and let stand for 30 minutes.

4. Attach the bowl and the bread hook to the mixer, add the salt, and mix on medium speed for 6 minutes. The dough should slap around the sides without sticking to them. If the dough is sticking at any time during the mixing, add a tablespoon or two of bread flour until the dough comes away from the sides of the bowl. The dough should be soft and supple, slightly tacky, with a beautiful sheeting effect.

AUTHOR'S NOTE

A dough is proofed once it has fully risen. How can you tell if a dough is proofed? Gently push a floured finger into the dough. If it springs back, the dough needs to proof longer. If a dimple remains, move on to the next step.

5. For the first rise, scrape the dough onto a lightly floured work surface and knead it a few times. Put the dough into the buttered bowl, cover with a towel, and leave it to rise for about 1 hour, or until it is doubled in size (see Author's Note).

6. To shape the dough, scrape the dough onto a lightly floured work surface. Press down on the dough, working it toward a square shape while depressing all of the bubbles. Fold the dough down from the top to the middle, then up from the bottom to the middle. Next bring the newly formed top and bottom edges together and pinch the seam in the middle, sealing the seam with your fingers. Pinch the sides together and roll the shaped dough back and forth, plumping it so that it's evenly formed and about the size of your loaf pan. Place the dough in the pan with the seam side down and press it gently into the corners of the pan.

7. For the second rise, cover the dough with a towel and let it rest in a warm place for about 1 hour, or until the dough rises to half again its size or puffs up barely or just over the edge of the pan. While the dough is rising, preheat the oven to 400°F.

8. When the dough has finished its final rise, sprinkle the top of the loaf with oats or bran, if desired.

9. Bake for about 40 minutes, rotating halfway through. The loaf is ready when the top crust is as dark as molasses and the bottom crust is dark brown. To see if the bread is ready, give the top of the loaf a thump to see if it sounds hollow. If the hollow sound isn't there and the bread isn't quite dark enough, bake for another 5 minutes. Remove the loaf from the pan and cool on a baking rack, preferably for a few hours, so that the crumb doesn't collapse when you cut into it and the flavor can develop.

The double hit of ginger—both fresh and crystallized—and the combination of whole-wheat and all-purpose flours make these muffins fragrant and cakey.

GINGER PEACH MUFFINS

MAKES 9 MUFFINS

Butter for the tins
- **2 tablespoons plus 1 teaspoon grated fresh ginger**

PEACH TOPPING
- **1 large or 2 small peaches, ripe but firm**
- **1 tablespoon unsalted butter**
- **1 tablespoon honey**

DRY MIX
- **1 cup oat flour**
- **¾ cup all-purpose flour**
- **½ cup whole-wheat flour**
- **¼ cup sugar**
- **¼ cup dark brown sugar**
- **1 teaspoon baking powder**
- **1 teaspoon baking soda**
- **¾ teaspoon kosher salt**

WET MIX
- **3 ounces (¾ stick) unsalted butter, melted and cooled slightly**
- **¾ cup whole milk**
- **½ cup sour cream**
- **1 egg**
- **3 tablespoons finely chopped crystallized ginger**

AUTHOR'S NOTE
To encourage even baking and to allow each muffin enough room to have an individual dome top, fill alternate cups in a 24-cup tin, or use two 12-cup tins.

1. Place a rack in the middle of the oven and preheat to 350°F. Rub muffin tins with a ⅓-cup capacity with butter.

2. Grate the ginger into a large bowl. Some will be used for the topping and the rest for the batter.

3. For the topping, halve the peach, remove the pit, and slice the halves into slices about ¼ inch thick. Add the butter, honey, and 1 teaspoon of the grated ginger to a medium-size skillet. Place the skillet over a medium flame to melt the mixture, stirring to combine. Cook until the syrup begins to bubble, about 2 minutes. Add the peaches, toss the pan to coat them with the syrup, and set aside.

4. Sift the dry ingredients into a large bowl, pouring back into the bowl any grain or other ingredients that may remain in the sifter. Add the wet ingredients to the bowl with the grated ginger and whisk until thoroughly combined. Using a spatula, mix the wet ingredients into the dry ingredients and gently combine.

5. Scoop the batter into 9 muffin cups, using a spoon or an ice cream scoop. The batter should be slightly mounded above the edge. Toss the pan of peaches to coat them with the pan juices. Lay one slice of peach over each of the muffins, tucking a second slice partway into the batter. Any extra peaches are delicious over yogurt or ice cream. Spoon the pan juices over the peaches.

6. Bake for 24 to 28 minutes, rotating the pans halfway through. The muffins are ready to come out when they smell nutty, their bottoms are golden in color (twist a muffin out of the pan to check), and the edges of the peaches are caramelized. Take the tins out of the oven, twist each muffin out, and place it on its side in the cup to cool. This ensures that the muffin stays crusty instead of getting soggy. These muffins are best eaten the same day they are made. They can also be kept in an airtight container for up to 2 days, or frozen and reheated.

These are the ultimate pretzels—tender, a little chewy and nicely salty—made with wholesome rye flour in addition to all-purpose flour.

SOFT RYE PRETZELS

MAKES 12

2 tablespoons unsalted butter, melted, for the bowl and the baking sheets

DOUGH

1 package active dry yeast
1 tablespoon honey
1 cup rye flour
2½ cups all-purpose flour
1 tablespoon kosher salt

BATH

½ cup baking soda

FINISH

Coarse sea salt, such as Maldon

These pretzels are soft, chewy, and flavorful, with a slight sourness that comes from boiling the pretzels in a baking soda bath. The baking soda also gives the pretzels their traditional dark mahogany color. Be sure to boil only a few pretzels at a time and to use the bath for only a single batch of the recipe—otherwise the baking soda water reduces too far and leaves a metallic bite to the dough. A simple dusting of sea salt, especially flaky Maldon salt, is the best finish to these. Serve a basket of the pretzels with a pot of whole-grain mustard.

1. Measure the yeast into a large bowl. Heat 1½ cups of water in a small saucepan over low heat to a temperature that is warm to the touch, about 100°F, and pour it over the yeast. Add the honey and stir to combine. Add the flours and salt and stir again.

2. Dump the sticky dough onto a floured surface and knead. Add up to ½ cup all-purpose flour, as needed, until the dough is tacky but not sticky. Knead for about 12 minutes, or until the dough is soft and supple.

3. Lightly brush a large bowl with melted butter. Using a dough scraper, scrape the dough into the bowl, cover with plastic wrap or a towel, and let rise for about 1½ hours, or until doubled in size (see Author's Note on page 27).

4. While the dough is rising, place two racks at the top and bottom thirds of the oven and preheat to 450°F. Brush two baking sheets generously with butter.

5. Once the dough has doubled, gently pour it from the bowl onto a lightly floured surface. Cut the dough into 12 pieces. Take each piece of dough and roll it into a snake about 17 inches long, with thinly tapered ends. Don't flour your surface as you roll; the slight stickiness enables you to roll the dough out evenly and quickly. Form the dough into a pretzel shape by folding one-third of the left side over the center of the snake, and then one-third of the right side over the left. Place the shaped pretzels onto the prepared baking sheets. Let the pretzels proof (rise) for 15 to 20 minutes.

6. Meanwhile, for the bath, fill a large pot with 10 cups of water and bring it to a boil. Once the pretzels are proofed and the water is boiling, add the baking soda to the water.

7. To poach the pretzels, lift 2 or 3 pretzels, depending on the surface area of your pot, into the bath. Boil each side for 30 seconds, use a strainer to remove the pretzels, pat any excess water with a towel, and transfer them back onto the buttered baking sheets. Boil the remaining pretzels. Sprinkle liberally with salt.

8. Bake for 15 to 18 minutes, rotating the sheets halfway through. The pretzels should be dark mahogany in color. Transfer them to a rack to cool. These pretzels are best eaten the day they're made, ideally within the hour.

Adding corn flour along with cornmeal to the crust gives these rustic rhubarb-hibiscus tarts their wonderful corn flavor and crunch.

RHUBARB TARTS

MAKES 10 INDIVIDUAL TARTS

Parchment for the baking sheets

DRY MIX

- 1 cup corn flour
- 1 cup all-purpose flour
- ½ cup fine cornmeal
- ¼ cup plus 2 tablespoons sugar
- 1 teaspoon kosher salt

WET MIX

- 4 ounces (1 stick) cold unsalted butter, cut into ½-inch pieces
- ¼ cup plus 2 tablespoons heavy cream
- 2 egg yolks

- 1 batch Rhubarb Hibiscus Compote (recipe follows)

Free-form tarts are my favorite way to showcase ripe fruit—they're delicious, easy and beautiful without being precious. Here, corn flour and rhubarb are paired for both their assertive flavor and their stunning color. You can also press the dough into a fluted tart shell for a larger, more formal dessert. Or, just make the dough (without the compote) and roll into simple cookies.

1. To make the dough, sift the dry ingredients into the bowl of a standing mixer, pouring back into the bowl any bits of grain or other ingredients that may remain in the sifter.

2. Attach the bowl and the paddle to the standing mixer. Add the butter, turn the mixer speed to low (so the flour doesn't go flying out of the bowl) and mix to break up the butter. Increase the speed to medium and mix until the butter is as coarse as cornmeal. Add the heavy cream and the egg yolks and mix until combined. The dough will appear crumbly, but when squeezed between your fingers it will become one mass. This dough is best shaped right after making, as it hardens when refrigerated. If the dough is chilled first, let it come to room temperature before shaping.

3. To shape the tarts, divide the dough into 10 equal pieces. Lightly flour a work surface. Grab one piece of dough and, using the heel of your hand, flatten the dough into a rough circle. Continue flattening until the circle is approximately 5 inches in diameter and of even thickness. If at any time the dough is sticking, flour the work surface and the dough. For an elegant finish, gently flatten the outer edge in a downward fashion, making it thinner than the rest of the dough.

4. Spoon ¼ cup of rhubarb compote into the center of the dough. Fold the edge of the dough toward the compote and up, to create a ruffled edge. Continue until an irregularly shaped ruffling happens. (Keep in mind that this is a rustic, handmade tart, so it shouldn't look like a machine made it.)

continued on page 34

rhubarb tarts continued

5. Slide a bench scraper or metal spatula underneath the tart and transfer it to a plate or baking sheet. Continue with the remaining dough. Slide the shaped tarts into the freezer to rest and harden for at least 1 hour, or up to 2 weeks if wrapped tightly in plastic.

6. Preheat the oven to 375°F. Line two baking sheets with parchment. Transfer the tarts onto the baking sheets.

7. Bake for about 35 minutes, or until the edges of the tarts are brown and the rhubarb is bubbling and thick.

8. The tarts can be eaten warm or at room temperature. They can also be wrapped tightly in plastic and kept for up to 2 days.

RHUBARB HIBISCUS COMPOTE

MAKES ABOUT 3 CUPS

- 2 pounds rhubarb stalks
- 1¼ cups dark brown sugar
- 8 dried hibiscus flowers

AUTHOR'S NOTE
In this recipe, fresh rhubarb is cooked down into a bright-colored compote. Dried hibiscus flowers are traditionally used in *jamaica,* a Mexican agua fresca, and to make tea. You can find hibiscus flowers in tea shops and many grocery stores, especially Latin markets. Here, they brighten the pink hue of the rhubarb. This compote fills the corn-flour Rhubarb Tarts and also makes a delicious filling for fruit crisps and cobblers.

1. Rinse the rhubarb stalks and trim off the very ends. Unless the stalks are very slender, cut them in half lengthwise. Cut the rhubarb on the diagonal into ¾-inch chunks. You'll have about 6 cups of rhubarb; set aside 2 cups and put the remaining 4 cups into a medium heavy-bottomed pot (with about a 5-quart capacity).

2. Add the brown sugar and hibiscus flowers to the pot, give the mixture a few stirs, cover, and turn the heat to medium-low. (It's important to begin slowly so the rhubarb warms up and begins to release its liquid.) Cook the rhubarb mixture for about 15 minutes, covered, until the mixture is saucy.

3. Remove the cover and increase the heat to medium. Cook for 15 to 17 minutes, stirring continuously, until the rhubarb is completely broken down and thick enough that a spoon leaves a trail at the bottom of the pan.

4. Add the remaining rhubarb chunks to the pot and stir to combine. Immediately pour the compote out onto a large plate or baking dish to cool. When the compote is cool, remove the hibiscus flowers, squeezing any juice from them into the compote, and discard. The compote will keep in the refrigerator for up to 1 week.

BEST OF THE BEST EXCLUSIVE

Boyce includes rye flour in the dough for her adorable, spiral-shaped scones; it's healthier than all-purpose flour and doesn't affect the texture of the pastry.

CHOCOLATE-ORANGE-PECAN SCONES

MAKES 12 SCONES

- ¾ cup pecans (about 3 ounces)
- 1 teaspoon vegetable oil
- 1 teaspoon kosher salt
- 1 cup heavy cream
- 1 large egg
- 2½ teaspoons finely grated orange zest
- 1½ cups all-purpose flour, plus more for dusting
- 1½ cups rye flour (see Note)
- ¼ cup granulated sugar
- 2½ teaspoons baking powder
- ⅓ cup plus 2 tablespoons dark brown sugar
- 1 stick cold unsalted butter, cubed
- 3½ ounces bittersweet chocolate, finely chopped
- ½ cup orange marmalade, at room temperature

1. Preheat the oven to 350°F and line 2 baking sheets with parchment paper. In a pie plate, toss the pecans with the oil and ¼ teaspoon of the salt. Toast in the oven for about 5 minutes, until fragrant; let cool completely. In a food processor, pulse the pecans until finely ground.

2. In a small bowl, whisk the cream with the egg and orange zest. In a large bowl, whisk both flours with the granulated sugar, baking powder, ½ cup of the ground pecans, ⅓ cup of the brown sugar, and the remaining ¾ teaspoon of salt. Using your fingertips, rub in the butter until the mixture resembles coarse meal. Stir in the cream mixture until the dough just comes together.

3. In a small bowl, combine the chopped chocolate with the remaining ground pecans and 2 tablespoons of brown sugar.

4. On a lightly floured surface, knead the dough until just smooth. Roll out the dough to an 11-by-16-inch rectangle, with a longer side facing you. Using an offset spatula or butter knife, spread the marmalade evenly over the dough. Sprinkle the chocolate-pecan mixture on top. Roll the dough, gently pressing, to form a 16-inch log. Cut the log in half and wrap each half in plastic. Freeze the logs until cold, about 10 minutes.

5. On a lightly floured surface, cut each log into 6 even pieces. Transfer the scones to the baking sheets, cut side down. Bake for about 30 minutes, until golden and risen; shift the pans halfway through baking. Let the scones cool before serving.

NOTE Rye flour is made from finely ground rye, a cereal grain with dark brown kernels. It's most commonly used in Eastern Europe and can be purchased at specialty markets, health-food stores or online.

MAKE AHEAD The scones can be stored in an airtight container overnight.

KIM BOYCE ONLINE

kimboycebakes.com

@KimBoyceBakes

Grilled chicken wings with homemade hot sauce and blue cheese, page 38

BROMBERG BROS. BLUE RIBBON COOKBOOK

→ 03

Bruce Bromberg, Eric Bromberg & Melissa Clark

Bruce and Eric Bromberg's Blue Ribbon empire (10 restaurants in total) stays true to no specific cuisine, and instead zigzags wildly between beef marrow and matzoh ball soup, paella and fried chicken. There is a philosophy, however: "To make the best versions possible of lovable classics." Their first cookbook takes you through their process with recipes that emphasize French technique and prime ingredients. Fiery chicken wings are still deliciously messy bar food, but with an innovative glaze of homemade habanero hot sauce, Chinese plum sauce and brown sugar. Salt-and-pepper shrimp, inspired by Manhattan's Chinatown, come with a citrusy Japanese *ponzu* sauce. These are recipes for cooks interested in "elevating [each dish] to its highest expression while still remaining true to its nature."

Published by Clarkson Potter, $35

These wings get exceptionally crispy because of the brown sugar added to the hot-sauce glaze, which caramelizes from the heat of the broiler or grill.

GRILLED CHICKEN WINGS

with homemade hot sauce & blue cheese

SERVES 2 TO 4

- 8 chicken wings (about 1¾ pounds)
- Kosher salt and freshly ground black pepper (see Editor's Note)
- 2 tablespoons Blue Ribbon Hot Sauce (recipe follows) or your favorite bottled hot sauce
- 2 tablespoons unsalted butter, melted
- 1 tablespoon Chinese plum sauce
- 1½ teaspoons light brown sugar
- ¼ cup sour cream
- ¼ cup crumbled blue cheese

EDITOR'S WINE CHOICE

Dry, rich Champagne
(see page 264)

EDITOR'S NOTE

The Brombergs like to season their chicken wings with a mix of salt, pepper and thyme.

At Blue Ribbon, one of our main culinary goals is to take all the dishes that we loved from childhood and elevate them. Chicken wings are no exception. Broiled or grilled instead of deep-fried, and seasoned with homemade hot sauce spiked with plum sauce and brown sugar, these crispy, tangy, spicy wings are like the best Buffalo chicken wings you've ever tasted, maybe even better.

1. Sprinkle the chicken wings with the seasoning. Let rest for 20 minutes.

2. In the meantime, preheat the broiler or grill.

3. In a small bowl, mix together the hot sauce, butter, plum sauce, and brown sugar. Set aside half of the hot sauce mixture.

4. Broil or grill the wings, turning once, for 20 minutes. Slather the wings with the remaining half of the hot sauce mixture, making sure to coat both sides of the wings. Broil or grill until glazed and crispy, 10 to 15 minutes longer, turning once. Using a clean utensil, brush the wings with the reserved hot sauce mixture before serving.

5. TO MAKE THE DRESSING Mix together the sour cream and blue cheese. Serve with the wings.

BLUE RIBBON HOT SAUCE

MAKES 4 CUPS

- 3 cups distilled white vinegar
- 3 to 4 red, orange, or yellow habanero chiles, to taste, trimmed and sliced
- 2 tablespoons salt
- 1 pound carrots, trimmed, peeled, and roughly chopped

When we opened Blue Ribbon Brooklyn with a much larger kitchen than we have in SoHo, we decided that we wanted to make everything we could from scratch—including all the ice creams and many of the condiments, like ketchup, pickles, even our own hot sauce and steak sauce. Well, after a lot of playing around, we realized that A1 was still better than any steak sauce we could make, Ciao Bella made superior vanilla ice cream, and Heinz had us beat on ketchup. But our partner and chef Mike Paritsky did manage to come up with excellent recipes for pickles and this killer hot sauce, which we think is better than anything you can buy. Our secret is the carrots, which make the bright-orange sauce just glow in its bottle. Carrots also add body and sweetness to temper the heat of the habanero chiles. Store the sauce in your refrigerator. It will last for years.

1. Combine the vinegar, chiles, and salt in a large nonreactive pot over medium-high heat. Bring to a boil. Let the mixture cool, then puree in a blender and strain.

2. While the peppers are cooking, in a separate pot combine the carrots with water to cover. Simmer until very tender but not overcooked, about 10 minutes. Drain well. Puree the carrots in the blender until smooth (you do not need to strain them), then stir into the strained vinegar mixture. If it's too spicy-hot, thin it down with a little water.

3. Use immediately, or transfer the hot sauce to airtight, sterile jars or bottles and refrigerate.

Pairing this Chinese dish with ponzu, *a Japanese citrus-based sauce, is inspired, if a bit unorthodox. Its tanginess is outstanding with the peppery shrimp.*

CRISPY FRIED SALT & PEPPER SHRIMP

with spicy wilted lettuce

SERVES 2 TO 4

- 2½ tablespoons coarse salt
- 1 tablespoon crushed red pepper flakes
- 1½ teaspoons black sesame seeds
- 5 ounces jumbo shrimp (about 6 pieces)
- 1 teaspoon canola oil, plus more for deep-frying
- 2 cups sliced iceberg lettuce
- 1 teaspoon chopped serrano chile
- ½ teaspoon salt and freshly ground white or black pepper (see Editor's Note)
- Ponzu Sauce (recipe follows)

EDITOR'S WINE CHOICE

Spicy American Gewürztraminer (see page 265)

EDITOR'S NOTE

For their salt-and-pepper seasoning, the Brombergs mix salt and finely ground white pepper in a proportion of 6 tablespoons salt to 1 teaspoon pepper.

When we were kids, on Saturday mornings we'd make the trip with our dad from New Jersey to the bustling streets of Chinatown in Manhattan. Going from quiet, tree-lined suburbia to the vibrant chaos of Mon Bo Rice Shop was like taking a day trip to another planet. Cooks yelled, glasses crashed, waiters zipped around carrying sizzling food high over their heads. We'd devour plump and crispy salt-and-pepper shrimp, shells and all. In our version, we use fresh Louisiana shrimp and serve them on wilted iceberg lettuce studded with serrano chiles.

1. In a small bowl, mix the salt, red pepper flakes and sesame seeds.

2. Using kitchen shears, cut through the shell on the back of each shrimp, and remove the thick black vein with the tip of a knife. Do not remove the shell.

3. Fill a medium pot halfway (about 3 inches) with canola oil; heat until a deep-fat thermometer reads 375°F. Fry the shrimp until golden and just cooked through, about 2 minutes. Transfer to a paper-towel-lined plate. Sprinkle with some of the spicy salt mixture.

4. While the shrimp fry, heat the teaspoon of oil in a medium skillet over medium-high heat. Add the lettuce, serrano chile, and salt and white or black pepper mixture. Cook, stirring, until the lettuce is wilted, about 45 seconds.

5. Arrange the lettuce on a platter. Top with the shrimp. Serve with Ponzu Sauce and pass the remaining spicy salt and pepper mixture.

PONZU SAUCE

MAKES ABOUT 2½ CUPS

- ¾ cup soy sauce
- ¾ cup rice wine vinegar
- 6 tablespoons mirin
- 3 tablespoons sake
- One 1-inch strip of kombu
- 1 tablespoon bonito flakes
- ¼ orange, peeled and cut into segments

Combine the soy sauce, vinegar, mirin, sake, kombu, bonito flakes, and orange in a jar and stir well. Cover and refrigerate for at least 2 days and up to a week.

These aren't exactly health food, but they have much less fat than regular fried doughnuts, and the cakey texture will satisfy any doughnut craving.

DOUGHNUT MUFFINS

MAKES 24 MINI MUFFINS OR 12 MINI BUNDT CAKES

MUFFINS

- 3 cups all-purpose flour
- 2½ teaspoons baking powder
- ¾ teaspoon salt
- ½ teaspoon freshly ground nutmeg
- ¼ teaspoon baking soda
- ¾ cup whole milk, at room temperature
- 2 tablespoons buttermilk, at room temperature
- 10 tablespoons (1¼ sticks) unsalted butter, at room temperature
- ¾ cup plus 2 tablespoons sugar
- 2 large eggs, at room temperature

COATING

- 1 cup sugar
- 1 tablespoon ground cinnamon
- 8 tablespoons (1 stick) unsalted butter, melted

AUTHOR'S NOTE

The batter will keep for three days in the fridge, so you can prepare it in advance and bake them up whenever a doughnut craving hits. And, if you just have to have a doughnut with a hole in the middle, you can bake them in mini Bundt pans.

These have all the nutmegy goodness and dunk-ability of a traditional doughnut, but without the frying. We think they're even better baked than fried, because these have a delicious sourness from the buttermilk, a subtle flavor that gets lost in the deep-fryer. Once you've devoured these warm, brushed with a little melted butter and sprinkled with cinnamon sugar, you'll never yearn for doughnuts any other way.

1. Preheat the oven to 375°F. Grease and flour two 12-cup mini muffin tins.

2. TO MAKE THE MUFFINS In a bowl, sift together the flour, baking powder, salt, nutmeg, and baking soda. In a separate bowl, whisk together the milk and buttermilk.

3. In the bowl of an electric mixer fitted with the paddle attachment, beat the butter and sugar until light and fluffy. Beat in the eggs, one at a time, until just combined.

4. With the mixer set on low speed, beat in one-fourth of the dry ingredients. Beat in one-third of the milk mixture. Continue to alternate until all of the remaining ingredients are incorporated, finishing with the dry ingredients. Do not overmix.

5. Fill the prepared muffin cups just to the rim with batter. Bake until lightly golden and firm to the touch, 15 to 20 minutes. Let the muffins cool in the pan for 5 minutes. Remove the muffins from the tins and transfer to a wire rack set over a baking sheet.

6. TO COAT THE MUFFINS Combine the sugar and cinnamon in a bowl. Brush each muffin generously with melted butter. Then sprinkle generously with cinnamon sugar. Serve warm or at room temperature.

VARIATION > JELLY DOUGHNUT MUFFINS

If jelly doughnuts are more your style, allow the muffins to cool and use a small pastry tip to make a hole in the bottom of each muffin. Fill the pastry bag with your favorite jam, jelly, or citrus curd, and squeeze into the muffin.

BEST OF THE BEST EXCLUSIVE

Instead of using unwieldy slices of beet and onions, the Brombergs chop the vegetables to create a tasty relish, which they top with creamy goat cheese.

WARM GOAT CHEESE SANDWICHES

with beet & red pepper relish

MAKES 8 SANDWICHES

- ½ pound small beets
- 1 large red onion, chopped
- 1 tablespoon extra-virgin olive oil
- Kosher salt and freshly ground pepper
- 1 roasted red bell pepper from a jar, coarsely chopped
- 1 tablespoon fresh lemon juice
- 8 small ciabatta rolls (about 2½ ounces each), halved
- 1 pound fresh goat cheese
- ½ pound watercress, thick stems discarded

EDITOR'S WINE CHOICE
Dry, crisp rosé (see page 267)

1. In a medium saucepan, cover the beets with water and bring to a boil. Reduce the heat to moderately low and simmer until the beets are tender, about 40 minutes. Drain, peel and coarsely chop the beets.

2. Meanwhile, preheat the broiler. On a small baking sheet, toss the onion with the olive oil and season with salt and pepper. Broil the onion for about 5 minutes, until golden brown.

3. Lower the oven temperature to 400°F. In a food processor, pulse the beets with the onion, roasted red pepper and lemon juice until finely chopped. Season the relish with salt and pepper.

4. Arrange the ciabatta halves on a baking sheet, cut side up. Spread about 2 tablespoons of the relish onto each top half. Spread ¼ cup of the goat cheese onto each bottom half and season with salt and pepper. Bake until the relish and goat cheese are heated through, about 5 minutes. Top the goat cheese with the watercress, close the sandwiches and serve.

MAKE AHEAD The relish can be refrigerated in an airtight container for up to 3 days.

THE BROMBERGS ONLINE

blueribbonrestaurants.com

Blue Ribbon Restaurants

@BlueRibbonNYC

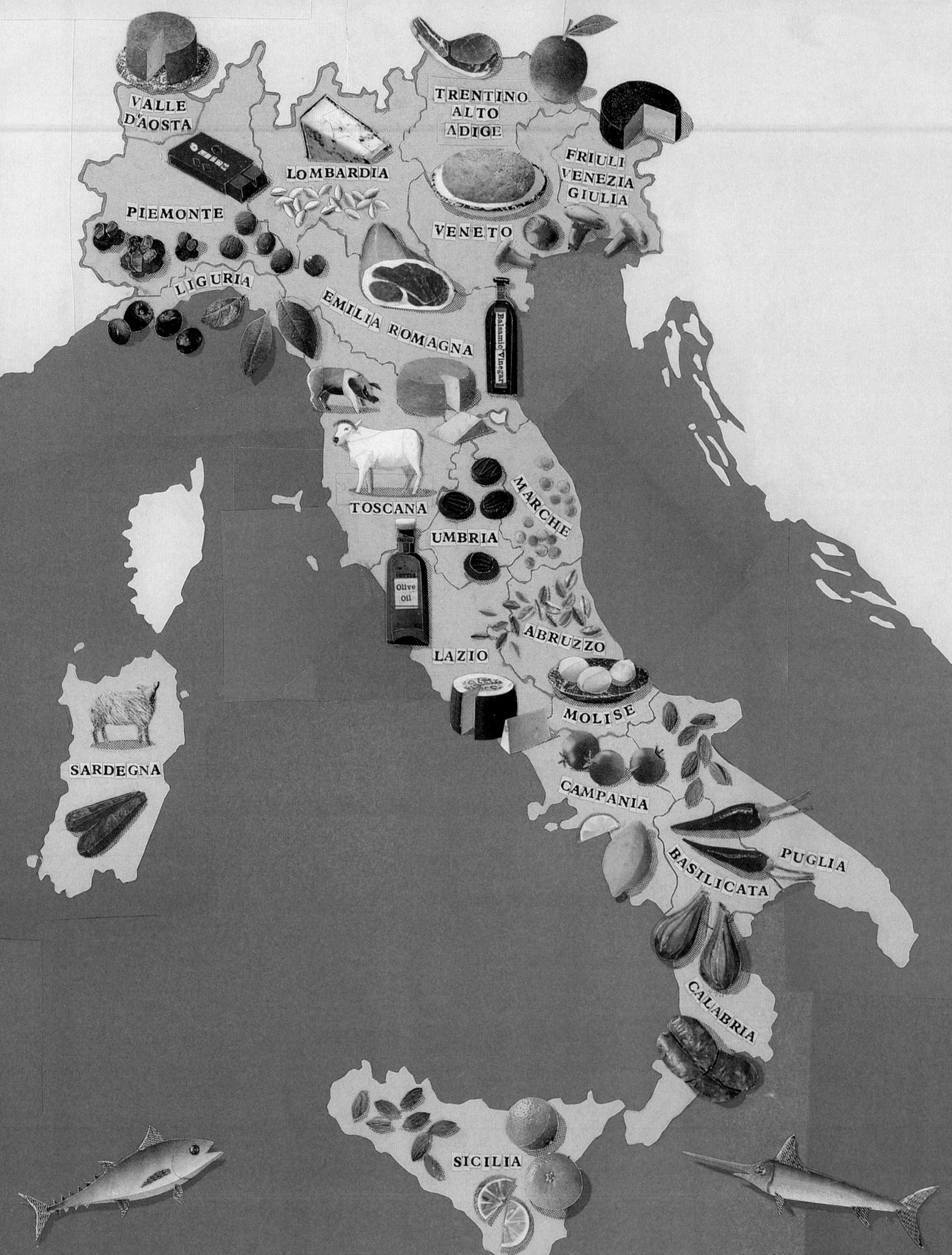

VALLE D'AOSTA
TRENTINO ALTO ADIGE
LOMBARDIA
FRIULI VENEZIA GIULIA
PIEMONTE
VENETO
LIGURIA
EMILIA ROMAGNA
Balsamic Vinegar
MARCHE
TOSCANA
UMBRIA
Olive Oil
ABRUZZO
LAZIO
SARDEGNA
MOLISE
CAMPANIA
PUGLIA
BASILICATA
CALABRIA
SICILIA

COOK ITALY

→ 04

Katie Caldesi

Why should you trust a British chef to teach traditional Italian recipes and techniques? Because Katie Caldesi has dedicated 12 years to the subject, traveling around all 20 Italian regions, living with local families, transcribing oral recipes from matriarchs and working alongside Italian chefs (including her Tuscan-born husband) in her two U.K. restaurants. *Cook Italy* is deep *and* wide, covering every aspect of the Italian meal and all of its famed dishes—there are recipes for nine different styles of ragù (meat sauce), including a white version simmered with cream and white wine. Caldesi's passion for the cuisine is obvious, and so is her zeal for educating; her book includes a helpful glossary and 40 photo-driven tutorials for tougher techniques, like boning and butterflying a leg of lamb, which she then stuffs with a delicious mix of pecorino, mint and artichokes. *Published by Kyle Books, $39.95*

Stuffing and rolling a boneless leg of lamb is an elegant way to showcase the inexpensive cut. The leftovers—if there are any—are terrific in a sandwich.

ROLLED LAMB
with pecorino, mint & artichoke stuffing

SERVES 6

- 4 to 5 pounds leg of lamb, boned and butterflied (you can ask your butcher to do this for you, or see Boning and Butterflying a Leg of Lamb)
- Salt and freshly ground black pepper
- 30 mint leaves
- 2 ounces semi-matured (*semi-stagionato*) pecorino, roughly cut into slivers
- One 10-ounce jar of marinated artichoke hearts in oil (6 ounces drained weight), halved
- 2 garlic cloves, sliced
- 3 tablespoons olive oil
- 2 cups dry white wine
- 1¼ cups water

EDITOR'S WINE CHOICE
Cherry-inflected, earthy Sangiovese (see page 269)

AUTHOR'S NOTE
A boned shoulder also works, but increase the cooking time by 30 minutes to 1 hour.

I ate this at Sora Lella in Rome. It's a cheap cut with the ingredients of the area added to it. I was impressed with the flavors and amused by the fact that—like the Brits—the Italians served mint with lamb. Use lightly cooked fresh artichoke hearts if you wish, but I prefer the flavor of marinated ones for this dish. I usually have a jar in my cupboard.

Preheat the oven to 475°F. Trim away any excess fat from the lamb and lay it out flat. Season well with salt and pepper. Place the mint, pecorino, artichokes, and garlic on the lamb and roll up. Secure with cotton string. Heat the oil in a large frying pan and sear the rolled lamb on all sides, then pour away the excess oil. Transfer the lamb to an ovenproof casserole, deglaze the pan with the wine, and then pour this into the casserole along with the water. Cover, place in the very hot oven for 15 minutes, then reduce to 325°F and cook for 30 minutes. Remove the lid to allow the sauce to reduce, and cook for another 30 minutes, or until cooked through.

Serve with new potatoes, wilted spinach, and plenty of crusty bread to mop up the juices.

BONING AND BUTTERFLYING A LEG OF LAMB Trim away large areas of solid fat, then cut away the bone from the leg by working the knife around it. Cut back the flesh on either side of the bone, keeping the knife as close to the bone as possible. Pass the knife under the bone to remove it completely. Open out the meat and cut away any excess fat and gristle—but don't remove all the fat, as most of the soft fat will break down during the cooking, making the meat tastier and more juicy.

To butterfly the lamb, slice the thick sides in half and open out. Then do the same again so the meat is twice its original size.

Using a sweet red pepper as the edible "bowl" for cheese soufflé is really smart. If you can find mini bell peppers, these would also make lovely hors d'oeuvres.

BAKED RED PEPPERS

filled with four-cheese soufflé

SERVES 4

- 4 red Romano or sweet bell peppers
- ⅔ cup whole milk
- Half a small onion, peeled
- 1 bay leaf
- A good pinch of nutmeg
- Salt and freshly ground pepper
- 2 tablespoons butter
- 3 tablespoons all-purpose flour
- ¾ cup finely grated Parmesan
- 2 ounces ricotta
- 2 ounces Taleggio, cut into chunks
- 3 ounces Gorgonzola, cut into chunks
- 2 eggs, separated

These peppers are light and easy to serve with dressed greens. Use any cheeses you have, but make sure one of them is blue for flavor.

Preheat the oven to 350°F. Cut the peppers in half lengthwise through the stem. Discard the seeds and membrane. Put on a baking sheet and bake for 7 minutes (not necessary for Romano peppers).

Put the milk, onion, bay leaf, nutmeg, pepper, and salt in a medium saucepan and bring to a boil. Melt the butter in a small pan and stir in the flour. Remove the bay leaf and onion. Cook for a few minutes, then add the mix to the milk and whisk. The mix will be very thick. When the mixtures are combined, replace the whisk with a wooden spoon, add the cheeses, and stir until melted.

Pour into a bowl and leave to cool for a few minutes, covered with plastic wrap. Whisk the egg whites in a bowl. Beat the yolks, add to the béchamel, then fold the egg whites into the rest of the ingredients in the bowl. Spoon the soufflé mixture into the peppers and bake for 25 minutes, until puffed and lightly browned.

Even with such an incredibly simple preparation, the cubes of lamb get very tender in this stew. The peas add a nice sweet note to the dish.

LAMB & PEA STEW

SERVES 4

- 1½ pounds boneless stewing lamb, cut into 2-inch cubes
- Salt and freshly ground black pepper
- 3 tablespoons oil
- 1 white onion, finely chopped
- 2 garlic cloves, sliced
- ⅔ cup dry white wine
- 10 ounces frozen peas
- 4 sprigs of rosemary
- 1 cup stock or water

EDITOR'S WINE CHOICE
Juicy, fresh Dolcetto
(see page 268)

This is a dish from the south of Italy, where cheaper cuts of lamb are stewed slowly on the stove or in the oven. Ask your butcher for a cut such as middle neck, shoulder, or scrag end that will stand up to the long cooking time and contains some fat to flavor the stew. Although this stew is slow to cook, it is very quick to prepare and so makes a good supper dish.

Season the lamb all over with salt and pepper. Heat the oil in a large lidded frying pan or heavy-bottomed flameproof casserole. When hot, add the onion and garlic. Cook until softened and then add the lamb and cook, turning the pieces, for about 10 minutes, until they are brown on all sides. Next pour in the wine and let it reduce for a couple of minutes. Then add the peas, rosemary, and stock or water and bring to a boil.

Cover the pan and let it simmer for 1 to 1½ hours, until the lamb is tender and the sauce has reduced. If you feel the stew is too watery, remove the lid and let the sauce bubble and reduce, as necessary.

An unusual cream-based ragù is a great alternative to the traditional tomato-based meat sauce. Try a mix of veal and pork for the richest flavor.

WHITE RAGÙ WITH RIGATONI

SERVES 4

- 4 tablespoons olive oil
- 1 small white onion, finely chopped
- 1 large garlic clove, finely chopped
- Salt and freshly ground black pepper
- 1 pound ground turkey, veal, pork, or chicken, raw or cooked
- 8 sage leaves, coarsely chopped
- ⅓ cup dry white wine
- 1 cup chicken stock
- 12 ounces rigatoni
- ⅓ cup cream

TO SERVE

- Olive oil
- ¼ cup grated Parmesan

EDITOR'S WINE CHOICE
Fresh, minerally Vermentino
(see page 267)

This is a simple dish that is quick to prepare and cook. My children like the big tube pasta, which they fill up with meat sauce. Leftovers can be reheated in an ovenproof dish with extra cream and Parmesan for delicious baked pasta. You can use leftover meat from a roast—simply pop chunks of cooked meat into a food processor and process to mince. Brown the meat in hot oil and then add the sage leaves and wine.

Bring a large saucepan of salted water to a boil. Heat the oil in a pan over medium heat and add the onion, garlic, and salt and pepper. Cook for about 2 minutes, then add the ground meat and reduce the heat. If using raw meat, allow the water to evaporate from it. Once the meat is browned, add half the sage leaves.

Next add the wine and allow to reduce for a couple of minutes. Add the stock, stir well, reduce the heat, and allow to simmer. Adjust the seasoning as necessary.

Meanwhile, put the pasta in the boiling water and cook until al dente. After 5 minutes, add the cream to the ragù and simmer gently, stirring frequently. When the pasta is cooked, drain, add to the ragù, and toss to combine. Serve with a drizzle of olive oil, the remaining sage, and a generous sprinkling of Parmesan.

BEST OF THE BEST EXCLUSIVE

After cooking chicken, Caldesi adds vinegar to the pan juices to create a warm, savory vinaigrette for dressing the accompanying arugula salad.

PANCETTA-WRAPPED CHICKEN BREASTS

SERVES 4

- 4 skinless, boneless chicken breast halves (1⅓ pounds total)
- 4 thin slices of Pecorino Toscano cheese (about 6 ounces)
- Salt and freshly ground pepper
- 12 very thin slices of pancetta (about 4 ounces)
- ¼ cup extra-virgin olive oil
- ½ cup dry white wine
- ¼ cup chicken stock or low-sodium broth
- 4 cups packed baby arugula (about 4 ounces)
- 1 tablespoon aged balsamic vinegar

EDITOR'S WINE CHOICE
Zippy, fresh Pinot Bianco (see page 266)

1. Preheat the oven to 350°F. Using a small knife, cut a deep, narrow pocket in the side of each chicken breast. Insert a slice of cheese into each pocket; press gently to close. Season the chicken with salt and pepper. Wrap each breast in 3 slightly overlapping slices of pancetta.

2. In a large ovenproof skillet, heat 2 tablespoons of the olive oil. Add the chicken breasts and cook over moderate heat until the pancetta is golden brown, about 3 minutes per side. Transfer the chicken to a platter and pour off the fat in the skillet.

3. Add the wine to the skillet and simmer over moderate heat, scraping up any browned bits, until reduced by half, about 2 minutes. Stir in the chicken stock and the remaining 2 tablespoons of olive oil and bring to a simmer. Return the chicken to the skillet and roast in the oven for 20 minutes, until just white throughout.

4. Transfer the chicken to a platter and mound the arugula alongside. Stir the vinegar into the pan juices and season with salt and pepper. Drizzle the sauce over the chicken and arugula and serve right away.

MAKE AHEAD The chicken can be prepared through Step 1 and refrigerated overnight. Bring to room temperature before cooking.

KATIE CALDESI ONLINE

caldesi.com

Katie Caldesi

@KatieCaldesi

Sandwiches
soup of the day
smoked turkey, cheddar, cranberry chutney
hummus, cucumber, radish sprouts,
applewood-smoked bacon, L&T
fresh mozzarella, basil pesto, tomato
curried tuna salad, apples, carrots, golden
roast lamb, tomato chutney, goat cheese
roast chicken, avocado, jicama
roast beef, horseradish, crispy onions,
grilled roast chicken, brie, arugula, peppers
grilled portobello melt, pesto, mozzarella,
simple mixed green salad
Chocolate Chip Brioche Loaf $9.00

FLOUR

→ 05

Joanne Chang with Christie Matheson

"In baking, as in life, simple things are best," says Joanne Chang, owner of Boston's Flour Bakery + Cafe. But simple is not the same as easy. "We strive for perfection with every recipe we prepare and item we serve," Chang adds. Ideal for the home baker looking to graduate beyond recipes on the back of the chocolate chip bag, *Flour* is rigorous in its approach. This is true whether Chang is tackling French pastry (croissants, éclairs), American classics (jam-topped granola bars, coconut cream pie) or upscale versions of nostalgic junk food (Homemade Pop-Tarts, Milky Way Tart). Yet Chang's superclear prose makes techniques like tempering and *fraisage* seem doable. She also reminds you that "the best thing about baking is that most of the time your mistakes are edible—and usually quite enjoyable!" *Published by Chronicle Books, $35*

This revamp of the childhood favorite is so good you'll never go back to store-bought. Chang suggests raspberry jam for the filling, but other flavors work, too.

HOMEMADE POP-TARTS

MAKES 8 PASTRIES

- 1 recipe Pâte Brisée (recipe follows)
- 1 egg, lightly beaten
- 1 cup (340 grams) raspberry jam

SIMPLE VANILLA GLAZE

- 1 cup (140 grams) confectioners' sugar
- ¼ teaspoon vanilla extract
- 2 to 3 tablespoons water

Rainbow sprinkles for sprinkling (optional)

I took the bus to elementary school every day with Linda, my best childhood friend and next-door neighbor. We always sat together in the third row and shared our breakfasts-on-the-go. Most of the time I had buttered toast or a traditional bao *(Chinese white steamed bun)—pretty boring. Linda's mom often sent her with foil-wrapped packets of Pop-Tarts, which I could never get her to trade with me. She shared bites with me occasionally, but I longed to have my own, and I could never convince my mom to buy them. When I started baking professionally, I dreamed of all the things I would offer at my own bakery. Those childhood tarts were high on my list, and I thought if I made them from scratch, they could surpass the packaged supermarket version I remembered. I was right. The tarts we make at Flour get steady attention from both our customers and the press. Making them is similar to making ravioli, but even if you've never done that, you'll find the process quite straightforward: First, you roll out flaky, buttery dough into a big sheet and score it into rectangles. Then, you spoon jam into the rectangles, lay another sheet of pastry dough on top, and press down to make little jam pockets. Finally, you cut the pockets apart and bake them to golden brown yumminess.*

Position a rack in the center of the oven, and heat the oven to 350°F.

Remove the dough from the refrigerator and divide it in half. Press each half into a rectangle. On a lightly floured surface, roll out each half into a 14-by-11-inch rectangle. Using a paring knife, lightly score one rectangle into eight 3½-by-5½-inch rectangles (about the size of an index card).

Brush the top surface of the entire scored rectangle with the egg. Spoon 2 tablespoons of the jam in a mound in the center of each scored rectangle. Lay the second large dough rectangle directly on top of the first. Using fingertips, carefully press down all around each jam mound, so the pastry sheets adhere to each other.

continued on page 58

homemade pop-tarts continued

Using a knife, a pizza roller (easier), or a fluted roller (easier and prettier), and following the scored lines, cut the layered dough into 8 rectangles. Place the rectangles, well spaced, on a baking sheet.

Bake for 40 to 45 minutes, or until the tops of the pastries are evenly golden brown. Let cool on the baking sheet on a wire rack for about 30 minutes.

TO MAKE THE GLAZE While the pastries are cooling, in a small bowl, whisk together the confectioners' sugar, vanilla, and enough of the water to make a smooth, pourable glaze. You should have about ½ cup. (The glaze can be made ahead and stored in an airtight container at room temperature for up to 1 week.)

When the pastries have cooled for 30 minutes, brush the tops evenly with the glaze, then sprinkle with the rainbow sprinkles (if using). Let stand for 10 to 15 minutes to allow the glaze to set before serving.

The pastries can be stored in an airtight container at room temperature for up to 2 days.

Pop-Tarts is a registered trademark of Kellogg Co.

PÂTE BRISÉE

MAKES ABOUT 18 OUNCES DOUGH, ENOUGH FOR 8 POP-TARTS OR ONE 9-INCH DOUBLE-CRUST OR LATTICE-TOP PIE

- 1¾ cups (245 grams) unbleached all-purpose flour
- 1 tablespoon sugar
- 1 teaspoon kosher salt
- 1 cup (2 sticks/228 grams) cold unsalted butter, cut into 12 pieces
- 2 egg yolks
- 3 tablespoons cold milk

Using a stand mixer fitted with the paddle attachment (or a handheld mixer), mix together the flour, sugar, and salt for 10 to 15 seconds, or until combined. Scatter the butter over the top. Mix on low speed for 1 to 1½ minutes, or just until the flour is no longer bright white and holds together when you clump it and lumps of butter the size of pecans are visible throughout.

In a small bowl, whisk together the egg yolks and milk until blended. Add to the flour mixture all at once. Mix on low speed for about 30 seconds, or until the dough just barely comes together. It will look really shaggy and more like a mess than a dough.

Dump the dough out onto an unfloured work surface, then gather it together into a tight mound. Using your palm and starting on one side of the mound, smear the dough bit by bit, starting at the top of the mound and then sliding your palm down the side and along the work surface (at Flour, we call this "going down the mountain"), until most of the butter chunks are smeared into the dough and the dough comes together. Do this once or twice on each part of the dough, moving through the mound until the whole mess has been smeared into a cohesive dough with streaks of butter.

Gather up the dough, wrap tightly in plastic wrap, and press down to flatten into a disk about 1 inch thick. Refrigerate for at least 4 hours before using. The dough will keep in the refrigerator for up to 4 days or in the freezer for up to 1 month.

Chang goes all out with her granola bar—it's packed with homemade jam, toasted nuts, shredded coconut and oats, then topped with crunchy seeds.

GRANOLA BARS

MAKES 12 BARS

GRANOLA JAM

- 1 cup (80 grams) dried apples
- 1 cup (160 grams) dried cranberries
- 1 cup (160 grams) dried apricots
- ⅓ cup (70 grams) granulated sugar
- 2 cups (480 grams) water

- 1 cup (100 grams) walnut halves
- 1¾ cups (245 grams) unbleached all-purpose flour
- 1½ cups (150 grams) old-fashioned rolled oats (not instant or quick cooking)
- ⅔ cup (150 grams) packed light brown sugar
- ⅔ cup (80 grams) sweetened shredded coconut
- 1 teaspoon kosher salt
- ¼ teaspoon ground cinnamon
- 1 cup (2 sticks/228 grams) unsalted butter, at room temperature, cut into 8 to 10 pieces
- 6 tablespoons (128 grams) honey
- 3 tablespoons flaxseeds
- 3 tablespoons sunflower seeds
- 3 tablespoons millet

Every so often, a Flour customer puts a request for more healthful items in our suggestion box . . . please! It's not that Flour is full of unhealthful items—I think our baked goods are healthful, in moderation—but we are a bakery, after all, which means that many of our offerings are necessarily indulgent. We came up with this bar as an option for customers seeking a good-for-you snack. You make a granola of oats, nuts, coconut, and honey for the base. Add a fruity filling made by blending a dried-fruit compote into a sweet, chunky jam. And finish off the bar with more of the granola base mixed with a handful of sunflower seeds, flaxseeds, and millet. The bars stay moist for several days and actually get better with age (I like them best after 2 or 3 days). We make huge trayfuls of these at Flour, and one of my favorite ways to snack at the bakery is to raid the pans after the bars have been cut for serving and enjoy a plateful of edge trimmings.

TO MAKE THE JAM In a medium saucepan, combine the apples, cranberries, apricots, granulated sugar, and water and bring to a boil over high heat. Remove from the heat and let sit for about 1 hour. Transfer to a food processor and pulse 8 to 10 times, or until a chunky jam forms. (The jam can be made in advance and stored in the refrigerator in an airtight container for up to 5 days or in the freezer for up to 1 month.)

Position a rack in the center of the oven, and heat the oven to 350°F. Spread the walnuts on a baking sheet and toast for about 10 minutes, or until lightly toasted and fragrant. Transfer to a plate and let cool.

Leave the oven set at 350°F. Line a 9-by-13-inch baking pan with parchment paper.

continued on page 62

granola bars continued

In the food processor, combine the walnuts, flour, oats, brown sugar, coconut, salt, cinnamon, and butter and pulse about 15 times, or until the mixture is evenly combined. Dump the mixture into a medium bowl and drizzle the honey on top. Work in the honey with your hands until the mixture comes together.

Press about two-thirds of the mixture into the bottom of the prepared pan. Place the remaining one-third of the mixture in the refrigerator.

Bake for 30 to 40 minutes, or until light golden brown throughout. Remove the pan from the oven, spoon the granola jam on top, and spread in an even layer with the spoon or with a rubber spatula, covering the surface. Remove the reserved granola mixture from the refrigerator, and break it up with your fingers into a small bowl. Add the flaxseeds, sunflower seeds, and millet and stir to combine. Sprinkle the mixture, like a crumb topping, evenly over the jam.

Return the pan to the oven and bake for 50 to 60 minutes, or until the top is golden brown. Let cool in the pan on a wire rack for 2 to 3 hours, or until cool enough to hold its shape when cut. Cut into 12 bars.

The bars can be stored in an airtight container at room temperature for up to 1 week.

Lots of pastry chefs riff on classic candy bars, but this is one of the ultimate interpretations. The tart is filled with caramel and a creamy milk chocolate mousse, drizzled with more caramel, then topped with milk chocolate curls.

MILKY WAY TART

MAKES ONE 10-INCH TART (SERVES 8 TO 10)

MILK CHOCOLATE MOUSSE

- 5 ounces (140 grams) milk chocolate, chopped
- 2 cups (480 grams) heavy cream
- 2 teaspoons instant coffee powder
- ⅛ teaspoon kosher salt

CARAMEL FILLING

- ¾ cup (150 grams) sugar
- ⅓ cup (80 grams) water
- ¾ cup (180 grams) heavy cream
- 2 tablespoons (¼ stick/28 grams) unsalted butter
- ¼ teaspoon kosher salt
- 2 teaspoons vanilla extract

Pâte Sucrée 10-inch tart shell (page 69)
3- to 4-inch slab milk chocolate, at warm room temperature, for decorating

I got the idea for this tart many years ago from Maury Rubin's Book of Tarts, *and it has become a favorite of Flour customers. In the book, Rubin offers myriad creative, unconventional fillings for tarts, including the idea of re-creating the popular Milky Way candy bar in tart form. For the Flour version, I make a buttery caramel (which is a pretty amazing ice cream or dessert sauce in its own right) and layer it on the bottom of a sweet tart shell. Then I pile on a mound of light, fluffy milk chocolate mousse that has a hint of coffee flavor to give it extra depth and to keep it from being too sweet. More caramel is drizzled on top, and a shower of milk chocolate curls finishes it off. Of course, the finished tart tastes far better than any candy bar!*

TO MAKE THE MOUSSE Place the chocolate in a small heatproof bowl. In a medium saucepan, combine the cream and instant coffee and scald over medium-high heat (bubbles start to form around the edge of the pan, but the cream is not boiling). Pour the hot cream mixture over the chocolate and let sit for about 1 minute, then whisk gently until the chocolate is completely melted and the mixture is smooth. Strain through a fine-mesh sieve into a small container, stir in the salt, cover tightly, and refrigerate for at least 8 hours, or until it is absolutely, completely chilled, or up to 3 days. A few hours is *not* enough here. Because the cream has been heated, it will not whip properly unless it is very cold.

TO MAKE THE CARAMEL FILLING Place the sugar in the bottom of a medium saucepan and slowly pour in the water. Stir gently to moisten the sugar. If any sugar crystals are clinging to the sides of the pan, brush them down with a pastry brush dipped in water. Place the pan over high heat and leave it undisturbed until the mixture comes to a rolling boil. (You want to avoid crystallization of the syrup, which can happen if the pan is disturbed before the sugar starts to color.) Then continue to boil rapidly without moving the pan until the sugar syrup starts to caramelize. This will take 3 to 4

continued on page 65

milky way tart continued

EDITOR'S NOTE

We found that chilling the tart for at least 4 hours yielded the best results.

minutes: the sugar syrup will boil furiously; then as it thickens, it will boil more languidly; and then you will see some of the syrup starting to color and darken around the edge of the pan.

When you start to see color in the pan, gently swirl it in a circular motion so the sugar caramelizes evenly. The syrup will start to turn golden brown, and then as you swirl the pan, the syrup will continue to get a bit darker and then darker still. To check the true color of the caramel, tilt the pan so you can see the syrup covering the bottom. This is the actual color of the caramel, and you want to keep cooking the caramel until this layer is a deep amber-brown. It takes just seconds for caramel to go from great to burnt, so be sure to tilt and check constantly.

As soon as the caramel is ready, slowly add the cream and then reduce the heat to low. Be careful, because the steam that rises when the cream hits the caramel is extremely hot. Let the caramel and cream sputter for a few seconds, then whisk to mix. Turn up the heat to medium and whisk the caramel and cream (the mixture will have hardened a bit) for 2 to 3 minutes, or until combined. Whisk in the butter, salt, and vanilla. Remove from the heat, pour into an airtight heatproof container, and refrigerate for at least 4 hours or up to 1 week.

Place the tart shell on a flat plate. Spread about three-fourths of the caramel filling evenly in the bottom. Using a stand mixer fitted with the whip attachment (or a handheld mixer or a whisk), whip the mousse on medium speed until it holds soft peaks. Mound the mousse in the shell, and spread it evenly over the filling. Drizzle the remaining caramel filling in a crisscross pattern on top of the mousse. Using the back of a small knife, shave curls from the milk chocolate slab. (Make sure the chocolate is slightly warm, or you will get splinters instead of curls.) Decorate the tart with the curls.

Chill for at least 30 minutes before serving.

The tart can be refrigerated in an airtight container for up to 8 hours.

Milky Way is a registered trademark of Mars, Inc.

Chang's version of the old-fashioned pie is dreamy and satisfying but not overly sweet, and topped with a zesty lime whipped cream.

TOASTED COCONUT CREAM PIE
with lime whipped cream

MAKES ONE 9-INCH PIE (SERVES 8)

- 1¼ cups (300 grams) heavy cream
- 1 teaspoon finely grated lime zest
- 1 can (14 ounces/400 grams) coconut milk
- ½ cup (120 grams) milk
- ⅔ cup (140 grams) granulated sugar
- ⅓ cup (40 grams) cake flour
- 1 egg
- 4 egg yolks
- ¼ teaspoon vanilla extract
- ½ teaspoon kosher salt
- 1 cup (120 grams) sweetened shredded coconut, lightly toasted
- Pâte Sucrée 9-inch pie shell (recipe follows)
- 3 tablespoons confectioners' sugar
- 1 tablespoon cornstarch

Flour is not a pie bakery (much to the dismay of my husband, who is a pie addict), but every year during the holidays we pull out all the stops and make pies in almost every flavor. This one is a late addition to our holiday roster that was prompted by the dessert menu at Myers+Chang, our pan-Asian restaurant. Coconut and lime are common Southeast Asian flavors, so I combined them in a made-to-order tart that has become the most popular dessert at the restaurant. I adapted the tart for this pie, and it became one of the most popular holiday pies at Flour. As with the tart, the components of the pie can be made in advance and then easily combined the day you want to eat it. That makes a great pie even better.

In a small saucepan, combine the cream and lime zest over medium-high heat and bring just to a boil. Remove from the heat, pour into a small airtight container, let cool, and refrigerate overnight.

In a medium saucepan, combine the coconut milk and milk and scald over medium-high heat (bubbles start to form around the edge of the pan, but the liquid is not boiling). While the milks are heating, in a small bowl, whisk together the granulated sugar and flour. (Mixing the flour with the sugar will prevent the flour from clumping when you add it to the eggs.) In a medium heatproof bowl, whisk together the egg and egg yolks until blended, then slowly whisk in the sugar-flour mixture. The mixture will be thick and pasty.

continued on page 68

coconut cream pie continued

Slowly pour the hot milk mixture into the egg-sugar mixture, a little at a time, whisking constantly. When all of the milk mixture has been incorporated, return the contents of the bowl to the saucepan, and return the saucepan to medium heat. Cook, whisking vigorously and continuously, for 4 to 5 minutes, or until the mixture thickens and comes to a boil. Make sure you get the whisk into the corners of the saucepan and that you are scraping the bottom often. First, the mixture will be thin and frothy; as it gets hotter and the eggs start to cook, it will get thicker and start to steam. Eventually, it will start to boil, but because you will be whisking continuously (don't forget to do that!) and because the mixture is so thick, it will be hard for you to know when it is boiling. Once it is thick, stop whisking for a few seconds and watch the surface to see if it starts to blub up. If it goes blub blub, you will know that it has come to a boil. When that happens, whisk even more vigorously for 30 seconds, then immediately take the custard off the stove and pour it through a fine-mesh sieve into a heatproof pitcher. Whisk in the vanilla, salt, and ¾ cup (90 grams) of the toasted coconut. Pour into the baked pie shell and refrigerate, uncovered, for about 4 hours, or until the filling is set.

Fit a stand mixer with the whip attachment (or use a handheld mixer) and whip together the lime zest–cream mixture, the confectioners' sugar, and the cornstarch until stiff peaks form.

Pile the whipped cream on top of the coconut filling, spreading it to the edges of the pie. Decorate the pie with the remaining ¼ cup (30 grams) toasted coconut.

The pie can be stored in an airtight container in the refrigerator for up to 2 days.

PÂTE SUCRÉE

MAKES ONE FULLY BAKED 9-INCH PIE SHELL OR 10-INCH TART SHELL

- ½ cup (1 stick/114 grams) unsalted butter, at room temperature, cut into 8 pieces
- ¼ cup (50 grams) sugar
- ½ teaspoon kosher salt
- 1 cup (140 grams) unbleached all-purpose flour
- 1 egg yolk

Using a stand mixer fitted with the paddle attachment, cream together the butter, sugar, and salt on medium speed for 2 to 3 minutes, or until pale and light. Scrape the sides and bottom of the bowl with a rubber spatula. Add the flour and beat on low speed for about 30 seconds, or until the flour mixes with the butter-sugar mixture. The mixture will look like wet sand. Add the egg yolk and continue to mix on low speed for about 30 seconds, or until the dough comes together.

Wrap the dough tightly in plastic wrap and refrigerate for about 1 hour. (At this point, the dough can be stored in the refrigerator for up to 5 days or in the freezer for up to 2 weeks. If frozen, thaw it in the refrigerator overnight before using.)

If making a pie shell, have ready a 9-inch pie pan dish. If making a tart shell, line a baking sheet with parchment paper and place a 10-inch tart ring on top. Remove the dough from the refrigerator and let soften at room temperature for about 30 minutes. Using a rolling pin, bang and flatten the dough into a disk about ½ inch thick. Flour the work surface, and sprinkle the dough disk with a little flour. Roll out the dough into a circle 10 to 11 inches in diameter and about ¼ inch thick for a 9-inch pie shell, or about 12 inches in diameter and just under ¼ inch thick for a 10-inch tart shell. Make sure the work surface is well floured so the dough doesn't stick to it, and make sure the disk itself is floured well enough to keep the rolling pin from sticking to it. Roll from the center of the disk outward, and gently rotate the disk a quarter turn after each roll to ensure the disk is evenly stretched into a nice circle. Don't worry if the dough breaks a bit, especially toward the edges. You can easily patch any tears once you have lined the pan.

continued on page 70

pâte sucrée continued

Roll the dough circle around the pin and then unfurl it on top of the 9-inch pie pan or the 10-inch tart ring. Press the dough well into the bottom and sides of the pan or ring, and use any scraps or odd pieces to patch up any tears or missing bits. Make sure the entire interior is well covered with dough, and then press one last time all the way around to ensure any holes have been patched. Trim the edge of the dough so it is even with the rim of the pan or ring.

Refrigerate the pastry shell for at least 30 minutes. The gluten needs a little time to relax so the pastry doesn't shrink in the oven. (The pastry shell can be tightly wrapped in plastic wrap and refrigerated for up to 1 day or frozen for up to 2 weeks. Bake directly from the refrigerator or freezer.)

Position a rack in the center of the oven, and heat the oven to 350°F.

Bake for 30 to 35 minutes, or until golden brown. Let cool to room temperature on a wire rack. If you are making a tart shell, remove the tart ring. Proceed as directed in individual recipes.

BEST OF THE BEST EXCLUSIVE

Chang is known as a dessert superstar, but she also makes fantastic savory baked goods. The custardlike texture of this casserole comes from soaking the bread in eggs, half-and-half and Parmesan.

ASPARAGUS, THYME & PARMESAN BREAD PUDDING

SERVES 8 TO 10

- 2 large eggs
- 6 large egg yolks
- ¼ cup all-purpose flour
- 1 quart half-and-half
- 1 teaspoon chopped thyme
- 1 cup freshly grated Parmigiano-Reggiano cheese
- Kosher salt and freshly ground pepper
- 12 ounces day-old baguette, cut into ½-inch cubes (about 6 cups)
- 1 pound asparagus
- 1 tablespoon vegetable oil

EDITOR'S WINE CHOICE
Dry, fruity sparkling wine (see page 264)

1. In a large bowl, whisk together the eggs, egg yolks, flour, half-and-half, thyme, ¾ cup of the Parmigiano-Reggiano, 1½ teaspoons of salt and ½ teaspoon of pepper. Add the bread cubes and stir until evenly moistened. Transfer the bread mixture to a 9-by-13-inch baking dish and let stand at room temperature for 2 hours.

2. Preheat the oven to 400°F. On a rimmed baking sheet, toss the asparagus with the oil and season with salt and pepper. Roast for about 10 minutes, until just tender; let cool.

3. Reduce the oven temperature to 350°F. Cut the asparagus into ½-inch pieces and stir them into the bread mixture. Sprinkle the remaining ¼ cup of Parmigiano-Reggiano on top and bake the bread pudding for about 35 minutes, until risen and set. Let stand for 15 minutes before serving.

MAKE AHEAD The bread pudding can be prepared through Step 1 and refrigerated overnight. Bring to room temperature before baking.

JOANNE CHANG ONLINE

flourbakery.com

 @jbchang

Pea pesto crostini, page 77

GIADA AT HOME →06

Giada De Laurentiis

A meal at Food Network star Giada De Laurentiis's house is a little bit Old World Italian, a little bit seasonal Californian and always very low-stress: "As long as the food tastes amazing . . . I know that even my most discerning friends will appreciate the effort I've made—as well as the fact that I'm not too tired to sit down and enjoy it with them!" Her fifth cookbook, *Giada at Home* features the kinds of dishes she serves to family and friends. (And because it's her first book since having a daughter in 2008, the recipes are more time-conscious than ever before.) On the traditional side there's Cheesy Baked Farro, earthy and rich with mushrooms and three types of cheese, while the innovative Pea Pesto Crostini are a distinctly American creation, blending frozen peas with olive oil, garlic and Parmesan for an appetizer that comes together in 10 minutes. *Published by Clarkson Potter, $35*

With its chewy texture, farro is a terrific replacement for pasta in this variation on mac and cheese. The acid in the tomatoes helps balance the richness.

CHEESY BAKED FARRO

4 TO 6 SERVINGS

Vegetable oil cooking spray

SAUCE

- 4 tablespoons (½ stick) unsalted butter
- ¼ cup all-purpose flour
- 2 cups warm milk

Salt and freshly ground black pepper

FARRO

- 6 cups (1½ quarts) low-sodium chicken broth
- 2 cups farro, rinsed and drained
- 2 tablespoons olive oil, plus more for drizzling
- 2 cups assorted mushrooms (such as button, cremini, or portobello), cleaned and sliced

Salt and freshly ground black pepper

- ¾ cup halved cherry or grape tomatoes
- 2½ cups freshly grated Parmesan cheese
- 1 cup (4 ounces) grated Gruyère cheese
- ½ cup (about 1 ounce) grated Fontina cheese
- 1 teaspoon chopped fresh thyme leaves
- ½ cup plain dried bread crumbs

EDITOR'S WINE CHOICE
Juicy, spicy Grenache (see page 268)

AUTHOR'S NOTE
Use farro in salads, pilafs, and soups as you would use barley, which is also a good substitute for farro.

We think of mac and cheese as a true-blue American invention, but this homey dish, made with nutty farro, is actually very traditional. Farro is one of the first cultivated grains and was ground to make bread, cereals, and pasta in ancient Italy. It's becoming more popular in this country, but you still may need to visit an Italian specialty store to find it.

Preheat the oven to 400°F. Spray a 9-by-13-inch baking dish with cooking spray.

FOR THE SAUCE In a 2-quart saucepan, melt the butter over medium heat. Add the flour and whisk until smooth. Gradually add the warm milk, whisking constantly to prevent lumps. Simmer over medium heat, whisking constantly, until the sauce is thick and smooth, about 8 minutes (do not allow the mixture to boil). Remove from the heat and season with salt and pepper.

FOR THE FARRO In an 8-quart stockpot, bring the chicken broth to a boil over medium-high heat. Add the farro, lower the heat, and simmer, stirring occasionally, until tender, about 25 minutes. Drain if necessary.

In a large skillet, heat the oil over medium-high heat. Add the mushrooms and season with salt and pepper. Cook the mushrooms, stirring occasionally, for 8 minutes or until tender. Add the tomatoes to the pan and cook for 2 to 3 minutes, until tender.

In a large bowl, combine the Parmesan cheese, Gruyère cheese, Fontina cheese, and thyme. Remove ½ cup of the mixture and set aside. Add the cooked farro, sauce, and mushroom mixture to the cheeses. Stir until combined. Season with salt and pepper. Pour the mixture into the prepared baking dish and sprinkle with the ½ cup reserved cheese mixture. Sprinkle the top with bread crumbs and drizzle with olive oil.

Bake until the top is golden brown and forms a crust, 25 to 30 minutes. Remove from the oven and let stand for 5 minutes before serving.

Who needs croutons when you can have cheesy crostini? They're delicious with a classic, refreshing salad like this one, which is served with a lemony dressing.

BIBB, BASIL & MINT SALAD

with parmesan butter crostini

4 TO 6 SERVINGS

CROSTINI

- ½ baguette loaf, cut into ½-inch-thick slices
- ¼ cup (½ stick) unsalted butter, at room temperature
- ⅓ cup freshly grated Parmesan cheese

SALAD

- 3 tablespoons fresh lemon juice (from 1 lemon)
- 3 tablespoons olive oil
- Salt and freshly ground black pepper
- 1 head Bibb or butter lettuce, leaves torn
- 1 medium fennel bulb, trimmed and thinly sliced
- ⅓ packed cup fresh basil leaves, chopped
- ⅓ packed cup fresh mint leaves, chopped

You always need a simple, elegant green salad in your repertoire. What I love are the buttery and cheesy crostini, so you get your healthy, leafy vegetable with a little indulgence.

FOR THE CROSTINI Place an oven rack in the lower third of the oven and preheat the oven to 375°F.

Arrange the bread slices in a single layer on a rimmed baking sheet. Bake for 10 to 12 minutes, until golden.

Meanwhile, in a small bowl, using a fork, mix the butter and cheese together until smooth.

FOR THE SALAD In a salad bowl, whisk together the lemon juice and oil until smooth. Season with salt and pepper. Add the lettuce, fennel, basil, and mint and toss well.

Spread the Parmesan butter on the crostini and serve alongside the salad.

GIADA DE LAURENTIIS ONLINE

giadadelaurentiis.com

Giada De Laurentiis

@GDeLaurentiis

Even top chefs will use frozen peas instead of fresh. The freezer staple and pantry ingredients come together here for a fun, quick appetizer.

PEA PESTO CROSTINI

4 TO 6 SERVINGS

- One 10-ounce package frozen peas, thawed
- 1 garlic clove
- ½ cup freshly grated Parmesan cheese
- 1 teaspoon salt, plus more to taste
- ¼ teaspoon freshly ground black pepper, plus more to taste
- ⅔ cup olive oil
- Eight ½-inch-thick slices whole-grain baguette or ciabatta bread, preferably day-old (see Author's Note)
- 8 cherry tomatoes, halved, or 1 small tomato, diced

EDITOR'S WINE CHOICE
Peppery, refreshing Grüner Veltliner (see page 265)

AUTHOR'S NOTE
Day-old bread works best here because it stands up to the pea puree and isn't too soft in the center. If you don't have any on hand, you can dry out fresh bread by putting the slices in a 300°F oven until slightly crisp, about 5 minutes.

I don't keep a lot in my freezer, but one thing you'll always find there is a package of frozen peas. They're sweet, they have a lovely green color, and when pureed they can satisfy a craving for a starchy food. If you're not a big fan of peas, at least give this a try. I think it's going to be your new favorite thing. I can't resist eating it straight out of the bowl!

FOR THE PEA PESTO Pulse together in a food processor the peas, garlic, Parmesan cheese, salt, and pepper. With the machine running, slowly add ⅓ cup of the olive oil and continue to mix until well combined, 1 to 2 minutes. Season with more salt and pepper, if needed. Transfer to a small bowl and set aside.

FOR THE CROSTINI Preheat a stovetop griddle or grill pan over medium-high.

Brush both sides of each of the bread slices with the remaining ⅓ cup olive oil and grill until golden, 1 to 2 minutes. Transfer the bread to a platter and spread 1 to 2 tablespoons pesto on each slice. Top each crostini with 2 tomato halves and serve.

Frank Falcinelli (left) and Frank Castronovo

PHOTOGRAPH BY SIMON WATSON

THE FRANKIES SPUNTINO KITCHEN COMPANION & COOKING MANUAL → 07

Frank Falcinelli, Frank Castronovo & Peter Meehan

Leather-bound and gilt-edged, the first cookbook from Frank Falcinelli and Frank Castronovo looks formal. But inside, it has a hip, casual feel. This homey companion to Falcinelli and Castronovo's pair of Frankies Spuntino restaurants (one in Manhattan, one in Brooklyn) is all about the chefs' modern take on Italian American food. The recipes mix nostalgia for their grandmothers' cooking with creative interpretations, as in their orecchiette with a pistachio pesto that emphasizes nuts over herbs, or the baked eggplant made sweet-and-sour with a caramel-spiked tomato sauce. Throughout, the Franks coach you with chef-y tips (use white pepper instead of black), ideas for keeping costs down (choose pecorino over Parmesan) and hippie-Zen wisdom like, "Grandma never broke a sweat. Neither should you."

Published by Artisan, $24.95

The large amount of parsley and drizzle of dark green pumpkinseed oil give this salad an unexpected mix of Italian and Central European flavors.

FENNEL, CELERY ROOT, PARSLEY & RED ONION SALAD *with lemon & olive oil*

SERVES 4

- ½ celery root
- 1 fennel bulb, with stems removed
- ⅔ cup sliced red onion
- 2 packed cups flat-leaf parsley leaves
- ¼ cup olive oil, or more to taste
- Juice of ½ lemon
- ½ teaspoon fine sea salt
- 16 turns white pepper
- Pumpkinseed oil, for drizzling (optional)
- Pecorino Romano, to taste

Although we make it all year round, this salad is really a godsend in the winter when you're looking for that refreshing fresh-vegetable crunch and something bright and light. The two things that make it stand out: the amount of parsley—it should practically be a parsley salad, with the other vegetables lending it texture—and the finishing touch of pumpkinseed oil, which, combined with the white pepper in the dressing, gives a depth of flavor to the salad.

1. Peel the celery root and cut it into fine julienne. Trim the fennel bulb, discarding tough stems and reserving any fresh, pert fronds to garnish the salad, and julienne. (You should have in the neighborhood of 2 cups of each.)

2. Toss the cut vegetables together with the parsley in a large bowl. Add the oil, lemon juice, salt, and white pepper and toss again. Taste and add more oil, salt, and/or lemon juice as needed.

3. Divide the salad among serving plates. Finish each with a drizzle of pumpkinseed oil and a few curls of Pecorino Romano (cut with a vegetable peeler) and serve.

The luscious sauce for this vegetarian dish gets its great sweet-and-sour taste from a caramel base made with sugar, water and wine vinegar.

SWEET & SOUR BAKED EGGPLANT

with mint & ricotta salata

SERVES 6 AS AN APPETIZER

- ¼ cup water
- ¼ cup sugar
- ¼ cup wine vinegar
- One 28-ounce can San Marzano tomatoes, crushed by hand
- 2 garlic cloves, thinly sliced
- ½ cup extra-virgin olive oil
- Fine sea salt and freshly ground white pepper
- 2 large eggplants (about 1¼ pounds each), sliced into ¾-inch-thick disks
- ½ cup shredded ricotta salata
- ¼ cup chopped mint

EDITOR'S WINE CHOICE
Juicy, fresh Dolcetto
(see page 268)

We picked up this preparation in Sicily, where they're totally attuned to the affinity that eggplant has for sugar. This is a good way to vary the routine when you burn out on the Eggplant Marinara.

1. Combine the water and sugar in a small saucepan and stir over high heat until the sugar dissolves. Cook without stirring until a light amber caramel forms. Off the heat, add the vinegar; be careful—it will bubble furiously. Cook over very low heat just until the caramel dissolves again, about 1 minute.

2. Add the crushed tomatoes, garlic, and ¼ cup of oil to the caramel. Season with salt and white pepper. Simmer over moderately low heat until the sauce is thickened, about 30 minutes.

3. Meanwhile, preheat the oven to 400°F. Brush a large baking sheet with 2 tablespoons of oil. Arrange the eggplant on the sheet, brush with the remaining 2 tablespoons oil, and season with salt and pepper. Roast the eggplant 10 minutes, then flip and roast for 10 minutes longer, or until tender and lightly golden. Remove from the oven (leaving the oven on).

4. Arrange the eggplant slices in slightly overlapping rows in an 8-by-11-inch baking dish. Spoon two-thirds of the tomato sauce on top and bake for 20 minutes, or until bubbling and browned around the edges.

5. Sprinkle with cheese and mint and serve, passing the remaining sauce on the side.

Instead of using beef round or another inexpensive cut, this recipe calls for top-quality rib-eye roast. The result: sensational roast beef.

SLOW-ROASTED RIB EYE, SLICED COLD

SERVES 6 TO 9, THOUGH YOU WOULDN'T WANT TO END UP WITHOUT LEFTOVERS

- 1 sprig rosemary, leaves stripped and finely chopped
- 1 tablespoon finely chopped thyme leaves
- 2 tablespoons finely chopped flat-leaf parsley
- 4 cloves garlic, finely chopped
- 2 tablespoons olive oil
- One 2½- to 3-pound boneless rib-eye roast
- 1 tablespoon fine sea salt
- Freshly ground white pepper

EDITOR'S WINE CHOICE

Complex, aromatic Nebbiolo (see page 269)

We slow roast the rib eye, let it rest, and then chill it. And then a very special thing happens: it magically becomes the best roast beef ever. Not your deli-variety roast beef, but a thoroughbred version of it.

Serve the beef with some kind of salad, or a few tomatoes and red onions simply sliced and seasoned with olive oil, salt, and black pepper.

1. Combine the herbs, garlic, and olive oil in a small bowl. Smear this mixture all over the beef. Put the beef in a baking dish, cover, and allow to season in the refrigerator for as long as 24 hours.

2. Heat the oven to 375°F. Put the beef in a roasting pan or on a rimmed baking sheet (it shouldn't render too much fat during cooking) and rub it all over with the salt and white pepper to taste.

3. Pop the beef into the oven. After 15 minutes, turn the heat down to 325°F. Roast for 45 minutes more, or until a thermometer inserted into the thickest part of the rib eye reads 118°F. Remove the beef from the pan and let it rest, uncovered, for at least 45 minutes.

4. Wrap the beef in plastic, put it in the fridge, and hold it for up to a couple of days before serving.

5. Cut the beef into ½-inch-thick slices and serve.

Ear-like orecchiette are ideal here because they scoop up the supernutty pistachio pesto sauce. This dish would be lovely served alongside prosciutto.

ORECCHIETTE WITH PISTACHIOS

SERVES 4

Fine sea salt
- 1½ cups shelled unsalted green pistachios, preferably Sicilian
- 1 clove minced garlic
- 2 tablespoons finely chopped mint
- ½ cup extra-virgin olive oil, plus extra for serving
- ½ cup grated Pecorino Romano
- 1 pound orecchiette
- 4 scallions, white and light green parts only, julienned long and fine

EDITOR'S WINE CHOICE
Fresh, lively Soave
(see page 267)

This pasta sauce is what we think of in the States as a pesto, but with the ratio of nuts to herbs flip-flopped. The main ingredients are Sicilian in emphasis: the Sicilian pistachios, which are incredibly sweet and fruity, not like the cheap ones we eat in front of the TV here; and some mint, which reflects the North African influence on Sicilian cuisine.

1. Put a large pot of water on to boil and salt it well.

2. Meanwhile, roughly chop the pistachios by hand or in a food processor. Toss the pistachios with the garlic, mint, and olive oil in a small mixing bowl. Add the cheese and a large pinch of salt and stir to combine.

3. Cook the pasta in the boiling water until al dente, following the package directions. Drain, reserving ½ cup of the pasta cooking water, and return the pasta to the pot over low heat.

4. Add the pesto to the pot, along with the reserved pasta cooking water, and heat, tossing constantly, until the orecchiette are coated with the sauce. Transfer to bowls or a serving platter, garnish with the scallions, and serve, passing additional olive oil at the table.

FRANKIES
17
clinton street • new york, ny

BEST OF THE BEST EXCLUSIVE

Using rabbit in a ragù is smart: It's tender and delicious and it doesn't dry out like chicken might. The olives bring a depth of flavor. Add them twice: first while the sauce is cooking and again right before serving.

RABBIT RAGÙ

with pappardelle & sicilian olives

SERVES 6

- ½ cup chopped flat-leaf parsley
- ½ cup Sicilian olives, pitted and halved (about 2 ounces)
- 2 tablespoons brine-packed capers with their liquid
- ¼ cup extra-virgin olive oil
- One 3½-pound rabbit, cut into 8 pieces
- Salt and freshly ground white pepper
- 1 fennel bulb—quartered, cored and thinly sliced
- 2 garlic cloves, smashed
- ¼ cup dry white wine
- 1 cup chicken stock or low-sodium broth
- One 28-ounce can crushed tomatoes
- 1 bay leaf
- 1 pound pappardelle, preferably fresh
- 2 tablespoons freshly grated Pecorino Romano cheese, plus more for serving

EDITOR'S WINE CHOICE
Cherry-inflected, earthy Sangiovese (see page 269)

FRANKIES ONLINE
frankiesspuntino.com
 @franksspuntino

1. Preheat the oven to 325°F. In a small bowl, combine the parsley, olives and capers with their liquid.

2. In a large enameled cast-iron casserole or Dutch oven, heat 2 tablespoons of the olive oil. Season the rabbit pieces with salt and pepper and add them to the casserole. Cook over moderately high heat, turning once, until golden brown, about 3 minutes per side. Transfer the rabbit pieces to a plate.

3. Pour off the fat from the casserole and wipe it clean with a paper towel. Heat the remaining 2 tablespoons of olive oil in the casserole and add the fennel. Cook over moderate heat, stirring, until just tender, about 5 minutes. Add the garlic and cook until fragrant, about 1 minute. Add the wine and chicken stock and bring to a boil, scraping up any browned bits from the bottom of the casserole. Add the tomatoes, bay leaf and half the parsley, olive and caper mixture and bring to a simmer. Nestle the rabbit in the sauce. Cover and braise in the oven for about 1 hour, until tender.

4. Transfer the rabbit to a plate and let cool slightly. Simmer the sauce over moderately low heat until thickened, about 15 minutes. Pull the rabbit meat from the bones and shred it. Return the meat to the sauce and add the remaining parsley, olive and caper mixture. Season the ragù with salt and pepper and keep warm.

5. In a large pot of boiling salted water, cook the pappardelle until al dente. Drain the pasta well and toss with the ragù and the 2 tablespoons of cheese. Serve with additional Pecorino Romano.

MAKE AHEAD The rabbit ragù can be prepared through Step 4 and refrigerated in an airtight container for up to 3 days or frozen for up to 1 month. Rewarm before serving.

Roast chicken with basil, scallion, lemon butter and potatoes, page 88

A BIRD IN THE OVEN & THEN SOME

→08

Mindy Fox

More chefs and home cooks are buying responsibly raised chickens, a trend that prompted food writer Mindy Fox to dedicate an entire cookbook to the bird. For a single-ingredient cookbook, *A Bird in the Oven* covers a huge amount of ground: the "Roasting the Bird" chapter has 20 recipes alone, from simple Roast Chicken with Basil, Scallion, Lemon Butter and Potatoes to variations that use Greek, Jamaican, Chinese and Peruvian flavors. After those basic preparations, Fox gets really creative, spinning out 80 additional ideas for sides and new main courses—ranging from pastas to stews to pizzas—using leftover meat. She tucks the chicken into steamed buns with sweet-and-spicy sauce and cool cucumbers, and folds it into winey, cheesy farro cooked slowly like risotto. *Published by Kyle Books, $24.95*

A few additions—basil, scallion and lemon—help upgrade the standard roast chicken. The bird is juicy and the potatoes soak up the lemony drippings.

ROAST CHICKEN

with basil, scallion, lemon butter & potatoes

SERVES 4

One 4-pound whole chicken
- 1 cup thinly sliced basil leaves
- 5 tablespoons unsalted butter, at room temperature
- 2 lemons
- 5 garlic cloves, very thinly sliced
- 2 scallions, very thinly sliced

Flaky coarse sea salt
Freshly ground black pepper
- 1¾ pounds small to medium potatoes (about 1½ inches in diameter), cut lengthwise into quarters
- 2 tablespoons extra-virgin olive oil

About ½ good-sized bunch parsley, stems trimmed to 1 inch (1½ packed cups)

EDITOR'S WINE CHOICE
Ripe, luxurious Chardonnay (see page 265)

I'll never tire of a butter-rubbed chicken roasted with rich, earthy potatoes tucked along its edges. Still, it's nice to update the classic pairing with a simple tweak or two. Here, when the bird is almost done, I sprinkle whole parsley leaves and squeeze a few lemon quarters over the potatoes, then pop the whole thing back into the oven. The herb leaves crisp up and the lemon pieces caramelize. Some might find the lemon rinds intense, but if you like that sort of thing, you'll enjoy sliced bits of them with the rest of the dish.

Preheat the oven to 450°F with the rack in the middle. Pull off excess fat around the cavities of the chicken and discard, then rinse the chicken and pat dry very well, inside and out. From the edge of the cavity, slip a finger under the skin of each of the breasts, then gently but thoroughly loosen the skin from the meat of the breasts and thighs.

Put the basil and butter in a bowl. Finely zest the lemons into the bowl, holding the zester close so that you capture the flavorful oil that sprays from the lemons as you zest. Add the garlic and scallions and mix together to thoroughly combine.

Using your hands and working with about 1 tablespoon of the butter mixture at a time, gently push the mixture into the spaces you created between the chicken skin and meat, being careful not to tear the skin. As you work the mixture in, gently rub your hand over the outside of the skin to smooth out the mixture and push it farther down between the skin and meat where you may not be able to reach with your hand.

Season the chicken all over, using 2 to 3 teaspoons coarse salt and generous pepper, then tie the legs together with kitchen string. In a large bowl, toss the potatoes with oil, ½ teaspoon salt, and a generous grind of pepper to coat well. Cut 1 lemon into quarters and set aside.

AUTHOR'S NOTE
My favorite potatoes to use for this dish are a mix of farmers' market varieties, including fingerlings, Adirondack Reds and Blues, yellow Carolas, and more. It's fine to purchase potatoes of different shapes and sizes; just be sure to cut them into roughly same-size pieces so that they cook through at the same rate.

Put a roasting pan (not nonstick) or 9-by-13-inch baking dish in the oven to heat for 10 minutes. Remove the pan from the oven and immediately put the potatoes and any oil left in the bowl into the pan, keeping them in as much of a single layer as possible, and pushed to the edges of the pan to make room for the chicken (it's fine if the bird sits on some of the potatoes); put the chicken into the pan, breast-side up.

Roast for 20 minutes, then remove the pan from the oven and turn the chicken breast-side down. Continue to roast for another 20 minutes, then remove the pan from the oven and turn the bird breast-side up again. Sprinkle the parsley over the potatoes, then stir the parsley and potatoes to coat with the pan drippings. Squeeze 3 pieces of the cut lemon over the chicken, and put the squeezed rinds into the roasting pan. Continue to roast until the juices of the chicken run clear when the thigh is pierced with a fork, 20 to 30 minutes more.

Remove from the oven and let the chicken rest in the pan for 15 minutes, then transfer to a cutting board. Let rest for another 5 minutes, then carve. Spoon the pan juices over the chicken and serve with the potatoes and roasted lemons.

The unconventional pesto for this pasta dish uses raw spinach and omits the Parmesan, which makes the sauce healthier and gives it a superfresh flavor.

STROZZAPRETI
with spinach-basil pesto & ricotta salata

SERVES 4

Good basic kitchen salt, like kosher (for water)
One 10-ounce bunch spinach, tough stems removed (about 5 cups packed)
1 cup packed fresh basil leaves
3 tablespoons pine nuts
1 garlic clove, peeled
Fine sea salt
6 tablespoons extra-virgin olive oil
1 pound strozzapreti, or other short pasta
2½ cups finely shredded roast chicken, at room temperature
Good-quality extra-virgin olive oil for drizzling
2 ounces ricotta salata cheese, thinly shaved

Strozzapreti, "priest strangler" in Italian, are fun twisty short pasta. Other short types, like farfalle, fusilli, orecchiette, and rotelle ("wagon wheels"), work well here, too. The combination of spinach and basil makes for a healthy, bright green pesto, and ricotta salata—a fresh-tasting, mildly salty cheese—adds a slightly nutty touch.

Bring a large pot of well-salted water to a boil.

In a food processor, combine the spinach, basil, pine nuts, garlic, and ½ teaspoon fine sea salt. With the machine running, add the oil in a slow and steady stream; puree until smooth.

Cook the pasta in the boiling water until al dente. Reserving ¼ cup of the cooking liquid, drain the pasta, then add it back to the pot off the heat. Immediately add the pesto and chicken, and stir to combine thoroughly. Moisten with 2 tablespoons of the pasta cooking liquid, or more, if desired.

Serve immediately, drizzled with a touch of good oil and topped with the cheese and extra salt to taste.

EDITOR'S WINE CHOICE
Zippy, fresh Pinot Bianco (see page 266)

AUTHOR'S NOTE
A great way to wash greens is to plug up the sink and fill it with cold water, then plunge in the greens and swish them around. Let the greens sit undisturbed for a few minutes, then carefully lift them out of the water without disturbing the grit, which will have fallen to the bottom of the sink. Drain and rinse out the sink, then repeat as necessary.

Making the steamed dough here is a bit of a project, but the buns are so fluffy, light and sweet, they're even good with store-bought roast chicken.

CHINESE ROAST CHICKEN BUNS

with scallion & spicy hoisin sauce

SERVES 4

- 1 cup unbleached all-purpose flour
- ½ cup cake flour
- 1½ teaspoons active dry yeast
- 1½ teaspoons sugar
- ⅛ teaspoon fine sea salt
- ½ cup warm water (around 105°F)
- 1 teaspoon vegetable oil, plus more for brushing dough
- 1 pound sliced roast chicken, white and/or dark meat, preferably with skin (3½ to 4 cups)
- Hoisin sauce
- Sriracha sauce
- 1 medium cucumber, thinly sliced crosswise
- 5 to 6 scallions, julienned or thinly sliced on a long diagonal

SPECIAL EQUIPMENT

A pasta pot with a deep perforated colander-steamer insert or a bamboo or metal steamer

EDITOR'S WINE CHOICE

Fruity, soft Chenin Blanc (see page 265)

Tender meat—often pork, though here, it's chicken—sweet, garlicky hoisin sauce, cooling cucumber, and scallion all tucked into soft pillowy steamed dough; no wonder everyone seems crazy for Chinese buns these days. Packaged buns can be purchased at Asian markets if you don't have time to make and steam your own dough.

In a large bowl, whisk together the flour, cake flour, yeast, sugar, and salt; add the water and oil. Using your hands, mix and then knead in the bowl until a dough forms (add up to ¼ cup more water by the tablespoonful, if necessary). Turn out the dough onto a lightly floured work surface and knead until smooth and elastic, about 5 minutes. Put the dough into an oiled bowl, turning the dough to coat it with oil, then cover with a clean dishtowel and let rise at a draft-free warm room temperature until doubled in size, 45 minutes to 1 hour. Meanwhile, cut out 12 (2½-by-2½-inch) squares of parchment paper.

Punch down the dough and form it into a 1¾-inch-thick rope. Cut into 12 equal pieces. Roll each piece into a ball. Place the balls on a baking sheet, cover loosely with plastic wrap, and let rise at warm room temperature for 30 minutes.

Pat each ball into a long oval, about 5 by 2 inches, ⅛ inch thick. Brush 1 oval with oil, then fold in half crosswise, place on a parchment square, and brush with oil. Place on a baking sheet and repeat with the remaining dough pieces. Loosely cover the buns with plastic wrap and let rise at a warm room temperature until nearly doubled in size, about 30 minutes.

Bring a few inches of water to a simmer in a pot so that the bottom of a steamer insert sits above the water. Arrange the buns, in batches, if necessary, about ½ inch apart, on the insert and steam over medium heat, covered, until the dough is slightly puffed and cooked through, about 10 minutes.

Layer each bun with chicken, hoisin, Sriracha, cucumber, and scallions.

This dish is reminiscent of risotto but has a wonderful chewy texture. The fresh herbs added at the end are excellent with the luxurious farrotto.

FARROTTO
with roast chicken & herbs

SERVES 4

- 2 tablespoons extra-virgin olive oil, plus more for drizzling
- 2 tablespoons unsalted butter
- 1 cup finely chopped onion (from 1 small to medium)
- 1 garlic clove, finely chopped
- Flaky coarse sea salt
- 2 cups farro
- ½ cup dry white wine
- 4½ cups chicken broth, preferably homemade, heated to a simmer
- ½ teaspoon fine sea salt
- ¾ cup freshly grated Parmigiano-Reggiano cheese, plus more for serving
- 1½ cups medium shreds roast chicken (dark and/or white meat)
- ⅓ cup chopped mixed fresh herbs, such as basil, marjoram, parsley, thyme, and chives
- Freshly ground black pepper

EDITOR'S WINE CHOICE
Bright, tart Barbera
(see page 267)

I love farrotto, a dish cooked like risotto, but with farro in place of rice. Hot broth is added to the grain little by little until it is tender, creamy, and deeply flavorful. A conscious eye and stirring as needed are all that's required. For proper cooking, keep the broth covered, and re-simmer it, if necessary, so it stays hot. You want a tender, yet firm to the bite (not overcooked, mushy), farrotto. Letting the finished dish sit covered for 5 minutes before serving completes the cooking. Trust the process and the dish will be perfect.

Heat the oil and butter in a heavy large saucepan or Dutch oven over medium heat until the butter is melted. Add the onion, garlic, and a generous pinch of salt. Reduce the heat to low and cook, stirring occasionally, until softened (do not brown), about 7 minutes. Add the farro, stir to coat with the oil mixture, and cook, stirring occasionally, for 2 minutes more.

Add the wine and cook, stirring frequently, until the wine evaporates, about 5 minutes. Then add ½ cup of the hot broth and cook, stirring occasionally, until the broth is almost fully evaporated (when the spoon scrapes the bottom of the pan, you should see hardly any liquid, though you do not want the farro to stick to the bottom). Cook this "low and slow." Each addition of broth should take about 7 minutes to fully evaporate; reduce the heat if necessary. Continue to add the broth, in ½ cupfuls, until the farrotto is tender, yet still firm to the bite (you should have about 1 cup broth left over), then remove from the heat, stir in the fine sea salt, cover, and let sit for 5 minutes.

Stir in the cheese, ¼ cup at a time, then stir in the chicken and herbs. Add ⅓ to ½ cup of the remaining broth to moisten the farrotto, then spoon into shallow bowls. Spoon a couple teaspoons broth over and around the edges of each serving, drizzle with oil, and sprinkle with more cheese, coarse salt, and pepper.

BEST OF THE BEST EXCLUSIVE

Two extra steps—roasting the onions and adding garlic and pistachios to the mayonnaise—turn an everyday chicken salad into something more interesting.

ROAST CHICKEN SALAD

with pistachio aioli & roasted red onion

SERVES 6

- ½ cup unsalted shelled pistachios (about 2 ounces)
- 2 large red onions, sliced into ¼-inch-thick rings
- ¼ cup extra-virgin olive oil
- Kosher salt and freshly ground pepper
- 2 garlic cloves
- ½ cup mayonnaise
- 2 tablespoons fresh lemon juice
- One 3- to 4-pound rotisserie chicken, skin and bones discarded, meat shredded (about 4 cups)
- 2 endives, halved lengthwise and cut crosswise into ½-inch-thick slices
- 2 cups packed mesclun (about 2 ounces)

EDITOR'S WINE CHOICE

Full-bodied, rich Pinot Gris (see page 266)

1. Preheat the oven to 425°F. Spread the pistachios in a pie plate and toast for about 5 minutes, until golden brown and fragrant; let cool completely. In a food processor, pulse all but 2 tablespoons of the pistachios until finely chopped.

2. On a large rimmed baking sheet, toss the onions with 2 tablespoons of the olive oil and season with salt and pepper. Spread the onions in an even layer and roast for about 25 minutes, tossing once, until golden brown. Transfer the onions to a plate and let cool.

3. On a work surface, using the flat side of a knife, crush the garlic with a pinch of salt, then smash to a smooth paste. In a medium bowl, whisk the garlic paste with the finely chopped pistachios, mayonnaise, 1 tablespoon of the lemon juice and 1 tablespoon of the olive oil. Add the shredded chicken and toss to coat. Season the chicken salad with salt and pepper.

4. In a medium bowl, toss the roasted onions with the endives, mesclun and the remaining 1 tablespoon each of lemon juice and olive oil. Season with salt and pepper. Mound the greens on plates and top with the chicken salad. Coarsely chop the remaining 2 tablespoons of pistachios, sprinkle over the salads and serve.

MAKE AHEAD The chicken salad can be prepared through Step 3 and refrigerated overnight.

Greenspan's go-to beef daube,
page 98

AROUND MY FRENCH TABLE

→ 09

Dorie Greenspan

Dorie Greenspan boils down over three decades of living and traveling in France into this fantastic cookbook—a thorough guide to cooking like the French do. Not at Michelin-starred restaurants, but at home, where old bistro standards (beef daube) meet simple finger food (salmon rillettes) and international flavors (this has to be the first French cookbook with recipes for guacamole, hummus and Asian-style spareribs). Greenspan mixes her own personal recipes, like a light vegetable pot-au-feu, with ones from her favorite Paris restaurants, close friends and a few famous chefs, including Daniel Boulud and Pierre Hermé. She aims at an American audience—for instance, by using Cornish hens instead of French *poussins*, which are tough to find. The satisfying results are "dishes you don't need a Grand Diplôme from Le Cordon Bleu to make." *Published by Houghton Mifflin Harcourt, $40*

It's worth letting the stew simmer for hours: The beef becomes wonderfully tender. Serve this daube with wide egg noodles to sop up the rich sauce.

MY GO-TO BEEF DAUBE

MAKES 6 SERVINGS

- 4 slices thick-cut bacon, cut crosswise into 1-inch-wide pieces
- One 3½-pound beef chuck roast, fat and any sinews removed, cut into 2- to 3-inch cubes
- 2 tablespoons mild oil (such as grapeseed or canola)
- Salt and freshly ground pepper
- 2 yellow onions or 1 Spanish onion, quartered and thinly sliced
- 6 shallots, thinly sliced
- 1 garlic head, halved horizontally, only loose papery peel removed
- 1½ pounds carrots, trimmed, peeled, halved crosswise, and halved or quartered lengthwise, depending on thickness
- ½ pound parsnips, trimmed, peeled, halved crosswise, and quartered lengthwise (optional)
- ¼ cup Cognac or other brandy
- One 750-ml bottle fruity red wine (I know this may sound sacrilegious, but a Central Coast Syrah is great here)
- A bouquet garni—2 thyme sprigs, 2 parsley sprigs, 1 rosemary sprig, and the leaves from 1 celery stalk, tied together in a dampened piece of cheesecloth

EDITOR'S WINE CHOICE
Firm, complex Cabernet Sauvignon (see page 268)

We all need a great beef stew in our cooking back pocket, and this one's mine. It's fairly classic in its preparation—the meat is browned, then piled into a sturdy pot and slow-roasted with a lot of red wine, a splash of brandy, and some onions, garlic, carrots, and a little herb bouquet to keep it company. It finishes spoon-tender, sweet and winey through and through, and burnished the color of great-grandma's armoire.

My first-choice cut for this stew is chuck, which I buy whole and cut into 2- to 3-inch cubes myself. Since the meat is going to cook leisurely and soften, it's good to have larger pieces—larger than the chunks that are usually cut for stews—that will hold their shape better. (If you've got a butcher, you can ask to have the meat cut at the shop.) My favorite go-alongs are mashed potatoes, celery root puree, or spaetzle.

If you're serving a crowd, you can certainly double the recipe, but if the crowd is larger than a dozen, I'd suggest you divide the daube between two pots, or put it in a large roasting pan and stir it a few times while it's in the oven.

Center a rack in the oven and preheat the oven to 350°F.

Put a Dutch oven over medium heat and toss in the bacon. Cook, stirring, just until the bacon browns, then transfer to a bowl.

Dry the beef between sheets of paper towels. Add 1 tablespoon of the oil to the bacon fat in the pot and warm it over medium-high heat, then brown the beef, in batches, on all sides. Don't crowd the pot—if you try to cook too many pieces at once, you'll steam the meat rather than brown it—and make sure that each piece gets good color. Transfer the browned meat to the bowl with the bacon and season lightly with salt and pepper.

Pour off the oil in the pot (don't remove any browned bits stuck to the bottom), add the remaining tablespoon of oil, and warm it over medium heat. Add the onions and shallots, season lightly with salt and pepper, and cook, stirring, until the onions soften, about 8

AUTHOR'S NOTE
I call this dish a *daube*, which means it's a stew cooked in wine and also means that it's made in a *daubière*, or a deep casserole, in my case, an enamel-coated cast-iron Dutch oven. However, a French friend took issue with the name and claimed that what I make, while *très délicieuse*, is not a *daube*, but *boeuf aux carottes*, or beef and carrots. She's not wrong, but I'm stubbornly sticking with *daube* because it gives me the leeway to play around.

minutes. Toss in the garlic, carrots, and parsnips, if you're using them, and give everything a few good turns to cover all the ingredients with a little oil. Pour in the brandy, turn up the heat, and stir well to loosen whatever may be clinging to the bottom of the pot. Let the brandy boil for a minute, then return the beef and bacon to the pot, pour in the wine, and toss in the bouquet garni. Once again, give everything a good stir.

When the wine comes to a boil, cover the pot tightly with a piece of aluminum foil and the lid. Slide the daube into the oven and allow it to braise undisturbed for 1 hour.

Pull the pot out of the oven, remove the lid and foil, and stir everything up once. If it looks as if the liquid is reducing by a great deal (unlikely), add just enough water to cover the ingredients. Re-cover the pot with the foil and lid, slip it back into the oven, and cook for another 1½ hours (total time is 2½ hours). At this point, the meat should be fork-tender—if it's not, give it another 30 minutes or so in the oven.

Taste the sauce. If you'd like it a little more concentrated (usually I think it's just fine as is), pour it into a saucepan, put it over high heat, and boil it down until it's just the way you like it. When the sauce meets your approval, taste it for salt and pepper. (If you're going to reduce the sauce, make certain not to salt it until it's reduced.) Fish out the bouquet garni and garlic and, using a large serving spoon, skim off the surface fat.

Serve the beef and vegetables moistened with the sauce.

SERVING I like to use shallow soup plates or small cast-iron *cocottes* for this stew. Spoon the daube out into the little casseroles and let each guest dig into one.

STORING Like all stews, this can be kept in the refrigerator for about 3 days or frozen for up to 2 months. If you are preparing the daube ahead, don't reduce the sauce, just cool the daube and chill it. Then, at serving time, lift off the fat (an easy job when the daube's been chilled), reduce the sauce, and season it one last time.

Rillettes is a rustic pâté, usually made with pork that's been slow-cooked in seasoned fat. Greenspan's spread is a lighter, faster alternative that mixes quickly poached fresh salmon with smoked salmon and plenty of lemon juice.

SALMON RILLETTES

MAKES ABOUT 2 CUPS OR 8 SERVINGS

- 1 lemon
- 1 small red chile pepper
- ½ cup dry white wine or white vermouth
- ½ cup water
- 1 bay leaf
- 5 white peppercorns
- 5 coriander seeds
- 2 small spring onions, trimmed and finely chopped, long green tops reserved, or 1 shallot, finely chopped, rinsed, and patted dry
- Salt
- ½ pound salmon fillet, cut into small (about ½-inch) cubes
- 4 to 6 ounces smoked salmon, cut into small (about ¼-inch) dice
- Freshly ground white pepper
- 3 tablespoons unsalted butter, at room temperature
- About ¼ teaspoon pink peppercorns, crushed

Bread, crackers, or toast, for serving

EDITOR'S WINE CHOICE
Creamy, supple Pinot Blanc (see page 266)

Using a vegetable peeler, remove a strip of zest from the lemon and toss it into a medium saucepan. Finely grate the rest of the zest, and set it and the lemon aside. With a small knife, cut away a sliver of the chile pepper; discard the seeds, and toss the sliver into the saucepan. Seed and finely chop the remainder of the chile pepper.

Pour the wine or vermouth and the water into the pan, add the bay leaf, white peppercorns, coriander, onion tops if you're using spring onions, and ½ teaspoon salt, and bring to a boil over medium heat. Lower the heat, cover, and simmer gently for 5 minutes.

Drop the cubes of fresh salmon into the pan, cover, and poach for just 1 minute. Turn everything into a strainer, drain, and transfer the cubes of salmon to a bowl. Discard herbs, spices, and vegetables.

With the back of a fork, lightly mash the poached salmon. Toss the smoked salmon, grated lemon zest, chile pepper, and chopped onions or shallot into the bowl, season with salt and white pepper, and give everything a good stir. Add the butter and use the fork to stir and mash it into the mixture until it's well incorporated and you have a thick spread. Squeeze about half of the lemon's juice into the bowl, stir it in, and season the rillettes again with salt and white pepper. Taste and add more lemon juice (it's nice when it's lemony) if you'd like, then stir in the pink peppercorns.

Pack the rillettes into a jar (a canning jar is traditional) or bowl, press a piece of plastic wrap against the surface, and chill for at least 2 hours—you want it to be firm.

Serve the rillettes with bread, crackers, or toast.

SERVING Rillettes is served as a spread, so have lots of bread, crackers, or toast available. If you'd like to dress it up, serve it on warm blini or spread it on small rounds of toasted brioche (think canapés) and top with salmon roe.

STORING Packed airtight, the rillettes will keep in the refrigerator for up to 2 days.

Cornish hens are so small that they take only about 40 minutes to roast—quick enough for a midweek meal. Try to find hens that still have their livers; mix them into the bread-and-sausage stuffing for a richer flavor.

SAUSAGE-STUFFED CORNISH HENS

MAKES 2 TO 4 SERVINGS

- 2 Cornish hens, preferably organic (livers reserved if included), at room temperature
- About 2 tablespoons olive oil
- About 1½ tablespoons unsalted butter, plus (optional) 1 tablespoon cold butter if making the sauce
- 1 garlic clove, split, germ removed, and finely chopped
- 1 shallot or ½ small onion, finely chopped, rinsed, and dried
- ¼ pound sausage, casings removed if necessary (you can use sweet or hot sausage or a mixture)
- ½ slice stale bread, crust removed, cut into small cubes
- 1 large egg, lightly beaten
- 2 tablespoons minced fresh parsley
- Salt and freshly ground pepper
- ½ cup dry white wine (optional)

EDITOR'S WINE CHOICE
Complex, elegant Pinot Noir
(see page 269)

Our readily available Cornish hens are perfect stand-ins for the slightly smaller French poussins, *or baby chickens. They're good little birds to cook on busy weeknights, since they're tasty, versatile, and in and out of the oven in about 40 minutes—and that's with stuffing (here a simple mix of bread and sausage). While a French cook might make even quicker work of this dish, because she can pick up her ready-made sausage stuffing from the butcher, this stuffing can still be put together in a flash, adding only a few extra minutes to your American kitchen time.*

A word on serving size: Depending on what else you've got on the menu, 1 hen will serve either 1 or 2 people. If you decide to make 2 hens for 4, roast the hens, then cut them in half along the breast and backbones. Of course, you can also double the recipe; in that case, use two skillets or a larger roaster.

Center a rack in the oven and preheat the oven to 425°F. Lightly butter or oil an oven-going skillet (I use my old cast-iron skillet) or a small roaster.

If you were lucky enough to get hens with livers, rinse and dry the livers, cut away any veins and green spots, and coarsely chop them.

Heat 2 teaspoons of the oil and ½ tablespoon of the butter in a medium skillet over medium heat. Toss in the garlic and shallot or onion and stir everything around for a minute or so. Add the livers, if you've got them, and stir for another minute. Toss in the sausage and cook for 1 to 2 minutes, breaking up any lumps. Remove from the heat and let cool for a couple of minutes, then stir in the bread, beaten egg, and parsley; season with salt and pepper.

Salt and pepper the insides of the hens and spoon in the stuffing, taking care not to pack it in too tightly or too fully. Rub the hens with a couple teaspoons of olive oil and a tablespoon or so of butter, then season them generously with salt and pepper.

Put them in the skillet and slide the pan into the oven—if you'd like, you can roast the hens using the side-side-back method: lay them on their sides in the skillet and give them 15 minutes of roasting time, turn them over onto their other sides and give them another 15 minutes, and then finish by roasting them for 10 minutes on their backs. However you roast them, cook for 40 minutes, or until the juices run clear when you prick their thighs at the thickest part.

When the hens are ready, give them a little feet-in-the-air rest: transfer them to a platter, put a bowl at one end of the platter, turn the birds over, breast side down, and rest their legs on the bowl. Cover them lightly with a foil tent and leave them like this for about 5 minutes, or while you make the sauce, if you'd like.

To make a pan *jus,* cut the tablespoon of cold butter into quarters. Pour off the fat in the skillet (or roaster) and put the pan over medium-high heat. When it's hot, pour in the wine and let it bubble away until it's reduced by about half. Pull the pan from the heat and swirl in the pieces of cold butter. Check for salt and pepper.

Serve the hens with the sauce, if you made it.

SERVING If you're going to split the hens, cut them in half along the breast and backbone with kitchen shears or a good strong knife, then tuck half the stuffing under each half. If you've made a pan sauce, just pour a little of it over each serving.

STORING If you've got leftovers, remove the stuffing from the hens and keep it and the bird(s) covered in the fridge—it makes for great next-day snacking.

This lighter take on French pot-au-feu (a stew of meat and root vegetables) is a stellar way to serve an assortment of spring or summer vegetables. Be sure to add the poached egg—when the yolk runs into the broth, it's heavenly.

WARM-WEATHER VEGETABLE POT-AU-FEU

MAKES 4 MAIN-COURSE SERVINGS

- 2 tablespoons extra-virgin olive oil
- 2 garlic cloves, split, germ removed, and thinly sliced
- 1 onion, preferably a spring or Texas onion, thinly sliced
- 1 leek, white and light green parts only, quartered lengthwise and rinsed
- Salt and freshly ground white pepper
- 6 small new potatoes, scrubbed and cut into ½-inch-thick slices
- 4 slender carrots, trimmed, peeled, and cut on the diagonal into ½-inch-thick pieces
- 3 cups vegetable broth or chicken broth
- 1 strip lemon or orange zest (optional)
- One 2-inch-long piece lemongrass, split lengthwise (optional)
- 8 asparagus stalks, trimmed and peeled
- 4 large shiitakes, stemmed, cleaned, and sliced
- ½ pound spinach, stemmed and washed
- 4 large eggs, poached or boiled

Basil, cilantro, or parsley coulis and/or chopped fresh herbs, for serving (optional)

EDITOR'S WINE CHOICE
Light, crisp white Burgundy (see page 264)

Traditional pot-au-feu, a mix of hearty cuts of meat, root vegetables, and a warming-down-to-your-toes broth, is an unequivocally wintry dish, perfect after a mountain hike or a day in the great outdoors. But it's a dish with too many possibilities to be shelved when the weather changes, which is why some form of pot-au-feu is made year-round, its concept remaining constant, the ingredients taking seasonal star turns: meat in fall and winter, fish or vegetables in spring and summer.

The underpinnings of classic pot-au-feu, the onions, carrots, leeks, and potatoes, are here, but in their young spring form. And in this can-be-vegetarian version, they cook briefly, keep their colors, and share their light broth with asparagus and spinach, harbingers of warmer times.

My recipe should be a jumping-off point for you. Choose whatever is young and fresh at your market. Because you add the vegetables in succession, you can easily use ingredients with widely different cooking times. Green beans or peas are a good addition, as are newly dug turnips, small pieces of squash (acorn, pattypan, or zucchini), tiny tomatoes, and corn cut from the cob.

You could omit the poached or soft-boiled eggs, but I hope you won't—they add richness to an otherwise lean but tasty broth. And, while the herb coulis is optional, again, I hope you'll include it—it tilts the dish a little toward Provence, and what could be nicer when the temperature registers sultry?

continued on page 106

vegetable pot-au-feu continued

In a large high-sided skillet or, if you've got one, a woklike stir-fry pan, warm the olive oil over medium-low heat. Toss in the garlic and cook for just 1 minute. Add the onion and leek, turning them in the oil, and season with salt and white pepper. Cook, stirring gently, just until the onion and leek soften slightly, about 5 minutes. Stir in the potatoes and carrots, then pour in the broth. If you're using zest and/or lemongrass, toss them in now too. Increase the heat and bring the broth to a boil, then lower the heat and simmer gently, uncovered, until the vegetables are just short of tender, about 10 minutes. *(You can make the pot-au-feu to this point up to 3 hours in advance; cover and refrigerate. When you're ready to continue, bring the broth back to a boil, lower the heat so that it simmers, and cook gently until everything is heated through.)*

While the vegetables are simmering, bring a skillet of water to a boil—you'll use the pan to reheat the eggs right before serving.

With the pot-au-feu at a gentle simmer, drop in the asparagus and shiitakes and cook until tender, about 4 minutes. Scatter the spinach over the vegetables and cook for another 2 minutes, just until slightly wilted. Taste for salt and white pepper.

Slip the eggs into the skillet of simmering water and give them just a couple of minutes to warm while you spoon out the pot-au-feu.

Ladle the vegetables and broth into shallow soup plates, dot with the basil, cilantro, or parsley puree and/or scatter with the chopped herbs, and finish each with a poached or boiled egg. Serve immediately.

SERVING This has to be piping hot—accompany the pot-au-feu with bread and the instruction that the egg should be cut into at once, so that the yolk can mix with the broth.

STORING This is not a dish for keeping.

BEST OF THE BEST EXCLUSIVE

This is a slightly sweet version of a traditional choucroute garnie, an Alsatian dish of sauerkraut garnished with potatoes and a variety of salted meats.

CHICKEN CHOUCROUTE

with apple & prunes

MAKES 4 SERVINGS

- 3 strips of bacon, chopped (about 3 ounces)
- One 3½- to 4-pound chicken, cut into 2 breast halves and 2 whole legs
- Salt and freshly ground pepper
- 1 onion, finely diced
- 3 cups drained and rinsed sauerkraut (about 1½ pounds)
- 1 tart apple, such as Granny Smith—peeled, cored and chopped
- 8 pitted prunes
- 1½ cups dry white wine
- ¼ cup chopped flat-leaf parsley
- ¼ cup heavy cream (optional)

EDITOR'S WINE CHOICE
Rich Alsace Gewürztraminer
(see page 265)

1. Preheat the oven to 400°F. In a large enameled cast-iron casserole or Dutch oven, cook the bacon over moderate heat until browned. Using a slotted spoon, transfer the bacon to paper towels.

2. Season the chicken with salt and pepper and add it to the casserole, skin side down. Cook over moderately high heat, turning, until browned all over, about 8 minutes. Transfer the chicken to a plate.

3. Pour off all but 2 tablespoons of the fat in the casserole. Add the onion to the casserole and season with salt and pepper. Cook over moderate heat, stirring, until softened but not browned, about 5 minutes. Add the sauerkraut, apple, prunes, wine and bacon and bring to a boil. Cook for 2 minutes. Return the chicken to the casserole, cover and braise in the oven until the chicken is white throughout, about 25 minutes.

4. Transfer the chicken to a plate. Stir the parsley and cream into the choucroute and season with salt and pepper. Spoon the choucroute onto a large, deep platter, top with the chicken and serve.

DORIE GREENSPAN ONLINE

doriegreenspan.com

Dorie Greenspan

@doriegreenspan

Beef and carrots in stout
with parsley and horseradish
dumplings, page 116

PLENTY

→10

Diana Henry

A cookbook dedicated to thrift and ethics doesn't sound very appetizing, but U.K. food writer Diana Henry's fourth recipe collection, *Plenty,* is exactly that. It's a sort of choose-your-own adventure: Almost every recipe comes with ideas for variations and leftovers (which she calls "the art of dovetailing meals"). You could make a roasted pork shoulder with stuffed squash, or, with just a few different ingredients, a mustardy *porc au four* or a Cuban-style *lechon asado.* Take any leftover pork and use it as the foundation for Indonesian *nasi goreng* (fried rice), Saigon crêpes or a pork-and-apple pie. It's all rustic, "what's in the fridge" food that uses seasonal produce and inexpensive cuts of meat to create dishes that Henry describes as "homely, humble . . . economical, but indulgent, too." *Published by Mitchell Beazley, $29.99*

A lovely rendition of crudités and dip, this is a quick spring and summer appetizer. Artisanal, authentic ricotta is a must, as are superfresh vegetables.

HERBED RICOTTA WITH SUMMER VEG

SERVES 4 TO 6 AS A STARTER OR LIGHT LUNCH DISH

FOR THE RICOTTA

1 pound fresh ricotta cheese
1 garlic clove, crushed or grated
1 tablespoon fresh chives, snipped
2 tablespoons fresh flat-leaf parsley, chopped
1 tablespoon fresh mint leaves, chopped
Finely grated zest of 1 lemon, plus a good squeeze of lemon juice
3 tablespoons extra-virgin olive oil, plus more to serve
Salt and pepper

FOR THE VEGETABLES

A selection from:
Raw peas
Raw fava beans
French breakfast radishes with fresh, perky leaves, trimmed
Baby carrots, trimmed
Cherry tomatoes
High-quality black olives
Toasted ciabatta, to serve

EDITOR'S WINE CHOICE
Dry, rich sparkling rosé
(see page 264)

Another variation on the theme of plain, raw vegetables. Fresh ricotta can be hard to get but the stuff sold in tubs in the supermarket just doesn't cut it here. Go to a good Italian deli or cheese shop to seek out the fresh version. It is milky, sweet-smelling, and almost crumbly.

1. Mash the ricotta together with all the other ingredients, cover with plastic wrap, and put in the refrigerator to allow the flavors to mingle (it needs at least an hour). Bring it out before you want to serve it to allow it to get to room temperature.

2. Divide the ricotta among four to six plates (or put in a bowl or mound on a wooden board and surround with the vegetables and olives).

3. If it's early in the season and the fava beans are young, serve them shelled but not cooked. If it's a little later, cook the shelled beans until tender and slip them out of their skins so you can see their beautiful color. Arrange the vegetables and olives beside the ricotta and drizzle olive oil over everything. Serve with toasted ciabatta.

Potatoes add heft to this fresh vegetable and herb dish, which could easily be served as a main course—especially topped with thick, garlicky Greek yogurt.

GREEK POTATOES, FRISÉE, SPINACH & LEEKS
with dill, mint & garlic yogurt

SERVES 6 AS A SIDE DISH

- ¼ cup olive oil
- 5 leeks, cut into chunks
- 1¼ pounds small waxy potatoes, halved
- Salt and pepper
- 10 ounces spinach
- 6 ounces frisée (curly endive) leaves, torn
- 3 tablespoons chopped fresh dill
- Leaves from 6 mint sprigs, torn
- Good squeeze of lemon juice
- Extra-virgin olive oil, to serve (optional)
- 2 garlic cloves, crushed
- 1 cup Greek yogurt

Greece truly makes the most of vegetables. This is a complete, delicious one-pot meal; you won't miss meat. Frisée cooks to softness and the bitterness is pacified. Arugula can also be used.

1. Put half the oil into a heavy saucepan and add the leeks and potatoes. Season, add a splash of water, cover, and sweat for 20 minutes. Add a bit of water every so often and stir.

2. Once the potatoes are almost tender, add the spinach, frisée, and remaining oil and turn gently. Add another splash of water, season, cover, and cook until the leaves have wilted—about 4 to 5 minutes. Add the herbs and lemon juice, put into a serving dish, and drizzle with the extra-virgin olive oil, if you want.

3. Mix the garlic into the yogurt and serve with the vegetables.

LEFTOVERS Make these into soup. Add chicken stock, heat, mash to break down the potatoes, and leave chunky or puree. Top with Greek yogurt and a drizzle of olive oil.

The tender pork shoulder here is excellent and affordable, but the best part of the dish is the buttery squash halves filled with earthy rice stuffing.

SLOW-ROASTED SHOULDER OF PORK *with Stuffed Squash*

SERVES 8

FOR THE PORK

- Sea salt and pepper
- 6 pounds boneless pork shoulder roast, rind scored
- ¼ cup olive oil
- 4 cups dry hard cider or white wine

FOR THE SQUASH

- 2 small winter squash or pumpkins
- ¼ cup butter
- 1 onion, finely chopped
- 3 ounces pancetta, chopped
- 8 ounces mushrooms, quartered
- 1 cup brown basmati, wild, and Camargue red rice (or just brown and wild)
- 2¼ cups chicken stock or water

EDITOR'S WINE CHOICE
Deep, velvety Merlot
(see page 268)

Sunday lunch can seem dauntingly expensive if you're trying to feed a crowd. But slow-cooked pork shoulder is one of the most satisfying roasts (so tender) and, relatively, very cheap. It also looks magnificent. You can vary the stuffing by using dried fruit instead of mushrooms, or add grated Parmesan or wilted spinach.

1. Preheat the oven to 400°F. Season the inside of the pork. Roll up and tie at intervals with kitchen string. Rub with oil and season well. Put in a roasting pan and roast in the oven for 25 minutes. Reduce the heat to 325°F and pour in half the alcohol. Cook for another 25 minutes per pound—about 2½ hours in total—basting and adding more cider or wine as you go.

2. Meanwhile, halve the winter squash and scoop out the fibers and seeds. Score a lattice on the flesh. Put in a roasting pan and smear with 1 tablespoon of the butter. Season and roast for 20 minutes. Remove from the oven.

3. Melt another 1 tablespoon of the butter in a saucepan and sauté the onion until quite soft. Add the pancetta, mushrooms, and remaining butter and sauté until colored. Stir in the rice to coat, season, and add the stock or water. Cover, bring to a boil, reduce the heat to low, and cook for 15 minutes.

4. When the pork is cooked (the juices should run clear, with no trace of pink, when you pierce the meat), take it from the oven and put on a heated platter. Cover with foil, insulate well, and rest for 30 minutes. Increase the oven temperature to 375°F.

5. Spoon the rice stuffing into the winter squash cavities, mixing it with the butter that has collected there. Return to the oven for 30 minutes. The flesh should become completely tender and the tops golden.

6. Meanwhile, pour the cooking juices from the pork into a pitcher and remove the fat. Deglaze the roasting pan with more hard cider, white wine, or water (only about ½ cup), add the pork juices, and bubble away until you have a thin, tasty gravy. Serve the pork with the gravy and squash.

Dumplings are a traditional stew ingredient. Henry's dumplings include horseradish, a clever way to add a kick to this rich, hearty dish.

BEEF & CARROTS IN STOUT
with parsley & horseradish dumplings

SERVES 4 TO 6

FOR THE BEEF

- 3 tablespoons peanut or sunflower oil
- 2¼ pounds braising beef, in large chunks
- 12 ounces carrots, sliced
- 12 ounces leeks, sliced
- 1¾ ounces pearl barley

One 12-ounce bottle stout
Salt and pepper

FOR THE DUMPLINGS

- ½ onion, very finely chopped
- 1 tablespoon butter
- ¼ cup finely chopped fresh parsley
- 1¾ cups fresh bread crumbs
- 1 large egg
- 3 generous tablespoons creamed horseradish

EDITOR'S WINE CHOICE
Intense, spicy Syrah
(see page 269)

The stout mellows in the oven to a lovely deep, chocolatey flavor. You don't need potatoes, making this dish very cook-friendly. Buttered cabbage is delicious with it.

1. Preheat the oven to 325°F. Heat 2 tablespoons of the oil in a heavy flameproof Dutch oven and brown the meat in batches. Remove and set aside. Add the remaining oil to the pan and fry the vegetables until lightly colored, then pour in the barley.

2. Add the stout and stir to deglaze the pan. Pour in 2¾ cups water, return the meat, and season. Bring to the boil, reduce the heat, cover, and put in the oven for 2 hours. Check to make sure the casserole hasn't become dry; add more water if needed.

3. Make the dumplings: sauté the onion in the butter, put into a bowl, and add the remaining ingredients. Bring the mixture together and form into 12 little golf ball–sized dumplings. The mixture will be rather loose, but persevere. Dot the dumplings on top of the beef. Cook, covered, for 20 minutes, then uncover and cook for another 10 minutes.

BEST OF THE BEST EXCLUSIVE

Jerusalem artichokes (also called sunchokes) are boiled and then pureed with cream and butter to create a fabulous accompaniment to the chicken here.

BRAISED CHICKEN

with endives, shallots & jerusalem artichoke puree

SERVES 4

- 1½ pounds Jerusalem artichokes, peeled and cut into 1-inch pieces (see Note)
- 2 tablespoons fresh lemon juice
- Salt
- ½ cup heavy cream
- 1 cup plus 2 tablespoons chicken stock or low-sodium broth
- 2 tablespoons unsalted butter
- Pinch of freshly grated nutmeg
- Freshly ground pepper
- 1 tablespoon canola oil
- 8 chicken thighs (about 6 ounces each)
- 4 endives, halved lengthwise
- 4 small shallots, halved lengthwise through the root ends
- 3 thyme sprigs

EDITOR'S WINE CHOICE

Complex, aromatic Chenin Blanc (see page 265)

1. In a medium saucepan, cover the Jerusalem artichokes with cool water. Add the lemon juice and season generously with salt. Bring to a boil and cook over moderately high heat until they are tender, about 15 minutes.

2. Drain the Jerusalem artichokes and return them to the saucepan. Add the cream, 2 tablespoons of the chicken stock, 1 tablespoon of the butter and the nutmeg and bring to a simmer. Transfer the Jerusalem artichoke mixture to a food processor and puree until very smooth. Season with salt and pepper. Return the puree to the saucepan and keep warm.

3. In a very large, deep skillet, melt the remaining 1 tablespoon of butter in the oil. Season the chicken with salt and pepper and add it to the skillet, skin side down. Cook over moderately high heat, turning once, until golden brown, about 10 minutes. Transfer the chicken to a platter.

4. Spoon off all but 2 tablespoons of the fat in the skillet. Add the endives and shallots, cut side down. Cook over moderate heat until golden, about 4 minutes. Transfer the endives and shallots to a plate. Add the remaining 1 cup of chicken stock to the skillet and bring to a boil, scraping up any browned bits from the bottom. Add the thyme sprigs and return the chicken to the skillet. Reduce the heat to low, cover and cook for 20 minutes.

5. Nestle the endives and shallots in the skillet, cover and cook for 15 minutes longer, until the chicken is white throughout and the endives are tender. Discard the thyme sprigs. Serve the chicken with the Jerusalem artichoke puree.

NOTE Jerusalem artichokes are small, knobby relatives of the sunflower. They resemble fresh ginger but have a jicama-like texture and taste sweet when raw, nutty and earthy when roasted. Look for larger ones, as they are easier to peel.

MAKE AHEAD The Jerusalem artichoke puree can be refrigerated overnight. Reheat gently before serving.

DIANA HENRY ONLINE

dianahenry.co.uk

PHOTOGRAPH BY SARAH SHATZ

THE ESSENTIAL NEW YORK TIMES COOKBOOK

→ 11

Amanda Hesser

With over 1,000 recipes from 150 years of the *New York Times*, this is an "eclectic panorama of both high-toned masterpieces and low-brow grub, a fever chart of culinary passions," writes former *Times* food columnist Amanda Hesser. The collection ranges from 19th-century curiosities like Snow Pudding (meringue puffs held aloft by vanilla custard) all the way to recent favorites from Mark Bittman's "The Minimalist" column (garlicky Shrimp in Green Sauce). Cooks can challenge themselves with "odysseys" like Paul Prudhomme's Cajun-Style Gumbo or take it easy with Hesser's own shockingly simple Chocolate Dump-It Cake. Hesser is a gently encouraging guide: "Be patient. Adapt. . . . And if you don't have the right size casserole dish for a gratin, I know you'll find some other dish and improvise." *Published by W. W. Norton & Company, $40*

This is a slight tweak of an Italian classic amped up with lots of lemon; serve plenty of crusty bread for the sauce that pools on the bottom of the bowl.

SPICY, LEMONY CLAMS WITH PASTA

SERVES 4 AS A MAIN COURSE

Salt
1 pound spaghetti, linguine, or other long pasta
½ cup extra-virgin olive oil
8 cloves garlic, thinly sliced
36 littleneck clams, well scrubbed
¾ cup dry white wine
½ to 1 tablespoon crushed red pepper flakes
Finely grated zest of 2 lemons
Juice of 1 lemon, or to taste
½ cup chopped flat-leaf parsley
Fresh ground black pepper

EDITOR'S WINE CHOICE
Zesty, fresh Albariño
(see page 264)

AUTHOR'S NOTE
One problem with spaghetti and clams is that long strands and small round bits don't like to mix evenly. You can accomplish the task in a large bowl with tongs in each hand, but it's like trying to mix beads into a pile of yarn. As an alternative, mix the spaghetti with the sauce, then scatter the clams on top.

This recipe had me at spicy, lemony clams. And it did not disappoint.

1. Fill a large pot with water, add 1 tablespoon salt, and bring to a boil over high heat. Add the pasta and boil until the pasta is al dente, 7 to 8 minutes; drain well.

2. Meanwhile, heat the olive oil in a large skillet over medium-low heat. Add the garlic and sauté just until translucent, about 2 minutes. Add the clams and wine, cover immediately, and raise the heat to medium-high. Shake the pan often, and check the clams after 4 minutes. If any have opened, transfer them to a bowl so they do not overcook. Simmer the remaining clams until all have opened.

3. Combine the clams and the broth from the pan in a large serving bowl. Add 1½ teaspoons pepper flakes, the lemon zest, lemon juice, parsley, and salt and pepper to taste. Mix well. Add the pasta and, using tongs, toss well. Add more red pepper flakes and lemon juice, if desired. Serve in soup bowls.

FROM THE *NEW YORK TIMES*, AUGUST 11, 1999
"Why Dig for Gold, if There Are Clams?" by Elaine Louie. Recipe adapted from the Lobster Club in New York City.

This dish requires very little investment in time but offers a big taste payoff; the sauce's intensity is thrilling for anyone who craves big flavors.

SHRIMP IN GREEN SAUCE

SERVES 4

- 6 cloves garlic
- ⅓ cup extra-virgin olive oil
- 6 scallions, chopped
- 1 cup flat-leaf parsley leaves and thin stems
- 2 pounds medium shrimp, peeled, deveined if desired

Salt and freshly ground black pepper

- 4 dried chiles, crushed, or a few pinches of crushed red pepper flakes, or to taste
- ⅓ cup broth (shrimp, fish, or chicken), dry white wine, or water

EDITOR'S WINE CHOICE
Fresh, fruity rosé (see page 267)

I love this technique: masking the shrimp in a paste-like sauce and blasting them in a 500-degree oven. I love the gutsy garlic-and-scallion-soaked sauce. And I love the resulting dish, which needs nothing but a loaf of good bread and an icy beer to constitute a perfect low-key dinner.

1. Heat the oven to 500°F. Combine the garlic and oil in a small food processor and blend until smooth, scraping down the sides as necessary. Add the scallions and parsley and pulse until minced. Toss with the shrimp, salt and pepper, and chiles.

2. Put the shrimp in a large roasting pan. Add the broth and place the pan in the oven. Roast, stirring once, until the mixture is bubbly and hot and the shrimp are all pink, 10 to 15 minutes.

FROM THE *NEW YORK TIMES*, MARCH 5, 2003
"The Minimalist: Too Much Garlic? Impossible," by Mark Bittman.

The secret to the succulent texture of this Jewish-style brisket is baking the meat, refrigerating it overnight, then reheating before serving.

BRISKET IN SWEET & SOUR SAUCE

SERVES 12

FOR THE SAUCE

- 1 medium onion, quartered
- One 2-inch piece fresh ginger, peeled
- 6 large cloves garlic
- ¼ cup Dijon mustard
- ½ cup dry red wine
- 1½ cups Coca-Cola or ginger ale
- 1 cup ketchup
- ¼ cup honey
- ¼ cup cider vinegar
- ¼ cup soy sauce
- ½ cup olive oil
- ¼ teaspoon ground cloves
- 1 tablespoon coarsely ground black pepper, or to taste

One 6- to 7-pound first-cut brisket, rinsed and patted thoroughly dry

EDITOR'S WINE CHOICE
Fruity, luscious Shiraz
(see page 269)

AMANDA HESSER ONLINE
food52.com
@amandahesser

This brisket has become something of a classic. It's bad karma to use Diet Coke in place of Coke for this recipe—or any other.

1. Heat the oven to 350°F. Place all the sauce ingredients in a food processor and process until smooth.

2. Place the brisket fat side up in a heavy flameproof roasting pan just large enough to hold it, and pour the sauce over it. Cover tightly and bake for 2 hours.

3. Turn the brisket over and bake, uncovered, for 1 hour, or until fork-tender. Cool, then cover the brisket and refrigerate overnight.

4. The next day, heat the oven to 350°F. Transfer the brisket to a cutting board, cut off the fat, and slice with a sharp knife, against the grain, to the desired thickness. Remove any congealed fat from the sauce, set the pan over 2 burners, and bring to a boil. Taste the sauce to see if it needs reducing. If so, boil it down for a few minutes, or as needed.

5. Return the meat to the sauce and warm in the oven for 20 minutes.

FROM THE *NEW YORK TIMES*, NOVEMBER 27, 2002
"Just Right for the First Night of Hanukkah," by Joan Nathan. Recipe adapted from Levana's Table, by Levana Kirschenbaum.

This cake is so moist and tender, you could skip the two-ingredient frosting and simply serve it with a dusting of powdered sugar and a dollop of whipped cream.

CHOCOLATE DUMP-IT CAKE

SERVES 10

FOR THE CAKE

- 2 cups sugar
- ¼ pound unsweetened chocolate, chopped
- 8 tablespoons (1 stick) unsalted butter
- 1 cup water
- 2 cups all-purpose flour
- 2 teaspoons baking soda
- 1 teaspoon baking powder
- 1 teaspoon salt
- 1 cup whole milk
- 1 teaspoon cider vinegar
- 2 large eggs
- 1 teaspoon vanilla extract

FOR THE ICING

- 1½ cups Nestlé's semisweet chocolate chips
- 1½ cups sour cream, at room temperature

AUTHOR'S NOTE

When I was growing up, my mother baked this cake for my birthdays. Now I make it for my husband's and children's birthdays. "Dump-it" doesn't have quite the appeal of "galette" or "confit," but it candidly lays out the cake's virtue.

This moist, bouncy chocolate cake is the easiest one you'll ever make: you mix the batter in a saucepan, stirring in one ingredient after the other, and when it's glassy and smooth, you dump the batter into the cake pan and slide it in the oven.

1. To make the cake, heat the oven to 375°F. Place a baking sheet on the lowest rack to catch any drips when the cake bakes on the middle rack. Mix the sugar, unsweetened chocolate, butter, and water in a 2- to 3-quart saucepan, place over medium heat, and stir occasionally until blended. Remove from the heat and let cool slightly.

2. Meanwhile, sift together the flour, baking soda, baking powder, and salt. Stir together the milk and vinegar in a small bowl (it will curdle, but that's OK). Grease and flour a 9-inch tube pan.

3. When the chocolate has cooled a bit, whisk in the milk mixture and eggs. In several additions, and without overmixing, whisk in the dry ingredients. When the mixture is smooth, add the vanilla and whisk once or twice to blend.

4. Pour the batter into the tube pan. Bake until a skewer inserted in the center comes out clean, about 30 to 35 minutes. Let the cake cool for 10 minutes, then remove from the pan and set on a rack. (This can be tricky; the cake is heavy and likes to break in half—if someone is around to help, enlist him.) Let cool completely.

5. To make the icing, melt the chocolate chips in a double boiler, then let cool to room temperature. Stir in the sour cream ¼ cup at a time until the mixture is smooth.

6. You can ice the cake as is, or cut it in half so that you have 2 layers, and fill and ice it. There will be extra icing whether you have 1 or 2 layers. My mother always uses it to make flowers on top. She makes a small rosette, or button, then uses toasted sliced almond as the petals, pushing them in around the base of the rosette.

FROM THE *NEW YORK TIMES*, MAY 12, 2002
"Food Diary: Personal Best," by Amanda Hesser.
Recipe adapted from Judith Hesser.

Provençal-style stuffed zucchini,
page 126

FARM TO FORK

→ 12

Emeril Lagasse

Little-known fact: Emeril Lagasse was an early proponent of locavore eating. As the chef at Commander's Palace in the '80s, he helped start a farm co-op that supplied much of the New Orleans restaurant's produce and meat, including hogs they'd use "every which way." Lagasse's 15th cookbook follows the mantra "buy fresh, eat local," with over 100 recipes that are more vegetable-focused than the rich Creole food he's known for. But the recipes are still full of bold flavor: The tomato, zucchini and leek galette uses two full heads of roasted garlic, and his stuffed zucchini has a sausage-enriched filling. There are plenty of Southern staples, too, from fried chicken to shrimp and grits. Organized smartly by themes—nightshades, winter fruits, leafy greens—*Farm to Fork* balances modern health concerns and locavore ethics with Emeril's brawny approach to cooking. *Published by HarperCollins, $24.99*

It's worth making your own crumbs here; use rye or pumpernickel bread to give the crunchy topping on this stuffed-zucchini dish a more assertive flavor.

PROVENÇAL-STYLE STUFFED ZUCCHINI

6 TO 8 SERVINGS

- 2 cups (about 2 ounces) diced French baguette or other crusty bread, preferably day-old (½-inch dice)
- ¼ cup finely grated Parmigiano-Reggiano cheese
- ¼ cup packed fresh parsley leaves
- 1 tablespoon minced garlic
- ½ teaspoon salt, plus more if needed
- ⅛ teaspoon freshly ground black pepper, plus more if needed
- 3 tablespoons extra-virgin olive oil
- 8 small zucchini (each about 7 inches long and 1¼ to 1½ inches wide)
- 4 ounces fresh lean mild pork sausage
- ¾ cup minced onions
- 1 cup finely chopped peeled and seeded tomatoes (about 2 medium tomatoes)

EDITOR'S WINE CHOICE
Dry, crisp rosé (see page 267)

Any gorgeous variety of zucchini from the market can work in this recipe. One day you may find the cylindrical shape; another, the round shape. I've tried both. And who doesn't love stuffed zucchini? We bake these until the zucchini is nicely cooked through. If you need the crumbs to brown a little more, fire up the broiler for a minute at the end.

1. Pulse the diced bread in a food processor until you have an even mix of fine and coarse crumbs. Add the Parmesan, parsley leaves, 1½ teaspoons of the minced garlic, ¼ teaspoon of the salt, and the ⅛ teaspoon of pepper, and process until evenly mixed. Reserve 2 tablespoons of the breadcrumb mixture for the filling. Mix 1½ tablespoons of the extra-virgin olive oil into the remaining breadcrumbs, transfer the mixture to a small container, and set it aside. (Alternatively, you can use store-bought fine fresh crumbs: Combine ¾ cup breadcrumbs with 1 tablespoon minced parsley, ½ teaspoon minced garlic, ¼ cup finely grated Parmesan, ¾ teaspoon salt, and ⅛ teaspoon freshly ground black pepper. Set aside 2 tablespoons, and mix 1½ tablespoons extra-virgin olive oil into the remainder.)

2. Lay the zucchini on a flat work surface, and using a sharp knife, slice off the top quarter of each squash lengthwise. Next, slice a sliver off the bottom of each squash to help keep it stable. Using a small melon baller or spoon, remove the inner flesh from the zucchini to form a small boat shape, leaving a shell that is approximately ¼ inch thick. Cut the zucchini pulp into ¼-inch dice, and reserve it separately. Lightly salt the inside of the zucchini shells with the remaining ¼ teaspoon salt. Set them, hollow side down, on paper towels to drain while you prepare the filling.

3. Heat 1 tablespoon of the olive oil in a 12-inch skillet. Add the sausage and sauté until it is golden, using a spoon to break it into small pieces, about 6 minutes. Add the onions and cook until they are soft, 3 to 4 minutes. Add the chopped zucchini and cook for 2 minutes. Add the tomatoes and the remaining 1½ teaspoons garlic, and cook, stirring, until the moisture has evaporated and the filling comes together, 2 minutes. Remove the skillet from the heat, stir in the reserved 2 tablespoons breadcrumb mixture, and season with additional salt and pepper if necessary.

4. Preheat the oven to 350°F.

5. Rub the outside of the zucchini with the remaining ½ tablespoon olive oil, and season them lightly with salt and pepper. Turn the zucchini hollow side up, and lightly pat the insides with paper towels. Using a tablespoon or other small spoon, fill the zucchini with the warm filling. Top with the reserved breadcrumbs. Lay the zucchini in a baking dish, and bake for 30 minutes, or until golden brown and crispy on top.

This tart looks like a lot of work, but using store-bought puff pastry is a terrific shortcut. A mandoline will make slicing and layering the zucchini easier.

TOMATO, ZUCCHINI & LEEK GALETTE
with roasted garlic goat cheese

4 SERVINGS

- 1 sheet frozen puff pastry, thawed
- 3 tablespoons olive oil
- 2 cups thinly sliced well-washed leeks (white part only)

Salt and freshly ground white pepper

- 1 pound medium heirloom tomatoes, stem ends trimmed
- 8 ounces zucchini, ends trimmed
- 5 tablespoons extra-virgin olive oil
- 5 ounces goat cheese, at room temperature
- 1 teaspoon fresh thyme leaves
- 2 heads roasted garlic
- ½ cup finely grated Parmigiano-Reggiano cheese
- 2 tablespoons thinly sliced fresh basil leaves

EDITOR'S WINE CHOICE
Fresh, fruity rosé (see page 267)

This is no ordinary pie. The vegetables roast beautifully on top of golden puff pastry, and in between there is a scrumptious goat cheese spread (which is also delicious served with your favorite toast, so make extra!). We like to use beautiful heirloom tomatoes, but any of the best medium-size ripe local tomatoes will do.

1. On a lightly floured surface, roll out the puff pastry dough to 1/16-inch thickness. Cut out a 12-inch round, and place it on a rimmed baking sheet lined with parchment paper. Chill the dough in the freezer for at least 15 minutes or up to an hour.

2. Preheat the oven to 450°F.

3. Heat the olive oil in a 10-inch sauté pan over medium to medium-low heat. Add the leeks, ½ teaspoon salt, and ⅛ teaspoon white pepper. Cook, stirring as needed, until the leeks have softened, 5 to 7 minutes. Remove the pan from the heat and transfer the leeks to a plate; let them cool until you're ready to assemble the galette.

4. Slice the tomatoes into ¼-inch-thick rounds, and arrange them in one even layer on a wire rack set over a baking sheet. Sprinkle with ¼ teaspoon salt, and set aside to drain for 10 minutes.

5. Meanwhile, slice the zucchini into ⅛-inch-thick rounds. In a small bowl, mix the zucchini slices with 1 tablespoon of the extra-virgin olive oil, ¼ teaspoon salt, and ⅛ teaspoon white pepper. Set aside.

6. In a medium-size bowl, combine the goat cheese, thyme, ½ teaspoon salt, ¼ teaspoon white pepper, and 2 tablespoons of the extra-virgin olive oil. Mix well with a rubber spatula. Squeeze each head of roasted garlic over the bowl, pressing the soft cloves out of the peel. Mix until the goat cheese is smooth and the mixture is uniform.

continued on page 130

galette continued

7. Remove the baking sheet from the freezer (it is okay if the dough is frozen—it will soften by the time you complete the assembly) and spread the goat cheese mixture evenly over the dough, leaving a 1-inch border around the edges. Spread the sautéed leeks evenly over the goat cheese. Blot the tomatoes dry and arrange them in a concentric pattern over the leeks. Arrange the zucchini slices in a concentric pattern over the tomatoes. Sprinkle the Parmesan evenly over the top. Fold the border of the pastry up and over the edge of the tomatoes.

8. Bake the galette for 20 minutes, or until the crust is golden and puffed.

9. Remove the galette from the oven, sprinkle the fresh basil over the top, and drizzle with the remaining 2 tablespoons extra-virgin olive oil. Set the galette aside for at least 15 minutes before slicing and serving.

Fresh herbs, cheddar and Parmigiano-Reggiano give these popovers superb flavor and a great melty texture, eliminating any need to butter them.

CHEESY HERBED POPOVERS

12 POPOVERS, 6 TO 8 SERVINGS

- 4 tablespoons (½ stick) butter, melted
- ½ cup grated Parmigiano-Reggiano cheese
- 4 eggs
- 1 teaspoon salt
- ½ teaspoon freshly ground black pepper
- 1½ cups whole milk
- 3 tablespoons heavy cream
- 1 cup all-purpose flour
- 2 tablespoons chopped mixed fresh herbs, such as parsley, thyme, rosemary, basil, or chives
- About 2 ounces medium cheddar cheese, grated (½ cup) or cut into 12 pieces

It's hard not to stare at the oven while these bake, and rise, and pop. The aroma alone will get 'em out of bed to come see the action. By no means do you want to open the oven until the popovers are finished. Don't worry—you won't ruin their gorgeous color. Leave them in until the last moment to be sure the inside is cooked.

1. Preheat the oven to 450°F.

2. Brush the cups of a standard 12-cup muffin tin with some of the melted butter. Divide the Parmesan evenly among the cups.

3. Combine the eggs, salt, pepper, milk, cream, and the remaining butter in a blender and blend until well combined. Add the flour and blend for 15 seconds, until smooth. Transfer the batter to a large mixing bowl. Stir in the fresh herbs.

4. Fill each muffin cup halfway with batter. Divide the cheddar among the cups, and then top with the remaining batter.

5. Bake the popovers for 15 minutes. Then reduce the heat to 350°F and bake for 10 minutes.

6. Remove the muffin tin from the oven and unmold the popovers onto a wire rack. Pierce the side of each popover with a small sharp knife to allow steam to escape. (This will help keep them from deflating.) Serve immediately.

This airy, sweet bread is an excellent way to use up an overabundance of zucchini from the garden. Try it topped with fresh whipped ricotta and honey.

SPICED ZUCCHINI BREAD

2 LOAVES

- 3 eggs
- ¾ cup vegetable oil
- 1½ cups sugar
- 2 cups grated unpeeled zucchini
- 2 teaspoons vanilla extract
- 2½ cups all-purpose flour
- 1 tablespoon ground cinnamon
- ¾ teaspoon baking soda
- ¾ teaspoon salt
- ¼ teaspoon baking powder
- ¾ cup chopped lightly toasted walnuts or pecans
- Cream cheese, at room temperature, for serving (optional)

AUTHOR'S NOTE
This bread is also great at room temperature or toasted, and it freezes well.

Though we call this a bread, it's really more of a spice cake that uses grated fresh zucchini as a surprise ingredient. Serve it warm for breakfast, with cream cheese or butter and honey.

1. Preheat the oven to 325°F, and grease two 8-by-4-by-2½-inch loaf pans.

2. In the bowl of an electric mixer, beat the eggs until foamy. Add the vegetable oil, sugar, zucchini, and vanilla extract and mix well. Add the flour, cinnamon, baking soda, salt, and baking powder, and mix until well blended. Stir in the nuts. Divide the batter evenly between the prepared loaf pans, and tap them gently on the counter to release any air bubbles.

3. Bake until the loaves have risen and are golden brown and a tester inserted into the center comes out clean, 55 to 60 minutes. Allow the bread to cool in the pans for 5 minutes; then turn the loaves out onto wire racks to cool.

4. Serve the bread warm, sliced and spread with cream cheese if desired.

EMERIL LAGASSE ONLINE

emerils.com

Emeril Lagasse

@Emeril

Monkey bubble bread, page 136

BAKED EXPLORATIONS

→ 13

Matt Lewis & Renato Poliafito

Based on research from many dessert-eating trips around the country, Matt Lewis and Renato Poliafito of the Brooklyn and South Carolina pastry shops Baked turn "regional gems, fading beauties and family secrets" into modern desserts in their second cookbook. "Give us your vintage recipes," they say, "and we'll—ever so lovingly—turn them on their head." They offer two versions of Mississippi Mud Pie: a dense, coffee-ice-cream-and-fudge-filled version and also a "dreamier, more elegant" take that layers flourless chocolate cake and chocolate pudding in an Oreo cookie crust. The New York Style–Crumb Cake is more traditional; it's an idealized version of the corner deli standby—a buttery cake topped with a hefty layer of cinnamon-sugar crumbs. "I obeyed the New York Crumb Commandments," says Lewis, "and am now a convert myself." *Published by Stewart, Tabori & Chang, $29.95*

This breakfast pastry is made from balls of sweet, yeasty dough baked in a Bundt pan with sticky cinnamon sugar. Pulling the pieces off is part of the fun.

MONKEY BUBBLE BREAD

YIELD: ONE 10-INCH BUNDT

FOR THE MONKEY BUBBLE BREAD

- 1¼ cups whole milk
- 2 teaspoons instant yeast
- 4 cups all-purpose flour
- 5 tablespoons sugar
- 1 teaspoon salt
- 1 egg
- 5 tablespoons unsalted butter, melted

FOR THE CINNAMON SUGAR COATING

- 1¼ cups firmly packed dark brown sugar
- 2 teaspoons cinnamon
- ½ cup (1 stick) unsalted butter, melted and cooled

I suggest only making this from-scratch bread if you are having a large gathering. Otherwise, you could end up (like me) eating more than you should. Simply put, this is addictive stuff. I liken these warm, gooey bread balls to the most amazing glazed doughnut hole you have ever had. There are several recipes floating about for monkey bread that use canned biscuit dough, but I ask you to kindly refrain from this expedient fix because the result won't be as tasty, and it is more expensive. The origin of the name monkey bread or monkey bubble bread is quite hard to pinpoint, and while many dubious answers exist (the bread resembles a monkey puzzle tree or monkeys love to pull things apart), none of them are definitive, and some are cloyingly cute. I hate cloyingly cute. Suffice it to say that the source of the name is just one of life's great mysteries, and we should leave it at that.

MAKE THE MONKEY BUBBLE BREAD Generously spray the inside of a 10-inch Bundt pan with nonstick cooking spray.

In a small saucepan, warm your milk to slightly above room temperature, then remove it from the heat, add the yeast, and whisk to dissolve. (Do not warm it beyond 110°F or you will kill the yeast).

In the bowl of a standing mixer fitted with the paddle attachment, beat the flour, sugar, and salt until combined.

In a small bowl, beat the egg with a fork and add it to the dry ingredients. Mix on low speed until combined.

Keeping the mixer on low, slowly stream in the milk until combined. Add the melted butter and mix until the dough comes together. Replace the paddle attachment with the dough hook attachment. Continue to mix on medium speed until the dough becomes silky and tacky, but not sticky, 8 to 10 minutes. The dough should mound together and easily come off the bottom of the mixing bowl. (If the dough is too wet, add some flour. If it is too dry, add a tiny bit of water.)

AUTHOR'S NOTE
There are a lot of monkey bread misconceptions, and I will do my darnedest to dispel them. First, you do not need an icing or topping for this bread—too sweet. Second, you can make the dough ahead of time. Once the dipped dough has been placed in the pan, wrap it tightly, refrigerate it, and bring it back to room temperature to "proof" the dough before baking. Lastly, this is one of those breads that exists to be eaten warm, straight from the oven. Once the caramel begins to cool, reheat the bread in the oven before serving.

Spray the bottom and sides of a large bowl with cooking spray. Place the dough in the bowl and roll it around to make sure it is completely covered in oil. Cover the bowl with plastic wrap or a dish towel and let it rest in a warm area until the dough has doubled in size, approximately 1 hour.

Line a sheet pan with parchment paper.

Use your clean hands to push down and deflate the dough. Remove it from the bowl and pat it into a rough circle approximately 8 inches diameter. Use a bench knife or serrated knife to cut dough into 1- to 1½-inch pieces (about ½ ounce each)—alternatively, use your hands to pinch apart the dough. Roll the pieces into balls (they don't have to be perfectly round). Place the balls on the sheet pan (you will get about 60 pieces in all). Cover the balls lightly with plastic wrap.

MAKE THE CINNAMON SUGAR COATING In a small bowl, stir together the sugar and cinnamon. Place the melted butter in a separate bowl.

ASSEMBLE THE BREAD Remove the plastic wrap from the dough balls and dip one ball in the melted butter. Let the excess butter drip back into the bowl, roll the ball in the brown sugar mixture, and place it in the Bundt pan. Continue this process with each ball, until you have several layers, arranging them as if you are building a brick wall.

Wrap the Bundt pan tightly in plastic wrap. Set it in a warm area of the house for about 1 hour, or until the dough balls have doubled in size and appear puffy.

Preheat the oven to 350°F. Remove the plastic and bake the Bundt until the top layer is deep brown and the caramel coating begins to bubble around the edges, about 30 minutes.

Cool the bread for 5 minutes, then turn it out directly onto a platter and serve warm. Should you have any leftovers (this is rare, I promise you), simply reheat them in a 300°F oven until warm to the touch.

Other than melting chocolate, this recipe is as simple as mixing the ingredients and pouring them into a cast-iron skillet. Though you could use a regular baking pan, the cast-iron is what gives the cake its great crust.

QUICK SKILLET SNACK CAKE

YIELD: ONE 10-INCH SKILLET CAKE

FOR THE CHOCOLATE CAKE

- ½ cup unsweetened dark cocoa powder (like Valrhona)
- 2 ounces good-quality dark chocolate (60 to 72 percent), coarsely chopped
- 1 teaspoon instant espresso powder
- 1½ cups all-purpose flour
- 1 teaspoon baking soda
- 1 teaspoon salt
- ½ cup (1 stick) unsalted butter, cut into 1-inch cubes, at room temperature
- 2 tablespoons vegetable shortening, at room temperature
- 1 cup firmly packed dark brown sugar
- ¼ cup granulated sugar
- 1 teaspoon pure vanilla extract
- 3 large eggs
- ¼ cup plus 2 tablespoons buttermilk, shaken vigorously

FOR THE CHOCOLATE FROSTING

- ½ cup (1 stick) unsalted butter, softened
- 1 cup confectioners' sugar, sifted
- 1 tablespoon pure vanilla extract
- 3 ounces good-quality dark chocolate (60 to 72 percent), melted and cooled

A good, solid, easy-to-put-together, and easy-to-bake snackin' cake should be part of every home baker's repertoire, and this is our go-to solution. It's a springy chocolate cake with a slathering of fudgy frosting and my favorite part: It's baked in a skillet, which gives the sides a fun crunch. This is the cake I make when I have a hankering for something less celebratory and more quick and dirty—the kind of cake I can throw together for an impromptu afternoon gathering. If I am toting the cake to a destination, I put the whole thing back in the skillet for ease in carrying.

MAKE THE CHOCOLATE CAKE Preheat the oven to 350°F.

Grease a 10-inch cast-iron skillet or ovenproof stainless-steel skillet with butter. (The heavy, dark-colored cast-iron skillet will make the sides of the cake more crispy than a stainless steel one.) Line the pan with parchment paper and butter the parchment. Dust the parchment with flour and knock out the excess.

In a small, heatproof bowl, whisk together the cocoa powder, chocolate, and espresso powder. Add ¾ cup very hot water, wait 1 minute, and then whisk the mixture until it is melted and smooth. Set aside to cool.

In another small bowl, whisk together the flour, baking soda, and salt.

In the bowl of a standing mixer fitted with the paddle attachment, beat the butter and shortening together on medium speed until creamy, 2 to 3 minutes. Add the sugars and vanilla and beat until fluffy, about 3 minutes. Scrape down the bowl, add the eggs one at a time, and beat until just combined. Turn the mixer to its lowest setting, and in a slow, steady stream, add the reserved chocolate mixture. Scrape down the bowl again, then turn the mixer to low. Add the flour mixture in three parts, alternating with the buttermilk, beginning and ending with the flour mixture. Scrape down the bowl, then mix for a few more seconds and pour the batter into the prepared skillet. Smooth the surface with a spatula.

AUTHOR'S NOTE
I often get asked about the necessity of using shortening in this recipe. Do you have to do it? Not really. Can you replace it with butter? Yes, I suppose. Just note that shortening gives the cake a really great springy texture, and shortening is not necessarily the devil it is made out to be. Crisco, the classic vegetable shortening, makes a trans-fat-free version, and Spectrum Naturals makes an organic trans-fat-free version.

Bake for 40 to 45 minutes, rotating the skillet halfway through the baking time, until a toothpick inserted in the center of the cake comes out clean. Transfer the pan to a wire rack to cool for about 15 minutes. Run a paring knife around the sides of the pan and flip the cake out onto a cooling rack. Turn the cake right side up and let it sit on the rack until completely cool.

MAKE THE CHOCOLATE FROSTING In the bowl of a standing mixer fitted with the paddle attachment, beat the butter on high speed until creamy, about 2 minutes. Add the confectioners' sugar all at once and beat until completely blended, about 2 minutes. Add the vanilla and beat for 15 seconds. Scrape down the bowl and add the melted, cooled chocolate. Beat until smooth, continuing to scrape down the sides of the bowl as needed until the frosting is uniform in color.

Transfer the skillet cake to a cake board or serving platter. Use an offset spatula to spread the frosting evenly across the top. Serve it immediately or refrigerate it, if necessary. Bring it back to room temperature before serving.

This epic pie features a crunchy Oreo cookie crust, fudgy flourless chocolate cake and airy chocolate pudding. Do as Lewis and Poliafito advise and make the pie over the course of two days to break up the lengthy process.

MISSISSIPPI MUD PIE

aka muddy mississippi cake

YIELD: ONE 9-INCH ROUND CAKE

FOR THE CHOCOLATE COOKIE CRUST

- 16 ounces chocolate sandwich cookies such as Oreos (35 to 40 cookes), crushed
- 5 tablespoons unsalted butter, melted

FOR THE FLOURLESS CHOCOLATE CAKE

- 4 tablespoons (½ stick) unsalted butter
- 6 ounces good-quality dark chocolate (60 to 70 percent), chopped
- 2 tablespoons plus 1 teaspoon instant espresso powder
- ¼ cup strong coffee, at room temperature
- ¼ teaspoon salt
- 1 tablespoon pure vanilla extract
- 6 large eggs, separated, at room temperature
- 1 cup sugar

FOR THE CHOCOLATE PUDDING

- ¾ cup sugar
- ½ cup dark unsweetened cocoa powder (like Valrhona)
- ¼ cup cornstarch
- ¼ teaspoon salt
- 4 large egg yolks
- 2½ cups whole milk
- 3 tablespoons unsalted butter
- 2 teaspoons pure vanilla extract
- 3 ounces good-quality dark chocolate (60 to 70 percent)

ASSEMBLY

Simple Whipped Cream (recipe follows)

Though Mississippi mud pie was a staple of Southern menus during my collegiate youth, there is no real indication that this dessert was created in Mississippi (or even the South). To further complicate matters, it seems that Mississippi mud pie (or cake) varies widely in interpretation and means many things to many people. If I had to identify the characteristics of a typical Mississippi mud, I'd say it is a very dense, very sweet chocolate cake. Fudgy comes to mind. It is also probably covered or made with marshmallows and topped with pecans and chocolate sauce. The usual Mississippi mud is far too sweet and strangely dense for my taste buds these days, so I created a dreamier, more elegant version. I bake a flourless chocolate cake inside a cookie crust and top it with a layer of silky chocolate pudding and whipped cream. It is, by far, the Baked staff favorite.

MAKE THE CHOCOLATE COOKIE CRUST Preheat the oven to 300°F. Lightly spray a 9-inch springform pan with nonstick cooking spray. Line the pan with parchment paper and lightly spray the parchment and sides of the pan.

In a food processor, grind the cookies to a very fine crumb. You should have about 3½ cups. Put the crumbs in a small bowl. Pour the melted butter over them and mix with a rubber spatula until well combined.

Turn the crumb mixture into the prepared pan and press it into the bottom and up the sides, leaving about ½ inch between the top of the crust and the top of the pan. Use the back of a large spoon to get an even layer of crust. Place the pan in the freezer and let the crust set for about 10 minutes.

Bake the crust in the oven until it is dry to the touch, about 10 minutes. Transfer the pan to a wire rack and let cool.

continued on page 142

mississippi mud pie continued

AUTHOR'S NOTE

This is an easy, though many-stepped, recipe. Don't fear, just break up the parts over the course of two days. Make the cookie crust and cake on day one, and make the pudding on the day you're going to serve the dessert. Keep in mind that the cake requires 3 hours to set before it can be cut. The whipped cream topping can be made 15 minutes before serving.

MAKE THE FLOURLESS CHOCOLATE CAKE Increase the oven temperature to 350°F.

Using a double boiler or microwave, melt the butter and chocolate together. Set aside to cool.

In a small bowl, whisk together the espresso powder, coffee, salt, and vanilla. Set aside.

In the bowl of a standing mixer fitted with the whisk attachment, beat the egg yolks with ½ cup of the sugar until the mixture is light and has almost doubled in volume, about 5 minutes. Add the chocolate mixture and beat until just combined. Scrape down the sides and bottom of the bowl and mix on low speed for 5 seconds. Add the coffee mixture and beat until just combined. Scrape down the sides and bottom of the bowl and mix on low for 5 seconds.

In a clean bowl fitted with the whisk attachment (or you can elect to do this step by hand if you are feeling strong), beat the egg whites until foamy. Gradually increase the speed to high and add the remaining ½ cup sugar, beating until soft peaks form.

Scoop 1 cup of the egg whites into the chocolate mixture. Use a rubber spatula to gently fold in the egg whites. After about 30 seconds of folding, add the remaining egg whites and continue folding until they are almost completely combined. Do not rush the folding process, work gently, and take care not to overmix. Pour the batter onto the cooled cookie crust and bake for 38 to 42 minutes, until the cake is set but still jiggles slightly. It might not appear to be completely cooked. Transfer it to a wire rack and cool completely. (As it cools, the cake will deflate in the center and look sunken. Do not despair, this is just the way it settles.) Tightly wrap and refrigerate the cake for at least 3 hours or overnight.

MAKE THE CHOCOLATE PUDDING In a medium saucepan, whisk together the sugar, cocoa powder, cornstarch, and salt. Add the egg yolks and whisk until combined. The mixture will look like a thick paste. Slowly pour in the milk, whisking constantly.

In a saucepan over medium heat, bring the mixture to a boil, whisking constantly to prevent it from burning on the bottom of the pan. Boil for 30 seconds, then transfer it to a medium bowl. Add the butter, vanilla, and chocolate and whisk until combined. Continue to whisk for a few more minutes to cool the mixture slightly. Let the pudding stand for 15 minutes at room temperature. Press a piece of plastic wrap directly onto the surface of the pudding to prevent a skin from forming, and chill it for at least 3 hours.

TO ASSEMBLE THE MISSISSIPPI MUD PIE Stir the pudding to loosen it, then pour it on top of the cake, making sure to stay inside the cookie-crust border. Use an offset spatula to spread the pudding into an even layer. Return the cake to the refrigerator for at least 30 minutes while you prepare the whipped cream topping. Spread whipped cream across the pudding layer, all the way out to the sides, unmold the cake, and serve it immediately.

The cake can be kept, covered, in the refrigerator for up to 2 days.

SIMPLE WHIPPED CREAM

YIELD: ABOUT 2 CUPS WHIPPED CREAM

- 1¼ cups heavy cream
- 2 tablespoons granulated sugar

Pour the cream into a chilled metal bowl and beat with a chilled whisk for about 1 minute or until soft peaks form. Sprinkle the sugar on the cream and continue whisking vigorously until stiff peaks form.

The Baked guys set out to satisfy everyone who finds the crunchy crumb topping as appealing as the cake by making both parts almost equal in size.

NEW YORK–STYLE CRUMB CAKE

YIELD: ONE 9-BY-13-INCH CAKE

FOR THE CRUMB TOPPING

- 1 cup firmly packed dark brown sugar
- ½ cup granulated sugar
- ½ teaspoon salt
- 1½ tablespoons cinnamon
- 1 cup (2 sticks) unsalted butter, melted and warm
- 2½ cups all-purpose flour

FOR THE CAKE

- 2½ cups all-purpose flour
- ¾ teaspoon baking powder
- 1 teaspoon baking soda
- ½ teaspoon salt
- 12 tablespoons (1½ sticks) unsalted butter
- 1½ cups granulated sugar
- 2 large eggs
- 1¼ cups sour cream
- 1 teaspoon pure vanilla extract

I learned the hard way: New York–style crumb cake is not to be confused with coffee cake—ever. A very passionate born and bred New Yorker (aka Renato Poliafito) informed me, quite brutally, about the not-so-subtle differences between the two. It was a dressing down I won't ever forget. It was as if I'd confused Picasso with Norman Rockwell. First and foremost, New York crumb cake is all about the crumb topping. It is obscenely large in proportion to the cake. In fact, the topping is nearly identical in thickness—or even thicker than—the cake. Second of all, the crumb should never contain nuts—no crushed nuts, no whole nuts, no hint of a nut whatsoever. Finally, a true New York crumb cake is swirl free. This was the hardest part for me to reconcile, as I love a chocolate nut swirl, and this cake seems like a natural swirl candidate. But I obeyed the New York Crumb Commandments and am now a convert myself.

Preheat the oven to 350°F and position the rack in the center. Butter the sides and bottom of a glass 9-by-13-inch pan. You can use a metal pan, but the edges of the cake may turn crispy (although that is not traditional, it is not an altogether bad thing).

MAKE THE CRUMB TOPPING In a medium bowl, stir together both sugars, the salt, and cinnamon. Add the melted butter and whisk until combined. Fold in the flour until it is absorbed and set the mixture aside.

MAKE THE CAKE Sift the flour, baking powder, baking soda, and salt together in a medium bowl. Set aside.

In the bowl of a standing mixer fitted with the paddle attachment, cream the butter until it is completely smooth and ribbonlike. Scrape down the bowl and add the sugar. Beat the mixture until it starts to look fluffy.

continued on page 146

crumb cake continued

AUTHOR'S NOTE
Renato likes this cake with really huge crumb chunks. To attain these gargantuan boulders of sugar, make sure you give the crumb time to rest. I sometimes cheat the process and spread the topping mixture on a parchment-lined baking sheet to make it dry a bit faster; however, you don't want it to dry out completely.

Add the eggs, one at a time, and beat until incorporated. Scrape down the sides of the bowl and mix again for 30 seconds. Add the sour cream and vanilla and beat just until incorporated. Add the dry ingredients in three parts, scraping down the bowl before each addition, beating only until it is just incorporated.

ASSEMBLE THE CAKE Pour the batter into the prepared pan. Use your hands to scoop up a handful of the topping and make a fist. The topping should hold together. Break off in chunks and drop them over the cake. Repeat to use all the topping. Remember, the topping layer will look outrageously thick.

Bake the cake for 45 to 55 minutes, or until a toothpick inserted in the middle comes out clean. Rotate the pan two times during the baking process. Cool the entire pan on a wire rack for about 30 minutes before serving.

The cake will last for 3 days, tightly covered, at room temperature.

BEST OF THE BEST EXCLUSIVE

The duo from Baked usually like intense desserts; this is a more restrained cookie that is rich in taste but light in texture. "These cookies will sneak up on you," they warn. "You'll find yourself munching on them morning, noon and night."

ULTIMATE CHOCOLATE CREAM CHEESE COOKIES

YIELD: 4½ DOZEN COOKIES

- 2¼ cups all-purpose flour
- ¼ cup unsweetened cocoa powder, preferably Valrhona
- 2 teaspoons baking soda
- ½ teaspoon salt
- 2 sticks unsalted butter, softened slightly
- 4 ounces cream cheese, at room temperature
- 1 cup granulated sugar
- ½ cup dark brown sugar
- 2 large eggs
- 2 tablespoons heavy cream
- 1 teaspoon pure vanilla extract
- 3 ounces bittersweet chocolate, melted and cooled
- 8 ounces semisweet chocolate chips

1. Preheat the oven to 350°F and line 2 baking sheets with parchment paper. In a medium bowl, sift the flour with the cocoa powder, baking soda and salt. In the bowl of a standing mixer fitted with the paddle, combine the butter, cream cheese, granulated sugar and brown sugar and beat until fluffy, about 3 minutes. Scrape down the side of the bowl. Beat in the eggs, heavy cream and vanilla until blended. At low speed, beat in the dry ingredients. Add the melted chocolate and chocolate chips and beat just until incorporated. Cover the bowl and refrigerate the dough for at least 15 minutes or up to 2 hours.

2. Scoop heaping tablespoons of cookie dough onto the prepared baking sheets, spacing them 2 inches apart. Bake for 12 minutes, until the cookies are just set; shift the baking sheets from top to bottom and front to back halfway through. Let the cookies cool on the baking sheets for 5 minutes, then transfer them to a rack to cool completely.

MAKE AHEAD The cookies can be stored in an airtight container for up to 3 days.

BAKED ONLINE

bakednyc.com

BAKED

@brooklynbaker

Salted peanut toffee cookies, page 150

CHEWY GOOEY CRISPY CRUNCHY MELT-IN-YOUR-MOUTH COOKIES

→ 14

Alice Medrich

In this nearly 400-page cookbook, pastry queen Alice Medrich brings some 40 years of writing and baking experience to bear as she reinvents the cookie. She asks: "What if cookies reflected our modern culinary sensibility—our spirit of adventure and passion for flavors and even our dietary concerns—without losing their universal friendly appeal?" So, while Medrich's book includes plenty of familiar recipes like buttery rugelach and miniature pecan rolls, she alters them for today's tastes with more salt, less butter and sugar and the use of herbs like thyme and saffron. Divided into chapter by texture, the book's recipes are hyperspecific and rigorously tested and range in difficulty from beginner (Caramel Cheesecake Bars) to advanced (authentic French *macarons*).

Published by Artisan, $25.95

This recipe is fabulous as is or with any of the upgrades Medrich suggests: white chocolate, jam, Thai-spiced cashews or even, amazingly, hot sauce.

SALTED PEANUT TOFFEE COOKIES

MAKES ABOUT FIFTY-SIX 1½-INCH COOKIES

- **1⅓ cups (6 ounces) unbleached all-purpose flour**
- **½ teaspoon baking soda**
- **1 teaspoon flaky sea salt or ¾ teaspoon fine sea salt**
- **8 tablespoons (1 stick) unsalted butter, melted**
- **½ cup (3.5 ounces) packed light or dark brown sugar**
- **½ cup (3.5 ounces) granulated sugar**
- **1 large egg**
- **1 teaspoon pure vanilla extract**
- **1 cup (9 ounces) natural (but *not* unsalted) chunky peanut butter—stir well to blend in the oil before measuring**
- **5 ounces store-bought Coconut Toffee Peanuts or Toffee Peanuts, coarsely chopped**

EQUIPMENT

Cookie sheets, lined with parchment paper or greased

Encrusted with toffee-coated peanuts and accented with flaky sea salt, these updated peanut butter cookies have a tender melt-in-your-mouth shortbread texture. They are festive enough for a party but easy enough for every day.

Combine the flour, baking soda, and salt in a medium bowl and mix together thoroughly with a whisk or fork.

In a large bowl, mix the melted butter with the sugars. Whisk in the egg, vanilla, and peanut butter, add the flour mixture, and mix with a rubber spatula or wooden spoon just until evenly incorporated.

Cover the dough and refrigerate for an hour or two and up to 2 days.

Preheat the oven to 325°F. Position racks in the upper and lower thirds of the oven.

Pour the chopped nuts into a shallow bowl. Scoop about 2 level teaspoons of dough for each cookie, shape into a 1-inch ball or a fat little log, and coat the top and sides heavily with the chopped nuts, pressing in any pieces that fall off so that there are no bald spots. Place 2 inches apart on the lined or greased pans.

Bake the cookies for 15 to 18 minutes, until they are lightly colored on top (and underneath). Rotate the sheets from top to bottom and from front to back halfway through the baking time to ensure even baking. The cookies will seem very soft to the touch (and the one you turn over to assess color may even fall apart), but they will firm up as they cool. For lined pans, set the pans or just the liners on racks to cool; for unlined pans, use a metal spatula to transfer the cookies to racks. Cool the cookies completely before storing. May be kept in an airtight container for at least 2 weeks.

UPGRADES

> SALTED PEANUT TOFFEE THUMBPRINTS WITH WHITE CHOCOLATE
Surprisingly, white chocolate tastes better than dark or milk chocolate in these cookies (and this from a huge fan of bittersweet chocolate!). And chopped pieces from a bar of "real" white chocolate taste better than white chocolate chips. Have ready 4 ounces white chocolate cut into little pieces or ⅔ cup (4 ounces) white chocolate chips. Bake the cookies in the shape of balls as described. As soon as the pans come out of the oven, press the back of a chopstick or dowel into the center of each hot cookie and move it around gently to widen the hole. Tuck pieces of chocolate (or chips) into each depression while the cookies are still hot.

> SALTED PEANUT TOFFEE THUMBPRINTS WITH JAM
Have ready about ½ cup (5.5 ounces) strawberry or other jam or preserves. Bake the cookies in the shape of balls as described. As soon as the pans come out of the oven, press the back of a chopstick or dowel into the center of each hot cookie and move it around gently to widen the hole. Cool the cookies. Just before serving, fill the depressions with jam.

> SALTED PEANUT COOKIES WITH THAI CURRY CASHEWS
Made by Sunridge Farms, Thai Curry Cashews can be found in bulk bins in some supermarkets. Substitute Thai Curry Cashews for the toffee peanuts.

> SPICY SALTED PEANUT TOFFEE COOKIES
Add ½ to 1 teaspoon Thai curry paste or other hot sauce to the dough with the peanut butter.

This recipe for miniature sticky buns offers two great time-saving ideas: using both a cream-based, yeast-free dough and mini muffin pans.

STICKY PECAN BITES

MAKES 24 ROLLS

- 24 pecan halves
- 1 cup (4.5 ounces) unbleached all-purpose flour
- 1 teaspoon baking powder
- ¼ teaspoon salt, plus additional for sprinkling
- ¾ cup heavy cream
- ½ cup (3.5 ounces) packed brown or muscovado sugar
- ½ teaspoon ground cinnamon
- 2 tablespoons unsalted butter, very soft

EQUIPMENT

- 1 miniature muffin pan with 24 cups, or 2 miniature muffin pans with 12 cups each

Rich, tender, cakey, with a bit of caramely brown sugar goop. Think bite-sized sticky buns without the time-consuming yeast dough. These little cheaters are made with a quick stirred-together cream biscuit concoction. Too simple for words.

Preheat the oven to 400°F. Position a rack in the lower third of the oven. Lightly grease the muffin cups unless they are nonstick pans.

Place a pecan half in each cup, top side down. Combine the flour, baking powder, and ¼ teaspoon salt in a medium bowl and mix together thoroughly with a whisk or fork. Make a well in the center. Pour the cream into the well. Use a rubber spatula to fold and stir the flour mixture and cream together just until the dry ingredients are entirely moistened and a soft dough is formed; it should not look perfectly smooth. Let the dough rest for 2 to 3 minutes to firm up. Meanwhile, mix the sugar with the cinnamon.

On a lightly floured surface, with a floured rolling pin, roll the dough to a rectangle 12 by 7 inches and ¼ inch thick. Spread the dough with the soft butter, and sprinkle with a pinch of salt and the brown sugar. Starting at one short end, roll the dough tightly. Gently stretch the dough to lengthen the roll. Cut the roll crosswise into 24 equal pieces. Place each piece in a muffin cup, cut side up.

Bake for 12 to 15 minutes, until well browned. Rotate the pan(s) from front to back halfway through the baking time to ensure even baking. Immediately turn the cookies out onto a sheet of parchment on a heatproof surface. Serve on the day you make them.

UPGRADE

> CHOCOLATE ROLL-UPS

Omit the pecans, cinnamon, and butter. Spread the dough with a mixture of ½ cup sour cream and ¼ cup packed brown sugar. Sprinkle evenly with 1¾ ounces finely chopped semisweet or bittersweet chocolate with 55 percent to 62 percent cacao.

Medrich's rugelach are traditional, if a bit bigger than the typical stubby cookies. The dough is flaky—thanks to lots of butter and cream cheese—and the filling is a not-too-sweet mix of walnuts, currants, cinnamon and brown sugar.

RUGELACH

MAKES 48 COOKIES

FOR THE DOUGH

- 2½ cups (11.25 ounces) unbleached all-purpose flour
- 2 tablespoons sugar
- ¼ teaspoon salt, plus additional for sprinkling
- ½ pound (2 sticks) unsalted butter, cold
- 8 ounces cream cheese, cold

FOR THE FILLING

- 2 tablespoons granulated sugar
- ½ cup (3.5 ounces) packed brown sugar
- 1 teaspoon ground cinnamon
- 1 cup (3.75 ounces) finely chopped walnuts
- ½ cup (2.5 ounces) currants

EQUIPMENT

Cookie sheets, lined with parchment paper or foil

Stand mixer with paddle attachment or food processor

Rugelach are miniature flaky pastries masquerading as cookies. Simple and fun to make, they can be filled with anything you can dream up, though the classic sugar, cinnamon, nuts, and currants combo is hard to beat. As children, my mother taught us to make primitive rugelach by rolling up cinnamon-sugar-sprinkled scraps of leftover pie dough. Which is just to say you can even get by without nuts or currants!

TO MAKE THE DOUGH Combine the flour, sugar, and ¼ teaspoon salt in the bowl of a stand mixer. Using the paddle attachment, mix briefly to distribute the ingredients. Cut each stick of butter into 8 pieces and add them to the bowl. Mix on low speed until most of the mixture resembles very coarse bread crumbs with a few larger pieces of butter the size of hazelnuts. Cut the cream cheese into 1-inch cubes and add them to the bowl. Mix on medium-low speed until the mixture is damp and shaggy looking and holds together when pressed with your fingers, 30 to 60 seconds. Dump the dough onto the work surface, scraping the bowl. Knead two or three times to incorporate any loose pieces. There should be large streaks of cream cheese.

Divide the dough into 4 pieces. Press each piece into a flat patty about 4 inches in diameter. Wrap and refrigerate until firm, at least 2 hours and up to 3 days.

Preheat the oven to 350°F. Position racks in the upper and lower thirds of the oven.

TO MAKE THE FILLING Combine the sugars, cinnamon, walnuts, and currants in a medium bowl and mix together thoroughly with a whisk or fork. Remove 1 piece of dough from the refrigerator. If necessary, let it stand at room temperature until pliable enough to roll, but not too soft. Roll into a 12-inch circle a scant ⅛ inch thick between sheets of wax paper. Peel the top sheet of wax paper from the dough and place it on the counter or a cutting board. Flip the dough over onto the paper and peel off the second sheet. Sprinkle a quarter of the filling over the dough, and then sprinkle with a tiny pinch of salt. Roll over the filling with a rolling pin to press it gently into the dough. Cut the dough like a pie into 12 equal wedges. Roll the wide outside edge up around the filling toward the point. Place the roll, with the dough point underneath to prevent it from unrolling, on the lined cookie sheets. Repeat with the remaining wedges, placing cookies 1½ inches apart. If at any time the dough becomes too soft to roll, return it to the refrigerator to firm up. Roll, cut, and fill the remaining pieces of dough.

Bake for about 25 minutes, until the cookies are light golden brown at the edges. Rotate the pans from top to bottom and from front to back halfway through the baking time to ensure even baking. Set the pans or just the liners on racks to cool. Cool the rugelach completely before storing or stacking. Rugelach are always most exquisite on the day they are baked, but they remain delicious, stored in an airtight container, for about 5 days.

UPGRADES

> APRICOT NUT RUGELACH
Process 1 cup apricot jam or preserves in a food processor if there are large pieces of fruit. Mix with ½ teaspoon ground cinnamon. Roll out the dough as described. In place of the filling, spread each piece with one-quarter of the jam mixture and then sprinkle with ¼ cup finely chopped walnuts. Sprinkle with salt, roll up, and bake as described.

> CHOCOLATE HAZELNUT RUGELACH
Combine ½ cup (3.5 ounces) sugar, 1 teaspoon pure vanilla extract, 1 cup (4 ounces) finely chopped toasted and skinned hazelnuts, and 1 cup (6 ounces) miniature chocolate chips. Use in place of the filling. Sprinkle with salt, roll up, and bake as directed.

It's worth buying artisanal caramel for this recipe, since it's a key ingredient. Adding salt to the caramel brings a bit of savory flavor to these gooey bars.

CARAMEL CHEESECAKE BARS

MAKES THIRTY-SIX 1½-BY-2-INCH BARS

- **1 recipe Shortbread Crust (recipe follows)**
- **½ cup (6 ounces) caramel sauce, purchased or homemade**
- **⅛ teaspoon salt**
- **1½ pounds cream cheese, at room temperature**
- **¼ cup (1.75 ounces) sugar**
- **1½ teaspoons pure vanilla extract**
- **2 large eggs, at room temperature**

EQUIPMENT

A 9-by-13-inch metal baking pan or an 8-by-12-inch quarter sheet pan, the bottom and all 4 sides lined with foil

Creamy and gooey! Rich vanilla cheesecake, slightly tangy, laced with sweet salted caramel. The flavor and texture of cheesecake only gets better, so make these a day or two ahead if you can.

Prepare the shortbread crust.

Preheat the oven to 325°F.

Stir the caramel sauce together with the salt. Set aside.

In a medium mixing bowl, with an electric mixer, beat the cream cheese just until smooth, about 30 seconds. Scrape the bowl and beaters. Add the sugar and vanilla and beat just until smooth and creamy, 1 to 2 minutes. Add 1 egg and beat just until incorporated. Scrape the bowl and beaters. Beat in the second egg. Stir 2 tablespoons of the batter into the caramel sauce. Pour the remaining batter over the prepared crust and smooth the top.

Spoon pools of the caramel mixture over the filling, leaving plenty of plain filling showing. If the caramel does not settle into the batter, jiggle the pan gently until the surface is level. Marble the caramel with a toothpick by stirring gently—being careful not to scrape the crust—in small loopy circles until the colors are marbled but not blended. Bake for 20 to 25 minutes, until the filling is puffed at the edges but still jiggles like Jell-O when the pan is nudged.

Set the pan on a cooling rack. When the bars are completely cool, cover and refrigerate the bars until set, at least 4 hours, but preferably 24 hours before serving. To serve, lift the edges of the foil liner and transfer to a cutting board. Use a long sharp knife to cut into bars 1½ by 2 inches. May be kept in an airtight container, refrigerated, for up to 4 days.

continued on page 158

Peanut caramel cheesecake bars,
page 158

caramel cheesecake bars continued

UPGRADES

> PEANUT CARAMEL CHEESECAKE BARS
Use only a scant ½ cup of caramel sauce. Mix ⅓ cup (3 ounces) well-stirred creamy natural peanut butter (see Note) into the sauce with the salt. Do not add any of the cheesecake batter to the caramel mixture. If the mixture is too thick or stiff to flow (slightly) from a spoon, warm it briefly in a pan of hot water or for a few seconds in the microwave. Use as directed.

> ALMOND OR HAZELNUT CARAMEL OR HONEY CHEESECAKE BARS
Use only a scant ½ cup of caramel sauce or substitute honey. Mix ⅓ cup (3 ounces) well-stirred roasted almond or hazelnut butter (see Note) into the sauce with the salt. Do not add any of the cheesecake batter to the caramel or honey mixture. Add a bit of extra salt to taste if the nut butters are unsalted. If the mixture is too thick or stiff to flow (slightly) from a spoon, warm it briefly in a pan of hot water or for a few seconds in the microwave. Use as directed.

NOTE A natural nut butter (peanut, almond, or hazelnut), without sugar or emulsifier, must be stirred before using in order to blend in any separated nut oils. Nevertheless, it is a better choice for this recipe than emulsified or no-stir nut butters.

SHORTBREAD CRUST

Tender, buttery, crunchy, this is a great base for cheesecake bars, pudding bars, and more.

MAKES ONE 9-BY-13-INCH OR 8-BY-12-INCH CRUST

- **14 tablespoons (1¾ sticks) unsalted butter, melted and still warm**
- **½ cup (3.5 ounces) sugar**
- **2 teaspoons pure vanilla extract**
- **⅜ teaspoon salt**
- **2 cups (9 ounces) unbleached all-purpose flour**

Preheat the oven to 350°F. Position a rack in the lower third of the oven. Line the pan as specified in the individual recipe with foil. In a medium bowl, mix the melted butter with the sugar, vanilla, and salt. Add the flour and mix just until incorporated. Don't worry if the dough seems too soft or oily. Press and smooth the dough evenly over the bottom of the pan. Bake for 20 to 25 minutes, until the crust is a rich golden brown with well-browned darker edges. Let cool on a rack before proceeding as directed in the recipe.

BEST OF THE BEST EXCLUSIVE

This torte was inspired by a recipe from Medrich's mother's copy of the 1948 Settlement Cook Book: The Way to a Man's Heart. *"It needs no frosting at all," Medrich says, "but is great with a dollop of whipped cream or mascarpone."*

not your mother's

FLOURLESS CARROT & ALMOND TORTE

SERVES 8 TO 10

- 1½ cups almonds (about 8 ounces)
- 4 large eggs, at room temperature, separated
- ⅛ teaspoon cream of tartar
- ¾ cup plus 2 tablespoons sugar
- 2 teaspoons finely grated orange zest
- ½ teaspoon cinnamon
- ¼ teaspoon pure almond extract
- ¼ teaspoon salt
- 2 cups finely grated carrots (about 1 pound), squeezed dry

Mascarpone cheese, for serving

1. Preheat the oven to 325°F. Butter an 8-inch springform pan. In a food processor, pulse the almonds until finely ground.

2. In a large bowl, using a handheld electric mixer, beat the egg whites with the cream of tartar at medium-high speed until soft peaks form. At medium speed, beat in 2 tablespoons of the sugar, then beat at high speed until stiff peaks form. Wipe the beaters clean.

3. In a medium bowl, beat the remaining ¾ cup of sugar with the egg yolks, orange zest, cinnamon, almond extract and salt until thickened and light in color, about 3 minutes. Using a rubber spatula, fold in the carrots and one-third of the beaten egg whites until incorporated, then fold in the remaining egg whites and the ground almonds.

4. Scrape the batter into the prepared pan and bake for about 45 minutes, until the torte is golden brown and just pulling away from the side of the pan. Transfer the torte to a rack to cool completely. Remove the ring and serve the torte with mascarpone cheese.

MAKE AHEAD The torte can be kept in an airtight container for up to 3 days.

ALICE MEDRICH ONLINE

alicemedrich.com

Alice Medrich

Roasted heirloom squash with sea salt and local honey, page 162

SUSTAINABLY DELICIOUS

→ 15

Michel Nischan with Mary Goodbody

Chef Michel Nischan of Dressing Room in Westport, Connecticut, knows the power of American classics like burgers, chicken pot pie and tomato soup in advancing the sustainability cause. In his third cookbook, he shares recipes that are both eco-conscious and satisfying, like a corn chowder that gets its rich flavor not from cream but from roasted native corn that simmers in a stock thickened with freshly squeezed corn juice. Throughout, there are smart, modern dishes like "Use a Spoon" Chopped Salad (a favorite of Paul Newman's, who launched Dressing Room with Nischan), combining quick-pickled vegetables, apple, goat cheese, almond slivers and greens. Nischan has an admirable mission: "to support the health of the planet . . . and of our families, both physically and spiritually." But this book is not just about sustainability. It's about pleasure, too. *Published by Rodale, $35*

In this supersimple preparation for squash, honey plays a big part. Seek out different types for varying effect, like tupelo, which adds a floral aroma, or buckwheat honey, which has a more earthy, molasses-like flavor.

ROASTED HEIRLOOM SQUASH

with sea salt & local honey

SERVES 6 TO 8

4 to 5 pounds hard winter squash in 2 varieties, such as butternut and kabocha, seeded (but not peeled) and cut into 1-inch slices or wedges, whichever shape best represents the original shape of the squash
2 tablespoons local honey
¼ cup extra-virgin olive oil
Sea salt and freshly ground black pepper
2 to 3 tablespoons chopped fresh herbs, such as sage, rosemary, thyme, oregano, and marjoram

Squash takes just about any kind of heat. When you cook it as I do here, the flesh dehydrates a little and turns meaty, so all it needs is a little drizzle of honey and a sprinkle of salt. Squash is forgiving no matter how you cook it, but only if you start with a good specimen. If you prefer, cook it to the texture you like best, and don't follow a prescribed time.

Preheat the oven to 375°F.

Lightly drizzle the squash with the honey and oil in a large bowl. Using your fingers, rub the honey and oil into the squash pieces to distribute evenly. Sprinkle with salt and pepper. Arrange the squash pieces, skin side down, on a baking sheet.

Bake the squash for 35 to 45 minutes, turning the pieces once or twice during cooking, or until the squash is fork-tender when pierced with a fork or a small, sharp knife.

Transfer the squash to a serving platter or bowl. Sprinkle with fresh herbs, a little more honey, and a little sea salt. Serve hot.

Nischan champions the use of old-fashioned yellow corn, which has a more pronounced corn taste than hybrids like Divinity and Alpine. He roasts half the kernels, then juices the rest to give this soup a wallop of corn flavor.

SWEET CORN CHOWDER

SERVES 6 TO 8

- 20 ears sweet corn, shucked
- ¼ cup grapeseed oil, plus more for brushing on corn
- 1 large Yukon Gold or other heirloom potato
- 2 carrots, diced
- 1 onion, diced
- 4 ounces celery root, peeled and diced
- 1 quart Savory Vegetable Stock (recipe follows)
- 2 tablespoons finely chopped fresh tarragon
- 2 tablespoons thinly chopped flat-leaf parsley
- 2 tablespoon unsalted butter, at room temperature
- 2 tablespoons goat's milk yogurt or any high-quality cow's milk yogurt, at room temperature
- Kosher salt and freshly ground black pepper

EDITOR'S WINE CHOICE

Ripe, luxurious Chardonnay (see page 265)

Over the years, we have come to value sweet corn as a special summertime treat. The best summer corn is not the silvery white stuff that tastes like sugar with only a hint of corn, rather than the other way around, but the yellow ears. These taste more of corn, and although they are disappearing in favor of sweeter varieties, they are important (though not critical) to this recipe. I juice the raw kernels to add to soup as a thickening agent. I believe the yellow kernels do this most successfully, so you will need a juicer for this recipe. Whichever kind of corn you use, you are in for a treat with this chowder.

Preheat the oven to 400°F.

Brush 10 ears of the corn with oil. Place on a baking sheet and roast, turning once or twice, for about 45 minutes, or until the kernels are slightly browned on at least 2 sides. Set aside to cool.

Put the potato in a saucepan with enough cold water to cover by about 1 inch. Bring to a boil and cook for about 20 minutes, or until the potato is tender when pierced with a fork. Drain and let the potato cool. Cut in half and set aside.

Heat the ¼ cup of oil in a large stockpot over medium-high heat. When hot, cook the carrots for 4 to 6 minutes, or until they begin to soften. Add the onion and celery root and cook for about 5 minutes longer, or until the onions are translucent and lightly browned. Cover and set aside.

With a sharp kitchen knife, cut the roasted kernels from the cobs and add them to the pot with the other vegetables. With the same knife, cut the uncooked kernels from the remaining 10 cobs. Run the raw kernels through a vegetable juicer and set the juice aside.

Heat the stock in a large saucepan over medium-high heat until simmering. Transfer half of the stock to a blender and add one potato half. Blend until smooth. Pour the thickened stock into a bowl and put the rest of the stock and the remaining potato half into the blender and puree. Add this to the rest of the thickened stock.

continued on page 165

Sweet corn chowder continued

Remove the lid from the stockpot and pour the slightly thickened stock over the vegetables. Add the sweet corn juice, making sure any cornstarch settled on the bottom of the container gets into the soup. Bring the soup to a simmer over medium heat. Immediately reduce the heat to medium-low and simmer very gently for about 5 minutes.

Stir in the tarragon and parsley. Remove the soup from the heat. Swirl in the butter and yogurt. Adjust the seasoning with salt and pepper and serve hot.

SAVORY VEGETABLE STOCK

MAKES ABOUT 4 QUARTS

- 1 fennel bulb, trimmed and quartered
- 3 large leeks, trimmed and coarsely chopped
- 3 large onions, peeled and quartered
- 1 rutabaga, peeled and coarsely chopped
- 1 pound mushroom stems or whole mushrooms

It's not uncommon to find ourselves in a "state of need" when it comes to stock, especially when we set about making soups, stews, and grain porridges. Vegetable stocks are very simple to make, as they use easy-to-obtain vegetables and do not require long cooking. Nothing could be more straightforward to make than one of these brews: You literally just add water and let the veggies simmer for an hour or so. Plus, these stocks are a safe bet if you have any worries about your guests' allergies or vegetarian tendencies.

Most recipes that call for stock have either a savory or sweet profile. For savory soups, you need a savory vegetable stock, such as this one. For a sweeter dish, you want a sweeter stock, made with root vegetables. For either of these stocks—or any other vegetable stock, for that matter—roasting the vegetables first will yield a richer, more flavorful broth. If you do this, cut the simmering time for the stock in half.

Combine the vegetables in a large stockpot. Add enough water to cover by an inch.

Bring to a boil over high heat. Immediately reduce the heat. Simmer gently for about 1½ hours, or until the stock is nicely flavored.

Strain the stock. Let it cool to room temperature. When cool, transfer to lidded containers and refrigerate for up to 1 week. (Save and refrigerate any vegetables that do not feel grossly overcooked. These veggies are a great addition to any hash recipe.)

The combination of fresh and pickled vegetables with goat cheese, almonds and apple makes this salad so appealing. When the ingredients are all jumbled together in small pieces, every single bite is a pleasant surprise.

"USE A SPOON" CHOPPED SALAD

SERVES 6

- 1½ cups Riesling vinegar or other white wine vinegar
- 3 celery ribs, cut into ¼-inch dice
- 2 carrots, peeled and cut into ¼-inch dice
- 1 large red bell pepper, seeded and cut into ¼-inch dice
- 1 heirloom apple, such as Cox's Orange Pippin or Roxbury Russet, peeled, cored, and cut into ¼-inch dice
- ½ large cucumber, peeled, seeded, and cut into ¼-inch dice
- 1 cup sliced treviso or radicchio
- 1 cup sliced arugula
- 1 cup thinly sliced Napa, Savoy, or other soft cabbage
- 3 tablespoons extra-virgin olive oil
- Sea salt and freshly ground black pepper
- 1½ cups crumbled local goat cheese
- ½ cup toasted almond slivers

When Paul [Newman] and I agreed to open Dressing Room, one of his first requests was that there always be a really good chopped salad on the menu. He loved an array of flavors and textures in each bite, and he could go on at length about what a pain it was to eat any salad that was not chopped!

In the spring we rely on raw peapods and asparagus, roasted nuts for crunch, and some kind of fruit such as strawberries and blueberries for the salad. We move to peaches in the summer and apples in the fall, looking for sweetness from both, and include some kind of great local cheese.

Bring the vinegar to a simmer in a saucepan over medium heat. Add the celery and carrots. Remove the pan from the heat. Set aside to cool.

When the vinegar is cool, add the bell pepper. Cover and refrigerate until cold.

Strain the chilled vegetables through a sieve. Reserve the vinegar and the vegetables separately.

Mix together the apple, cucumber, treviso, arugula, cabbage, and the reserved vegetables in a large bowl. Add ¼ cup of the reserved vinegar and the oil and toss well. Season to taste with salt and pepper. Add the goat cheese and almonds to the bowl and toss to mix. Divide among 6 small bowls or plates.

These soft, herby fish cakes get nice and crisp on the edges. They're lovely served with a salad or smashed on a roll with lettuce and tomato.

LINE-CAUGHT CHATHAM COD CAKES

MAKES 8 COD CAKES; SERVES 4

- 2 tablespoons coarse sea salt
- 1½ pounds Yukon Gold or corolla potatoes, peeled and cut into 2-inch chunks
- 1½ pounds boneless, skinless cod fillets, cut into 1½-inch cubes
- 2 tablespoons grated onion
- 2 tablespoons unsalted butter, at room temperature
- 1 tablespoon finely chopped flat-leaf parsley
- 1 tablespoon finely chopped fresh chervil, dill, or additional flat-leaf parsley (if you cannot find chervil or dill)
- 1 tablespoon finely chopped fresh chives
- 1 large organic egg plus 1 large organic egg yolk
- 1 to 2 cups coarse fresh bread crumbs (see Author's Note)
- ¼ cup grapeseed oil

EDITOR'S WINE CHOICE
Minerally, complex Sauvignon Blanc (see page 266)

AUTHOR'S NOTE
To make the bread crumbs, whiz 4 slices of country-style or artisan bread in a food processor or blender.

In the early days of cod fishing, the Atlantic waters off New England were so populated with codfish that sailors and fishermen could never have imagined they would one day face extinction. Fishermen spent months at sea, bringing home huge amounts of cod.

Today, factory trawlers wreak environmental havoc on the remaining cod supply. Their methods pick up so much bycatch that a lot more than just cod die. Hook-and-line-caught cod, on the other hand, is sustainable. It's a challenge to find line-caught fish, but it's worth the trouble. Look for it in fish markets that sell wild-caught salmon and sustainably farmed shrimp. Not only will you put a good piece of cod on the family table, you will also support an artisan fishing culture that once guaranteed the survival of numerous New England communities and could one day do so again. Cod cakes with fresh cod are easier to make than salt cod cakes, as the fresh fish is easier to handle—and you will be keeping a lid on your sodium intake.

Fill a large pot about halfway with water and add the salt. Add the potatoes and bring to a boil. Reduce the heat and simmer briskly for 25 to 35 minutes, or until the potatoes are nearly tender. Add the cod. Return to a simmer and cook, partially covered, for about 6 minutes longer, or until the fish is soft. Drain well. Transfer both the fish and potatoes to a colander to cool for 8 to 10 minutes.

When cool, transfer to a large mixing bowl. Add the onion, butter, herbs, egg, and egg yolk. With your hands or a potato masher, mash the mixture until thoroughly mixed. You will have about 6 cups. Form the mixture into 8 patties about 4 inches across.

Spread the bread crumbs in a shallow dish. Dip the patties in the crumbs to coat both sides. Use care, as the patties will be delicate.

Heat 2 tablespoons of the oil until hot in a large skillet over medium-high heat. Fry the patties for 4 to 5 minutes on each side, or until golden brown and heated all the way through. You will have to do this in batches. Wipe the crumbs from the pan between batches, and add more oil as needed. Drain on paper towels before serving.

BEST OF THE BEST EXCLUSIVE

If you happen to have leftover cooked salmon, this filling frittata is a great way to use it. When entertaining guests, serve the dish with a dollop of trout caviar.

WILD SALMON, SHIITAKE & ARUGULA FRITTATA

SERVES 6

- 3 tablespoons grapeseed oil
- 12 ounces skinless wild salmon fillets
- Salt and freshly ground pepper
- 1 dozen large eggs
- 3 tablespoons heavy cream
- 2 tablespoons unsalted butter
- 1 small shallot, halved and thinly sliced
- 8 ounces shiitake mushrooms, stems discarded, caps sliced
- 4 cups packed arugula (about 5 ounces), chopped
- ¼ cup fresh bread crumbs
- 3 tablespoons snipped chives
- 3 tablespoons crème fraîche
- 2 ounces trout caviar (optional)

EDITOR'S WINE CHOICE
Dry, rich Champagne
(see page 264)

1. Preheat the oven to 450°F. In an 8-inch cast-iron skillet, heat 2 tablespoons of the grapeseed oil until shimmering. Season the salmon with salt and pepper. Add the fillets to the skillet and cook over moderately high heat until golden brown, about 3 minutes per side. Transfer the salmon to a plate and let cool slightly. Flake the salmon with a fork. Wipe out the skillet.

2. In a large bowl, whisk the eggs with the cream and a generous pinch each of salt and pepper.

3. In the skillet, melt the butter in the remaining 1 tablespoon of grapeseed oil. Add the shallot and cook over moderate heat until softened, about 2 minutes. Add the mushrooms, season with salt and pepper and cook until the mushrooms are softened and all of their liquid has evaporated, about 5 minutes. Stir in the arugula and cook until just wilted, about 1 minute. Scatter the salmon in the skillet and pour in the beaten eggs. Stir gently to evenly distribute the ingredients. Cook over moderately low heat until the eggs are just set around the edge, about 4 minutes. Sprinkle with the bread crumbs.

4. Transfer the skillet to the oven and bake the frittata for 7 minutes, until just set and lightly browned on top. Remove from the oven and let the frittata stand for 5 minutes. Cut into wedges and serve with the chives, crème fraîche and trout caviar.

MAKE AHEAD The frittata can stand at room temperature for up to 1 hour.

MICHEL NISCHAN ONLINE

michelnischan.com

Michel Nischan

@michelnischan

Burger and slider, page 179

JAMIE'S AMERICA

→ 16

Jamie Oliver

On his Emmy-winning TV show, *Jamie Oliver's Food Revolution*, the star British chef focuses on what's wrong with American food, not what's right about it. Oliver makes peace with the U.S. in his latest cookbook, celebrating the "old-school, accessible, and affordable comfort classics that make the country tick." Organized around visits to New York, Louisiana, Arizona, L.A., Georgia, Wyoming and Montana, *Jamie's America* is a collection of dishes based on regional specialties (Spicy Meat Gumbo), ethnic immigrant food (Sher Ping Pancakes, stuffed with gingery pork) and "classic American showstoppers" like hamburgers and fried chicken. Oliver isn't scared to mess with tradition—his gumbo has sweet potato in it. And he hasn't abandoned his passion for healthy eating, modifying some recipes to be "less excessive in the sugar and fat department." *Published by Hyperion, $37.50*

Oliver's gumbo calls for the very nontraditional addition of sweet potato. It mellows the heat of the Cajun spices and helps thicken the stew.

LOUISIANA

SPICY MEAT GUMBO

SERVES 6 TO 8

- 4 chicken thighs, skin on, preferably free-range or organic
- 4 chicken drumsticks, skin on, preferably free-range or organic
- Sea salt and freshly ground black pepper
- 1 teaspoon paprika
- 1 teaspoon cayenne pepper
- Olive oil
- 14 ounces smoked sausage, such as andouille or fresh chorizo, thickly sliced
- 4 slices of smoked bacon, the best quality you can afford, roughly chopped
- 1 large onion, peeled and diced
- 1 green bell pepper, seeded and chopped
- 1 yellow bell pepper, seeded and chopped
- 4 celery stalks, trimmed and diced
- 3 heaping tablespoons all-purpose flour
- 6 cloves garlic, peeled and minced
- 2¼ pounds sweet potatoes, peeled and roughly chopped
- 6 sprigs of fresh thyme, leaves picked
- 4 fresh bay leaves
- 1½ quarts hot chicken broth, preferably organic
- A small bunch of fresh curly parsley
- 4 scallions, trimmed and finely sliced

AUTHOR'S WINE CHOICE
Italian red—a Barbera d'Alba or d'Asti

If there's one thing I've learned from the people I met in New Orleans, it's that everyone has their own take on gumbo. It's definitely more of a philosophy than a recipe. As long as you don't mess with the roux of fat and flour or the "holy trinity" of onions, bell peppers, and celery that you'll find in so many of Louisiana's recipes, you can add all sorts of tasty stuff.

Season your chicken with salt, pepper, paprika, and cayenne. Put a large saucepan on a high heat, add a little olive oil, and fry your chicken, sausage, and bacon for around 15 minutes, or until it is all golden brown and crispy. Remove the browned pieces of meat to a dish, leaving the flavorful fat in the pan, as you'll be using this to make that all-important roux.

Turn the heat down and add your holy trinity of onion, bell peppers, and celery. Slowly stir and fry for 10 minutes, until softened, then stir in the flour. This is the time to dedicate a bit of love to your roux, so keep stirring the vegetables and flour so the mixture cooks evenly and gets nice and dark. It might take around 10 minutes to get it to the right darkness. Peanut butter color is a good starting point, but you can take it even darker if you prefer by stirring and cooking it for another 20 to 30 minutes.

At this point, add your garlic, sweet potatoes, browned meats, thyme, and bay leaves and stir and fry for a further minute. Pour in the hot chicken broth, bring everything to a boil, then turn the heat down and simmer on a medium heat for 45 minutes, or until the chicken pulls apart easily. The fantastic flavors will mix together and the sweet potato will break down and help thicken the gumbo.

Before serving, I like to scoop the chicken pieces out, shred the meat from the bone with a fork, and put all the meat back into the pan, discarding the bones and skin.

Taste the gumbo and season if necessary. Seasoning is important to the folk from New Orleans, so work it, baby! Roughly chop your parsley and stir it in, then divide your gumbo into bowls over some fluffy rice. Scatter over some sliced scallions and enjoy.

Oliver's turkey stew is similar to Southern chicken-and-dumplings, with a couple of exceptions: He rolls his dumplings flat and adds lemon zest at the end, providing a zingy contrast to the creamy, mushroom-rich broth.

GEORGIA

COMFORTING TURKEY STEW

SERVES 6 TO 8

- 3 onions, peeled and diced
- Olive oil
- 1¾ pounds skinless turkey breast, preferably free-range or organic, cut into ½-inch slices
- 1¼ quarts chicken broth, preferably organic
- ½ pound small white or cremini mushrooms, thinly sliced
- ⅔ cup heavy cream
- A small bunch of fresh flat-leaf parsley
- 1 lemon
- ½ clove garlic, peeled

FOR THE DUMPLINGS

- 1¼ cups all-purpose flour, plus extra for dusting
- 1 large egg, preferably free-range or organic
- Sea salt and freshly ground black pepper
- Whole nutmeg

AUTHOR'S WINE CHOICE

French dry white—
a Côtes du Rhône, from either the Marsanne or Roussanne grape or a blend

I was treated to some seriously delicious Southern food at a family get-together in the town of Gray. The mother of the household, Miss Betty, made a bloody tasty and comforting stew, and this is my take on it.

Put a large frying pan on a medium high heat and add your diced onions and a lug of olive oil. Fry gently for 10 minutes or so, but don't let the onions color. Add your sliced turkey and pour in 1 quart of chicken broth to cover the turkey completely. Don't worry if it looks like a lot of liquid, because your dumplings will soak up a fair amount. Bring to a boil, then turn down the heat and simmer gently for 30 minutes with the lid on.

Meanwhile, make your dumplings. Put your flour into a mixing bowl, make a well in the middle, and crack in your egg. Add a good pinch of salt and pepper and 5 or 6 gratings of nutmeg. Mix together with a fork, add 2 to 3 tablespoons of the simmering broth from the pan, a splash at a time, and knead until you have a smooth dough. Cover the bowl with plastic wrap and pop the bowl into the refrigerator.

When the turkey is ready, shred the meat apart with 2 forks, then add the mushrooms to the pan with the cream and stir. Have a taste and season to your liking with salt and pepper, then let it tick away while you get on with finishing the dumplings.

Dust a clean worktop and a rolling pin with flour and roll the dough out until it's roughly the size of this open book and the thickness of a quarter. Slice into 18 to 20 ribbons about ¾ inch wide and stir these into your stew. They suck up quite a bit of moisture, so add a splash more broth if and when needed. Bring back to a boil, then turn down and simmer gently for 10 minutes.

At this stage your dumplings should be soft and cooked through, so roughly chop your parsley leaves and add them to the stew. Finely grate over the fragrant lemon zest and ½ clove of garlic right at the end. Stir, then check the seasoning one last time. Divide everything between your bowls and serve right away with a fresh green salad and some hot crispy bread.

These are like scallion pancakes stuffed with ground pork, cabbage and fresh cilantro. They get crisp on the outside while remaining chewy on the inside.

NEW YORK

SHER PING PANCAKES

SERVES 4 (MAKES 8 PANCAKES)

FOR THE DOUGH

- 3¾ cups white bread flour, plus extra for dusting
- Scant 1 cup water
- ¼ cup vegetable oil
- Sea salt and freshly ground black pepper

FOR THE FILLING

- 14 ounces ground pork, the best quality you can afford
- A handful of finely grated white cabbage
- A small bunch of fresh cilantro, leaves and stalks finely chopped
- A thumb-sized piece of root ginger, peeled and finely grated
- 4 scallions, trimmed and finely chopped
- 1 clove garlic, peeled and finely grated
- Sea salt
- Freshly ground Szechuan pepper

TO SERVE

- Sweet chile or hot chile sauce
- Soy sauce
- 2 limes, cut into wedges

AUTHOR'S WINE CHOICE
New Zealand red—
a Marlborough Pinot Noir

Sher ping *translates as "pan-cooked filled pancake," and they are one of the best things I've eaten in ages. A lovely lady from the north of China taught me how to make them at her food counter in the Roosevelt Food Court. It sounds like a cheat to explain how to make these pancakes, but it's well worth mastering, because you can swap the pork for other delicious fillings like chicken or seafood.*

Make the dough by mixing the flour, water, vegetable oil, a bit of pepper, and a pinch of salt with a fork. Then use your hands to knead it until smooth and elastic. Cover it with plastic wrap and let it rest for a couple of hours.

When you're ready to make your pancakes, mix all your filling ingredients together in a large bowl. Use your hands to really scrunch everything together, and season well with a good pinch of salt and Szechuan pepper.

Dust a clean surface with flour and cut the dough into 8. Divide your filling into 8 even piles. Oil a sheet pan and your hands. Pick up a piece of dough and create a patty like a mini pizza about 4¾ inches across and ½ inch thick.

Take one of your piles of filling and pop it into the middle of the dough. Pat it flat with your fingers, then slowly stretch the edges of the dough out, folding them back in over the pork mixture. Do this all the way around and, once closed, press down on the stuffed pancake with your hand. It should be about 1 inch thick and 3¼ inches across.

continued on page 178

sher ping pancakes continued

Do the same with the other 7 pancakes, then lay them on your oiled sheet pan and put them into the refrigerator for about 20 minutes or so. After that, get a large dry frying pan on a medium heat. Add a tiny drizzle of vegetable oil and lay each pancake, folded side down, in the pan. Gently push down on them with a spatula slice to flatten them slightly. Keep doing this until they're about ½ inch thick and about 4 inches wide. Be careful that the pan's not too hot, though, otherwise your pancakes will brown before they're properly cooked through.

After about 4 minutes you'll have a nice golden color happening, so turn the pancakes over, push them down lightly, and cook them for 4 minutes on the other side. Only push down once on this side. When they're golden and crisp, the meat should be perfectly cooked, but you can always break one open to check.

To serve, pour some chile sauce into one bowl and some soy sauce into another. Pop a few wedges of lime on the side for squeezing over, and dunk away in your sauces. These pancakes hit all the right spots!

Onions and bread crumbs in the patty make this hamburger reminiscent of a meat loaf. The spicy mayo is so good, you might want to double the batch.

NEW YORK

BURGERS & SLIDERS

SERVES 6

FOR THE BURGER MIX

Olive oil
- 2 medium red onions, peeled and finely chopped
- 4 slices of bread, crusts removed
- 1¼ pounds good-quality lean ground beef
- 1 teaspoon kosher salt
- 1 heaped teaspoon freshly ground black pepper
- 1 large egg, preferably free-range or organic, beaten

A handful of freshly grated Parmesan cheese

FOR THE SPICY MAYO
- 4 teaspoons mayonnaise
- 1 teaspoon ketchup

A good pinch of smoked paprika or cayenne pepper

Juice of ½ lemon

TO SERVE
- 12 slices of smoked bacon, the best quality you can afford
- 6 large or 8 small burger buns
- 1 butterhead lettuce, leaves washed and spun dry
- 4 tomatoes, sliced
- 6 gherkins, sliced

A few pickled chiles

EDITOR'S WINE CHOICE

Earthy, medium-bodied Tempranillo (see page 269)

I couldn't possibly leave the great American burger out of this book. Sadly, the classic burger has gone from humble beginnings (as something brought over by German immigrants) to becoming a symbol of fast food and junk. But when made at home with quality ingredients, it's an absolute joy. So, introducing my great American burger, and its little cousin, the "slider," or mini burger...

You can make these burgers or sliders in an oven at full whack, on the grill, or in a hot pan. If you're using the oven or grill, preheat it now.

Put a splash of olive oil into a large frying pan on a low heat and add your chopped onions. Fry for 10 minutes, or until the onions have softened, then put to one side and let cool completely. Blitz your bread in a food processor until you get a fine consistency. Oil a clean sheet pan and put aside. Put the cooled onions into a large bowl with the rest of the burger ingredients. Use clean hands to scrunch the mixture together, then divide into 6 equal balls for burgers and 18 equal balls for sliders. Wet your hands and roll the balls into burger-shaped patties about ¾ inch thick. Put your burgers or sliders on the oiled sheet pan and pat with a little olive oil. Cover with plastic wrap and put the pan into the refrigerator for at least an hour, or until the patties firm up. This is a good time to make your spicy mayo, so put all the ingredients into a bowl, mix well, and put to one side.

If using a frying pan or grill pan, put it on a high heat now and let it get really hot. However you decide to cook your burgers, they'll want around 3 or 4 minutes per side—you may have to cook them in batches if your pan isn't big enough. When your burgers or sliders are nearly cooked on one side, add the slices of bacon—whichever way you're cooking them—then flip the burgers and cook the bacon until golden and crisp. When the burgers are cooked to your liking and it's all looking really good, halve your burger buns and warm them through. Put the bacon on a plate lined with paper towels to drain.

When everything comes together pop your burgers or sliders onto their buns, add all your lovely toppings and your spicy mayo (you know how to put a burger together!), then tuck in with a lovely fresh salad and baked potatoes or potato wedges.

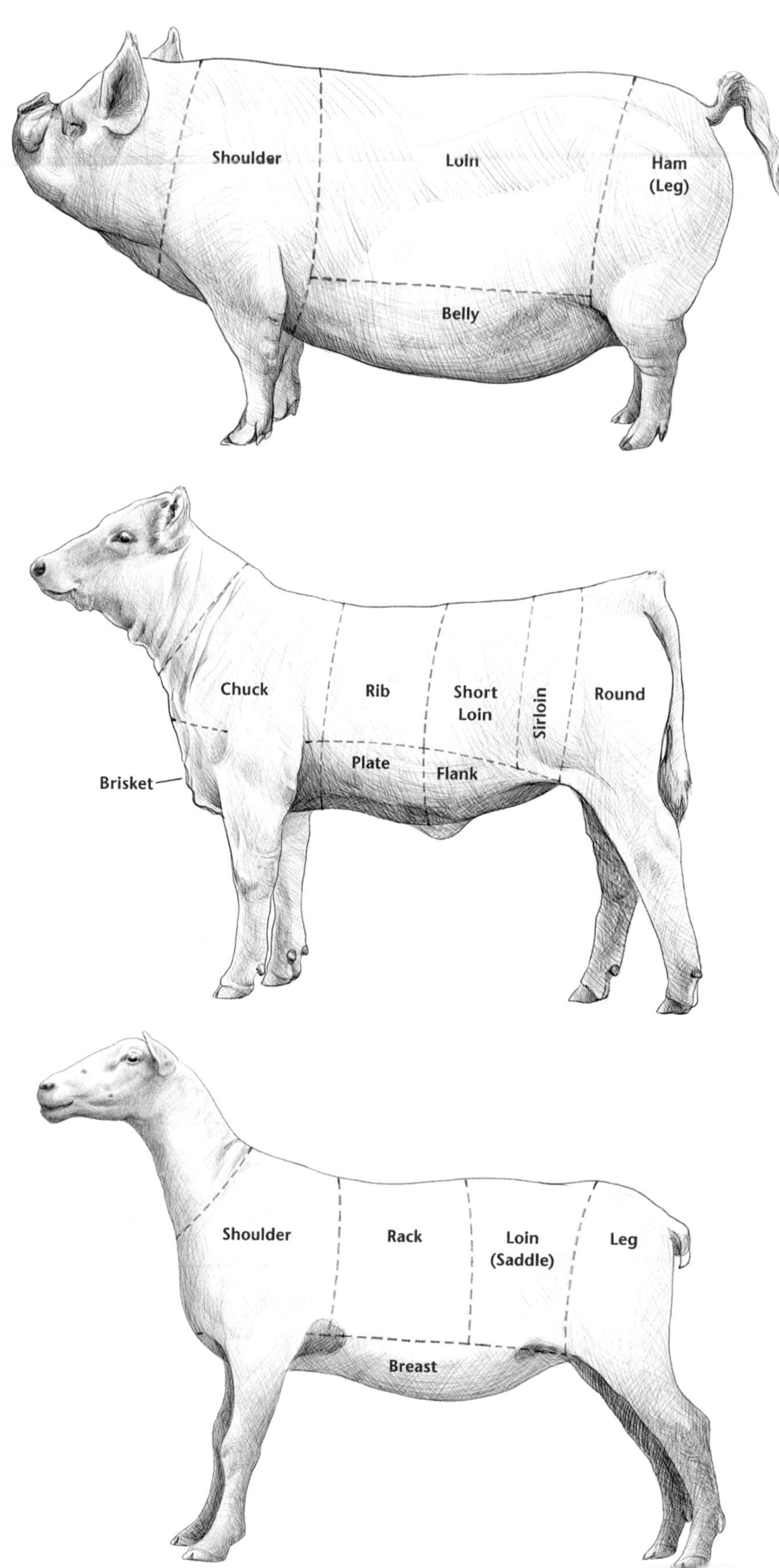

Shoulder
Loin
Ham
(Leg)
Belly
Chuck
Rib
Short
Loin
Sirloin
Round
Brisket
Plate
Flank
Shoulder
Rack
Loin
(Saddle)
Leg
Breast

MEAT

→17

James Peterson

As butchers become celebrities and more home cooks aspire to do things like break down a whole lamb, a book like this—a crash course for the carnivore—is very much of the moment. James Peterson, the author of 10 previous cookbooks, tells how to prepare all kinds of meat recipes, using step-by-step photographs that show, for instance, how to stuff ricotta and sage under the skin of a chicken to keep the breast meat from overcooking. Cooks who want to attempt foie gras terrines or homemade chorizo will get excellent instructions here, but beginners will find plenty of approachable comfort food, too, like Peterson's superrich meat loaf made with pork, veal, beef and mushrooms and wrapped in bacon. *Published by Ten Speed Press, $35*

Fajitas usually include just meat, peppers and onions. Peterson adds grilled shiitake mushrooms to give the Tex-Mex classic another layer of flavor.

FAJITAS

MAKES 6 MAIN-COURSE SERVINGS

- 2 skirt steaks, about 1 pound each
- 3 tablespoons red wine vinegar or fresh lime juice
- Salt
- Pepper
- 2 bell peppers, seeded and cut lengthwise into narrow strips
- ½ pound shiitake mushrooms, stems removed and caps sliced
- 1 onion, thinly sliced
- 1 Cuban or poblano chile, seeded and cut lengthwise into narrow strips
- 2 jalapeño chiles, seeded and chopped
- 3 tablespoons chopped fresh cilantro
- Olive oil
- 6 flour tortillas, 8 inches in diameter
- Sour cream for serving
- Salsa for serving

EDITOR'S WINE CHOICE
Rustic, peppery Malbec
(see page 268)

This Tex-Mex favorite of grilled meat wrapped in tortillas calls for skirt steak, an underappreciated, tasty, long, thin cut from the plate, or belly, of the steer. When shopping for skirt steak, keep in mind that two types are sold, the inside and the outside. The inside is thinner and generally smaller and is considered the more desirable of the two, primarily because it contains less tough membrane.

Cut each steak crosswise into 4 pieces. In a shallow bowl, combine the vinegar and a generous pinch each salt and pepper. Add the steaks, turn to coat, and marinate at room temperature for up to 1 hour or in the refrigerator for up to 4 hours.

Place a stove-top grill pan over high heat and heat until hot. Add the bell peppers, mushrooms, onion, and chiles and grill, turning all the while, for about 10 minutes, or until nicely browned. Transfer the vegetables to a bowl, add the cilantro, season with salt and pepper, and toss to mix. Cover to keep warm.

Remove the steaks from the marinade. With the grill pan still over high heat and working in batches to avoid crowding, add the steaks and cook for about 4 minutes, or until well browned. Turn the steaks over and continue to cook for about 3 minutes longer, or until well browned on the second side and firm to the touch. The steaks should be medium-rare. Transfer to a plate and let rest in a warm spot.

Coat a small skillet with a light film of olive oil and place over medium heat. One at a time, add the tortillas and heat, turning once, for about 1 minute on each side, or until very lightly browned but still flexible. As each tortilla is ready, transfer to a plate and cover to keep warm.

Cut the steaks into long, thin slices across the grain on the diagonal. Divide the meat evenly among the tortillas. Top the meat with the grilled vegetables, again dividing evenly. Roll up the tortillas and place a rolled tortilla on each warmed plate. Serve at once. Pass the sour cream and salsa at the table.

Spice fanatics will love the fire of this beefy, bean-free chili. Be sure to have sour cream (or ice-cold beer) on hand to help tame the smoky heat.

POBLANO CHILI CON CARNE

MAKES 6 MAIN-COURSE SERVINGS

- 8 poblano chiles
- 3 pounds boneless beef stew meat from the chuck, cut into 1-inch cubes
- Salt
- Pepper
- 5 tablespoons olive oil, or as needed
- 1 large onion, sliced
- 4 cloves garlic, minced
- 10 tomatoes, about 5 pounds total weight, peeled, seeded, and chopped
- 1 tablespoon dried oregano
- 1 tablespoon ground cumin
- 1 chipotle chile in adobo sauce, rinsed, seeded, and chopped
- 3 tablespoons chopped fresh cilantro
- Sour cream

EDITOR'S WINE CHOICE
Intense, fruity Zinfandel (see page 269)

Most people think of chili as consisting mostly of beans, but in New Mexico and Texas, chili is made by stewing meat with chiles. Because many cooks don't have access to the wide variety of chiles found in the Southwest, this recipe calls for the easily found poblano, which can range from mild to hot.

If you have a gas stove, put the poblano chiles over the flame and turn as needed to blacken evenly. If you don't have a gas stove, preheat the broiler, put the poblano chiles on a sheet pan, slip under the broiler, and broil, turning as needed to blacken evenly. Transfer the chiles to a bowl, cover with plastic wrap, and let stand for about 15 minutes to steam to simplify peeling. Rinse the peppers under cold running water and peel away the skin with your fingertips. Scrape off any stubborn patches with a small knife. Seed the chiles and cut lengthwise into ¼-inch-wide strips.

Season the meat all over with salt and pepper. In a heavy sauté pan, heat 3 tablespoons of the olive oil over high heat. When the oil begins to smoke, working in batches if needed to avoid crowding, add the beef and brown well on all sides. Transfer the beef to a plate. Pour the fat out of the pan.

In a pot just large enough to hold the meat, heat the remaining 2 tablespoons olive oil over medium heat. Add the onion and garlic and sweat them, stirring occasionally, for about 15 minutes, or until the onion and garlic have softened. Add the browned meat, tomatoes, oregano, and cumin to the pot and stir well. Cover, adjust the heat to maintain a gentle simmer, and cook for about 1½ hours, or until the meat is just tender.

Add the poblanos, re-cover, and simmer for 30 minutes longer, or until the meat is easily penetrated with a fork. Add the chipotle chile and cilantro and stir well. Spoon the chili into warmed soup plates and serve. Pass the sour cream at the table.

This is a fantastic way to prepare roast chicken. Peterson stuffs ricotta cheese under the skin, which keeps the bird succulent—even the breast meat.

ROAST CHICKEN
with ricotta & sage

MAKES 4 MAIN-COURSE BREAST SERVINGS AND 4 MAIN-COURSE LEFTOVER THIGH SERVINGS

Two 15-ounce tubs ricotta cheese
Salt
Pepper
- **8 fresh sage leaves, chopped, or 1 tablespoon chopped fresh marjoram**
- **2 chickens, about 4 pounds each**

EDITOR'S WINE CHOICE
Lush, fragrant Viognier
(see page 267)

Any number of ingredients can be stuffed under the skin of a chicken: chopped mushrooms (sautéed until tender and the moisture has evaporated), spinach (blanched and coarsely chopped), fresh cheeses, mornay sauce (thick béchamel with cheese), herb sprigs. All of these stuffings, except the herbs, help to protect the breast meat from overcooking.

Line a fine-mesh strainer with paper towels, place over a bowl, and spoon the ricotta into the strainer. Cover and refrigerate for at least 4 hours or up to overnight. Transfer the drained cheese to a bowl, season with salt and pepper, and stir in the sage.

Preheat the oven to 450°F. Select a heavy roasting pan or pans just large enough to hold the chickens without crowding. Using your fingers and starting at the cavity, carefully loosen the skin over the breasts of 1 chicken. Gently slide half of the ricotta mixture under the skin, covering the meat evenly, then pat the skin back into place. Repeat with the remaining ricotta mixture and the second chicken. Season the chickens on the outside with salt and pepper. If the giblets have been included with the chickens, place the neck and gizzard from each one in the roasting pan, and place the chickens on top.

Roast the chickens for about 1 hour, or until an instant-read thermometer slid between a thigh and breast without touching bone reads 145°F. If you do not have a thermometer, tilt a chicken slightly so some of the juices run out of the cavity. The chicken is ready if the juices are clear but streaked with red.

Remove the pan(s) from the oven and transfer the chickens to a cutting board (preferably one with a moat to catch juices) in a warm spot. Tent loosely with foil and let rest for 15 minutes before carving. Cut off the thighs and reserve for leftovers. Slide a knife along the breastbone, carefully lifting off the breast meat with its stuffing and crispy skin. Serve each diner a breast.

This ultratraditional meat loaf is incredibly juicy and intensely flavored. The secret is wrapping it in bacon, which keeps the meat moist as it cooks.

MEAT LOAF

MAKES 8 MAIN-COURSE SERVINGS

- 2 tablespoons olive oil or butter, plus more for the pan
- 1 onion, minced
- ¼ pound cremini mushrooms, finely chopped
- 1 teaspoon chopped fresh thyme, or 1 tablespoon chopped fresh marjoram
- 3 slices dense-crumb white bread, crusts removed
- ¼ cup milk
- ½ pound ground chuck
- ¾ pound ground pork shoulder
- ¾ pound ground veal
- 1 egg, beaten
- 1½ tablespoons salt
- 1½ teaspoons pepper
- 8 slices bacon

EDITOR'S WINE CHOICE
Juicy, spicy Grenache
(see page 268)

A meat loaf is more or less a rough-hewn pâté. Ground meat is typically mixed with seasonings, some raw onion, and one or more herbs and then shaped into a loaf and baked. Some meat loaf recipes include pork and/or veal, but many standard meat loaves are made with ground beef alone. Eggs are usually included to bind the meat loaf together.

Grease a roasting pan that is about 12 inches long.

In a medium sauté pan, heat the olive oil over medium heat. Add the onion and sauté for about 10 minutes, or until lightly browned. Raise the heat to high, add the mushrooms, and cook, stirring the mushrooms every couple of minutes until all the water they release evaporates. This should take about 5 minutes. Add the thyme and remove from the heat.

In a large bowl, combine the bread and milk and work together to form a paste. Add the cooked mushroom mixture, ground meats, egg, salt, and pepper and work together with your hands until all the ingredients are evenly distributed. Form the mixture into a loaf about 10 inches long and 4 inches wide. Wrap the bacon slices crosswise around the loaf, tucking the ends of the slices under the loaf, then place the loaf in the prepared pan.

Slide the pan into the oven, turn on the oven to 350°F (there is no need to preheat), and bake the meat loaf for about 1¼ hours, or until an instant-read thermometer inserted into the center of the loaf reads 145°F. Do not cook it any longer or the meat will dry out.

Transfer to a platter and let rest for 15 minutes. Cut into slices ½ inch thick and serve the slices wrapped with the bacon.

BEST OF THE BEST EXCLUSIVE

What makes these gratins great is that the thin strands of vermicelli noodles stay creamy in the ramekins as they bake while the tops get supercrunchy.

VERMICELLI GRATINS

MAKES 8 SIDE-DISH SERVINGS

- ½ pound vermicelli
- 1 teaspoon extra-virgin olive oil
- 1 cup freshly grated Parmigiano-Reggiano cheese
- Kosher salt and freshly ground pepper
- 2 cups heavy cream

1. Preheat the oven to 350°F. Butter eight 5-ounce ramekins and place them on a sturdy rimmed baking sheet.

2. In a large pot of boiling salted water, cook the vermicelli until just al dente; drain well. In a medium bowl, toss the pasta with the olive oil. Add ¾ cup of the Parmigiano-Reggiano cheese and toss to coat. Season with salt and pepper.

3. Divide the pasta evenly among the ramekins and pour ¼ cup of the cream into each one. Sprinkle the remaining ¼ cup of Parmigiano-Reggiano on top. Bake for about 40 minutes, until the cream is bubbling and the gratins are golden brown on top. Let cool slightly before serving in the ramekins.

JAMES PETERSON ONLINE

jimcooks.com
jamespetersonstudios.com

James Nicholas Peterson

AVEC ERIC

→ 18

Eric Ripert with Angie Mosier & Soa Davies

Eric Ripert is one of America's most astonishing chefs and a seafood genius. But while his flagship Manhattan restaurant, Le Bernardin, has maintained four stars from the *New York Times* for 25 years, Ripert is also brilliant at creating recipes for home cooks. A companion book to the public television show of the same name, *Avec Eric* follows the chef as he searches for inspiration around the world—boar hunting in Tuscany, harvesting honey in Sonoma—then translates those experiences into refined, immaculate dishes. The results are impressive, as in a whole roasted red snapper bright with Thai spices and a Cod Basquaise with a concentrated bell-pepper-and-red-wine sauce. There are a few complex entries (one recipe requires over 25 ingredients), but the emphasis here is on making Ripert accessible to amateurs, not on showing amateurs how hard it is to cook like Ripert. *Published by John Wiley & Sons, $34.95*

Tarragon lovers will delight in this salad; it's as much about the delicate anise-scented herb as the fresh leaves of butter lettuce and tart-sweet dressing.

BUTTER LETTUCE SALAD
with tarragon & citrus-honey vinaigrette

SERVES 4

- 1 lemon, zested and juiced
- 1 lime, zested and juiced
- 1 tablespoon honey
- 1 teaspoon Dijon mustard
- Fine sea salt and freshly ground black pepper
- 6 tablespoons canola oil
- 3 heads butter lettuce (also known as Boston lettuce or Bibb lettuce)
- ½ cup cut fresh tarragon leaves

Butter lettuce is such a delicious variety of lettuce. The sturdy green leaves are sold in individual heads that are so small each diner can eat an entire head. All that is needed is a well-seasoned, well-balanced vinaigrette to complement it.

Whisk the lemon zest and juice, lime zest and juice, honey and mustard in a bowl and season to taste with salt and pepper. Slowly drizzle in the canola oil while whisking constantly until completely emulsified.

Trim off the core from each head of lettuce and separate the leaves, discarding the tough outer leaves. Rinse the lettuce leaves in a bowl of cold water and spin dry. Place the lettuce leaves in a large bowl and season with salt and pepper. Add the tarragon leaves and gently toss the lettuce with enough vinaigrette to coat lightly.

Stack the lettuce leaves on 4 plates, starting each stack with the large outer leaves on the bottom and ending with the small inner leaves on top. Serve immediately.

These crisp portobello mushroom fries are nicely dressed up with the accompanying truffle aïoli, but they could also be served with just ketchup or mayonnaise. A squirt of fresh lemon juice on the fries adds zing.

PORTOBELLO "FRIES"

with truffled aïoli

SERVES 4

TRUFFLE AÏOLI

- **2 large egg yolks**
- **2 tablespoons fresh lemon juice**
- **1 teaspoon minced garlic**
- **½ cup canola oil**
- **½ cup olive oil**
- **2 tablespoons white truffle oil, approximately**
- **Fine sea salt and freshly ground white pepper**

PORTOBELLO "FRIES"

- **4 portobello mushrooms**
- **1½ cups fine dried bread crumbs**
- **½ cup grated Pecorino Romano cheese**
- **1 teaspoon freshly ground black pepper**
- **¾ teaspoon fine sea salt**
- **½ teaspoon dried thyme**
- **¼ cup all-purpose flour**
- **2 large eggs, lightly beaten**
- **Canola oil for frying**

Thick strips of portobello mushrooms are breaded and fried to create a flavorful alternative to potato fries.

Combine the yolks, lemon juice and garlic in a blender. With the blender on medium speed, drizzle the canola oil and olive oil into the yolk mixture in a slow steady stream until the aïoli is emulsified and well blended. Season with the truffle oil, salt and pepper. Transfer the aïoli to a small bowl and set aside.

Trim the stems from the mushrooms, scrape out the gills and gently wipe the mushroom caps with a damp cloth. Cut the mushroom caps into ½-inch-wide strips.

Combine the bread crumbs, cheese, pepper, salt and thyme in a shallow dish. Place the flour and eggs in separate shallow dishes. Toss the mushroom strips in the flour to coat evenly, then dip them into the eggs and roll them in the bread crumb mixture.

Heat about 1 inch of oil in a large skillet over medium heat. Working in batches, place the breaded mushroom strips in the hot oil and cook on all sides until golden brown, 3 to 4 minutes. Transfer to a tray lined with paper towels. Serve hot with the aïoli.

Baking a whole fish on the bone is an excellent way to keep the flesh moist. Serve the snapper with fragrant coconut rice for a terrific meal.

WHOLE ROASTED RED SNAPPER
with thai spices & coconut rice

SERVES 4

RED SNAPPER

One 4-pound whole red snapper, head on, scales removed and cleaned
Fine sea salt and freshly ground black pepper
- ⅓ cup canola oil
- 3 tablespoons unsweetened coconut milk
- 2 limes, 1 zested and juiced, 1 cut in half
- 1 tablespoon grated ginger
- 1 tablespoon ground coriander seeds
- 1 garlic clove, sliced
- ½ teaspoon chili flakes
- ¼ cup basil chiffonade
- ¼ cup cilantro chiffonade

COCONUT RICE

- 1 cup jasmine rice
- 1½ cups water
- ½ stalk lemongrass

Fine sea salt and freshly ground white pepper
- 1 cup unsweetened coconut milk
- 1 tablespoon cilantro chiffonade
- 1 lime

AUTHOR'S WINE CHOICES

The Johann's Garden 2008
Henschke Barossa, Australia

Dr. Loosen Blue Slate Estate
Kabinett Riesling 2007
Mosel-Saar-Ruwer, Germany

I really love cooking whole fish, and you can impart lots of great flavor by stuffing the cavity with herbs and lemons. This dish incorporates flavors inspired by the food of Southeast Asia.

Preheat the oven to 400°F. Generously season inside the belly and both sides of the fish with salt and pepper. Place the fish in a roasting pan.

Combine the canola oil with the coconut milk, lime zest and juice, ginger, coriander, garlic and chili flakes in a bowl and stir to blend. Spoon the spice mixture over the snapper and bake, basting frequently, for 25 to 30 minutes, or until a metal skewer can easily be inserted into the fish and, when left in for 5 seconds, feels warm.

Meanwhile, prepare the rice. Place the rice in a fine-mesh sieve and rinse under cool water until the water begins to run clear. Transfer the rice to a medium pot and add 1½ cups of water, lemongrass and a pinch of salt. Bring to a boil over medium-high heat, then lower the heat and simmer for 10 minutes. Remove the rice from the heat, cover and let sit for another 10 minutes. When the rice is cooked, remove and discard the lemongrass. Gently stir in the coconut milk and cilantro and season to taste with lime juice, salt and pepper. Make sure the rice is creamy.

Spoon the coconut rice into the middle of 4 plates. Fillet the snapper, running a knife lengthwise down the fish at about the center to separate the side into 2 fillets, and then under the flesh to separate the fillets from the bones. Carefully lift off each fillet and place it on top of the rice. When the top fillets have been removed, lift off the fish bones and portion the bottom fillets in the same manner. Plate the remaining fillets and spoon some of the sauce from the roasting pan over each portion. Finish each dish with a squeeze of fresh lime juice and garnish with the chiffonade of basil and cilantro.

The key ingredient in this dish is piment d'Espelette, a smoky red chile powder made from the Espelette pepper, a cornerstone of Basque cooking.

COD BASQUAISE

SERVES 4

BASQUAISE

- 3 tablespoons olive oil
- ½ cup finely diced yellow onion
- 1 teaspoon minced garlic
- ¼ cup small diced serrano ham
- ½ cup small diced red bell pepper
- ½ cup small diced yellow bell pepper
- 1 cup diced seeded peeled tomato
- 1 teaspoon chopped fresh thyme leaves
- ½ cup dry red wine
- 1 tablespoon chopped fresh Italian parsley
- Fine sea salt and freshly ground white pepper
- Piment d'Espelette

COD

- 2 tablespoons canola oil
- Four 6-ounce cod fillets
- Fine sea salt and freshly ground white pepper
- 2 thyme sprigs
- 2 garlic cloves, peeled and halved

AUTHOR'S WINE CHOICES

Château Haut-Bergey, Pessac-Léognan 2005 Bordeaux, France

Paul Cluver Pinot Noir 2008 Elgin Valley, South Africa

Cod is a delicious, sturdy, white-fleshed fish. So many people only know salted cod, but codfish is very versatile and can stand up to hearty sauces and strong cooking techniques. Inspired by the cacciucco I ate in Italy and my memory of the sauces of the Basque country, where I spent some time as a child, I developed this dish using a sauce with a tomato and red wine base.

Heat the olive oil in a heavy large sauté pan over medium-low heat. Add the onion and sauté until tender, about 5 minutes. Add the garlic and continue cooking until tender, about 2 minutes. Add the ham and bell peppers and sauté until the peppers are soft, about 5 minutes. Reduce the heat to low. Add the diced tomato and thyme and simmer, stirring often, until slightly thickened, about 20 minutes. Add the red wine and cook out the alcohol, about 10 to 15 minutes. Stir in the chopped parsley and season to taste with salt, white pepper and piment d'Espelette. This Basquaise can be made 1 day ahead; cool, then cover and refrigerate.

Heat a griddle or a griddle pan over medium-high heat until it is very hot, then add the canola oil. Season the cod on both sides with salt and pepper. Add the cod to the pan along with the thyme and garlic. Lower the heat to medium and cook until the fish is golden brown on the bottom, 6 to 8 minutes. Turn the fish over and finish cooking until a metal skewer can be easily inserted into the fish and, when left in the fish for 5 seconds, feels just warm when touched to the lip, another 2 to 3 minutes.

Meanwhile, heat the Basquaise until hot. Spoon the Basquaise onto plates, place the cod in the center and serve immediately.

BEST OF THE BEST EXCLUSIVE

This pretty, summery dish is served with a clever Japanese ponzu *vinaigrette made with two kinds of citrus, rice vinegar, soy sauce and mirin.*

FLASH-SEARED TUNA

with herb salad & ponzu vinaigrette

SERVES 4

- 1 tablespoon soy sauce
- 1 tablespoon mirin
- 1½ tablespoons unseasoned rice vinegar
- ¼ teaspoon finely grated lime zest plus 1½ tablespoons fresh lime juice
- ¼ teaspoon finely grated orange zest plus 1 tablespoon fresh orange juice
- 2 tablespoons extra-virgin olive oil
- ¼ cup canola oil
- Fine sea salt and freshly ground pepper
- Two 10-ounce tuna steaks, cut 1 inch thick
- 3 cups packed mesclun (about 3 ounces)
- ⅓ cup packed basil leaves, torn
- ⅓ cup packed mint leaves
- ⅓ cup packed cilantro leaves

EDITOR'S WINE CHOICE

Full-bodied, minerally Riesling (see page 266)

ERIC RIPERT ONLINE

aveceric.com

chefericripert

@ericripert

1. In a small glass or stainless steel bowl, whisk the soy sauce, mirin and rice vinegar with the lime and orange zests and juices. Whisk in the olive oil and 2 tablespoons of the canola oil. Season the *ponzu* vinaigrette with salt and pepper.

2. In a large nonstick skillet, heat the remaining 2 tablespoons of canola oil over high heat until shimmering. Season the tuna with salt and pepper, add to the skillet and cook for 1 minute per side, until golden. Transfer the tuna to a platter and let rest for 3 minutes. Slice the tuna steaks ½ inch thick.

3. In a large bowl, combine the mesclun, basil, mint and cilantro and toss with 3 tablespoons of the vinaigrette. Transfer the salad to plates and arrange the tuna alongside. Drizzle the remaining vinaigrette over the tuna and serve.

Roasted fingerling potatoes and artichokes with garlic and thyme, page 200

ETHAN STOWELL'S NEW ITALIAN KITCHEN

→ 19

Ethan Stowell & Leslie Miller

In his first cookbook, Seattle chef Ethan Stowell collects brash, gutsy, nose-to-tail recipes that show off his Pacific Northwest take on Italian cuisine. "Do what scares you," Stowell urges, and coaches home cooks through making oxtail soup, polenta with tripe, spaghetti with sea urchin, geoduck clam crudo and a panzanella with crispy pig's ears. There are also plenty of accessible, non-scary recipes that deliver Stowell's intense flavors, like a hearty salad of greens and pickled mackerel; seared duck breast with sugared figs and arugula; and a farro and artichoke soup, which he recommends making without chicken stock, preferring the "cleaner flavor" of a water-based broth. *Published by Ten Speed Press, $35*

Cooking the fingerling potatoes cut side down in a single layer on the stove before roasting them in the oven gives them an especially crunchy crust.

ROASTED FINGERLING POTATOES & ARTICHOKES
with garlic & thyme

SERVES 4

- 1 pound fingerling potatoes
- 8 cloves garlic
- 2 tablespoons unsalted butter
- 2 tablespoons extra-virgin olive oil
- 2 artichokes, trimmed (for instructions on trimming artichokes, see Farro & Artichoke Soup on page 204)
- ½ bunch thyme

Kosher salt and freshly ground pepper

This dish is one of the simple joys that comes from freshly dug new potatoes and the inimitable artichoke. You need nothing more than garlic and a hit of thyme to create a side that totally speaks of the earth and that would make even a simple grilled steak sublime.

Preheat the oven to 400°F.

Halve the potatoes lengthwise. Peel and halve the garlic cloves.

Heat the butter and oil together in a large, ovenproof sauté pan over medium-high heat. Add the potatoes, cut-side down, in a single layer. Cook until the potatoes are golden, 4 to 5 minutes.

Turn the potatoes and add the artichokes, cut-side down. Nestle the garlic and thyme amid the vegetables. Pop into the oven and roast until the artichokes and potatoes are tender, 10 to 12 minutes. Season to taste with salt and pepper and serve.

Caramelized figs drizzled with wine vinegar become deliciously sweet and sour—an excellent accompaniment to the simply prepared duck breast.

SEARED DUCK BREAST

with sugared figs & arugula

SERVES 4

12 Kadota or Mission figs
6 tablespoons extra-virgin olive oil
Rock or turbinado sugar, for sprinkling
1 teaspoon Chianti vinegar
Four 5- or 6-ounce duck breasts, skin on
1 bunch arugula
1 teaspoon fresh lemon juice
Kosher salt and freshly ground pepper

EDITOR'S WINE CHOICE
Bright, tart Barbera
(see page 267)

For those of you who crave the ubiquitous duck breast all dressed up for company, I offer you my version, the little ducky paired with sweet-and-sour roasted figs and given a little edge from the arugula. I won't lie—it's good.

Preheat the oven to 400°F.

Wipe the figs clean, remove the stems, then halve them lengthwise. Place the figs, cut-side up, on a wire rack set on a foil-lined baking sheet. Drizzle the figs with 2 tablespoons of the olive oil, then sprinkle with the sugar. Roast in the oven for about 15 minutes, or until soft. Drizzle with the vinegar as soon as they come out of the oven. Decrease the oven temperature to 375°F.

Film the bottom of a large, ovenproof sauté pan with 2 tablespoons olive oil and heat over medium-low heat. Add the duck breasts, skin-side down, and cook for 8 to 10 minutes, or until most of the fat renders and the skin crisps. As the breasts sear, spoon off the excess fat as it pools in the pan. When the fat has rendered, transfer the breasts to a plate and pour off all the accumulated fat. Return the breasts, skin-side up, to the pan and transfer the pan to the oven. Roast for no more than 2 to 3 minutes, then remove the breasts from the pan and allow to rest while you make and dress the salad.

Pick off the smallest and most tender arugula leaves and wash well. Pat dry. Toss with the remaining 2 tablespoons olive oil and the lemon juice; season with salt and pepper.

Lay 3 figs out on each of 4 plates. Slice each duck breast on the diagonal and fan out over the figs, then nestle the arugula salad next to it.

Mackerel is the unsung hero of the fish world: It's inexpensive and packed with good-for-you fatty acids. Pickling the fish is easier than you'd think; just simmer it in white vinegar with vegetables and spices, then let cool.

PICKLED MACKEREL SALAD
with watercress, radish & pistachio

SERVES 4

PICKLED MACKEREL

- 1 pound mackerel fillets
- 1 carrot, peeled and cut into coins
- 2 cloves garlic, sliced
- 1 small red onion, peeled and thinly sliced
- 1 cup white vinegar
- 1 cup water
- 2 tablespoons black peppercorns
- 1 tablespoon coriander seeds
- 1 tablespoon mustard seeds
- 3 fresh bay leaves

SALAD

- 2 bunches watercress
- 1 bunch radishes
- 1 shallot, thinly sliced
- ¼ cup toasted pistachios

Kosher salt and freshly cracked pepper

- 1½ tablespoons extra-virgin olive oil

EDITOR'S WINE CHOICE
Fresh, lively Soave
(see page 267)

This delicious salad makes a solid first course or a hearty addition to a small-plate menu. Mackerel is a fantastic fish, with rich flesh and a deep flavor that is tamed and enhanced by a quick pickling treatment. Crisp radishes and assertive watercress hold up to the forward flavors, while a sprinkling of toasted pistachios adds nice texture and crunch. For a fun variation, use the same pickling liquid on sardines. Because sardine fillets are much thinner, they can be cooked simply by heating the liquid to boiling and pouring it over the fillets. Continue as directed with the rest of the recipe.

To make the mackerel, prepare the fish by removing any bones with tweezers. Remove the skin by laying the fillet, skin-side down, on your work surface. Insert a sharp knife between the skin and flesh. Grasping the skin with your fingers, gently saw the knife back and forth, keeping it parallel to the cutting board. Discard the bones and skin. You should end up with about ¾ pound trimmed fish.

In a large nonreactive saucepan over high heat, combine the carrot, garlic, onion, vinegar, water, and spices. Bring to a boil, then lower the heat and simmer for 5 minutes to blend the flavors. Decrease the heat to maintain a bare simmer, add the fish, and poach until just cooked through, 6 to 8 minutes. Pour the fish and the liquid into a nonreactive container (glass is best) and allow to cool for 10 minutes. For best flavor, refrigerate overnight, though the fish can be used as soon as it has cooled. When ready to use the fish, remove from the liquid and flake into large chunks. Reserve 2 tablespoons of the pickling liquid for use in the salad and discard the rest.

To make the salad, wash and dry the watercress, then pick off the tenderest leaves and place in a large bowl. Trim and thinly slice the radishes and add to the bowl, along with the shallot, nuts, and fish. Season to taste with salt and cracked pepper. Combine the olive oil and reserved pickling liquid, then add to the bowl and toss the mixture gently so as not to break up the fish. Divide among 4 plates and serve.

It has only a few ingredients, yet this is a very sophisticated soup. If you can't find fresh artichokes—or don't feel like trimming them—use frozen artichoke hearts.

FARRO & ARTICHOKE SOUP

SERVES 6 TO 8

- 1 lemon, halved
- 4 large artichokes
- 2 tablespoons good-quality olive oil, plus more for drizzling
- 3 cloves garlic, thinly sliced
- 1 cup farro
- 6 cups water

Kosher salt and freshly cracked pepper

- 2 tablespoons chopped fresh parsley

I don't generally use chicken stock in soups. I prefer the cleaner flavor that water brings to the soup, especially with such a fantastic vegetable as the artichoke. Farro is a chewy Italian grain somewhat like spelt, but with a firmer texture.

If you want to prepare the soup ahead of time, be sure to chill it immediately after cooking, transferring it to a shallow container so that it cools quickly. You'll need to adjust the water levels when you reheat the soup because the farro will absorb some of the water as it sits. For a nice variation, you could add some fava beans or peas.

Fill a medium-size bowl with cool water. Squeeze the lemon juice into the bowl, then add the halves.

To prepare the artichokes, first peel the fibrous outer covering from the stems, trimming only the very bottom and leaving as much stem intact as possible. Cut off the top of each artichoke with a very sharp chef's knife. Next, pull off all the tough outer leaves. Use kitchen shears to snip off the tops of the tender inner leaves. Quarter the artichoke and remove the choke from each quarter. Slice thickly. Place the artichokes in the acidulated water and set aside.

Heat the olive oil in a stockpot or Dutch oven. Add the garlic and sauté until soft. Add the farro and stir to coat the grains with the oil. Add 2 cups of the water and bring to a boil. Decrease the heat to a simmer and cook until the water almost runs dry, about 10 minutes. The farro won't be completely cooked at this point, but this prevents it from overcooking as you finish the soup.

Add the artichokes and the remaining 4 cups water to the pot along with a good pinch of salt and a couple of grinds of cracked pepper. Simmer until the vegetables are just tender, 8 to 10 minutes. Add the parsley and stir. Serve in deep bowls, drizzled with olive oil.

BEST OF THE BEST EXCLUSIVE

Cooks usually make gnocchi with potato, but Stowell prepares them here with fresh whole-milk ricotta instead, resulting in an extra-creamy texture.

RICOTTA GNOCCHI

with veal ragù

SERVES 6

RAGÙ

- 2 tablespoons extra-virgin olive oil, plus more for drizzling
- ¾ pound ground veal
- 1 small onion, finely diced
- 1 carrot, finely diced
- 1 celery rib, finely diced
- 2 garlic cloves, thinly sliced
- Kosher salt and freshly ground pepper
- 1 cup dry white wine
- One 28-ounce can crushed Italian tomatoes
- 2 bay leaves
- 2 tablespoons chopped parsley
- 2 tablespoons chopped oregano
- 2 tablespoons chopped mint

GNOCCHI

- 1 pound fresh whole-milk ricotta cheese, drained overnight
- 3 large egg yolks
- Kosher salt
- ¾ cup all-purpose flour, plus more for dusting

EDITOR'S WINE CHOICE

Juicy, fresh Dolcetto (see page 268)

1. MAKE THE RAGÙ In a large, deep skillet, heat the 2 tablespoons of olive oil. Add the veal and cook over moderately high heat, stirring occasionally, until browned, about 10 minutes. Add the onion, carrot, celery and garlic and season with salt and pepper. Cook over moderate heat, stirring, until the vegetables are softened, about 5 minutes. Stir in the wine and simmer until reduced to ½ cup, about 3 minutes. Add the tomatoes and bay leaves and bring to a boil. Simmer over low heat until thickened, about 1½ hours. Discard the bay leaves and season the ragù with salt and pepper.

2. MEANWHILE, MAKE THE GNOCCHI In a large bowl, stir the ricotta with the egg yolks and season with salt. Add the ¾ cup of flour and stir gently until a very soft, slightly sticky dough forms. Turn the dough out onto a floured work surface and knead gently, dusting with as little flour as necessary, until no longer sticky.

3. Line a baking sheet with wax paper and dust with flour. On a floured surface, cut the gnocchi dough into 4 pieces and roll each piece into a ¾-inch-thick rope. Cut the ropes into 1-inch pieces. Roll each piece into a ball and gently press your thumb in the center to create an indentation. Transfer the gnocchi to the prepared baking sheet.

4. In a large pot of simmering salted water, cook the gnocchi in batches until they rise to the surface, then simmer for 1 minute longer. Using a slotted spoon, transfer the gnocchi to a serving dish.

5. Reheat the veal ragù if necessary. Stir in the parsley, oregano and mint. Spoon 2 cups of the ragù over the gnocchi and toss gently to coat. Drizzle with olive oil and serve immediately, passing the remaining ragù on the side.

MAKE AHEAD The ragù can be refrigerated for up to 3 days. Add the herbs just before serving. The uncooked gnocchi can be frozen on the prepared baking sheet, then transferred to a resealable plastic bag and frozen for up to 1 month. Boil without defrosting.

ETHAN STOWELL ONLINE

ethanstowellrestaurants.com

@ESRseattle

Grilled cauliflower steaks with tahini sauce, page 213

EATING LOCAL →20

Sur La Table with Janet Fletcher

What do you do with a five-pound crate of cauliflower? Grill cauliflower "steaks" and brush them with a tahini sauce, suggests food writer Janet Fletcher. She's written this book for farmers' market lovers and home cooks who've joined Community Supported Agriculture (CSA) groups to get seasonal produce directly from a local farm. CSA members often find themselves in desperate need of ideas for what to do with, say, an overabundance of rutabagas; Fletcher, who trained at Berkeley's locavore temple Chez Panisse, aims to help. Here she provides 150 recipes for just about every fruit and vegetable. For green garlic, she suggests a bracing, Parmesan-powered soufflé; for yellow tomatoes, a mellow gazpacho. Thoughtfully organized by dominant ingredient, *Eating Local* is essential for anyone who belongs to a CSA or just hangs out at the farmers' market. *Published by Andrews McMeel, $35*

A shallow dish gives this savory soufflé plenty of golden brown crust. Green garlic, the young, milder form of garlic, adds a subtle but distinctive flavor.

GREEN-GARLIC SOUFFLÉ

SERVES 6

- 6 tablespoons unsalted butter, plus more for the baking dish
- ¼ cup plus 5 tablespoons freshly grated Parmigiano-Reggiano cheese
- About 2 pounds green garlic, enough to yield 4 cups sliced
- Kosher or sea salt and freshly ground black pepper
- 3 tablespoons unbleached all-purpose flour
- 1 cup whole milk
- 4 thyme sprigs
- ¼ teaspoon freshly grated nutmeg
- 4 large egg yolks
- 5 large egg whites

EDITOR'S WINE CHOICE
Dry, fruity sparkling wine (see page 264)

1. Preheat the oven to 425°F. Generously butter the bottom and sides of a 13-by-9-inch oval gratin dish. Sprinkle the buttered dish evenly with 3 tablespoons of the cheese.

2. To trim the green garlic, cut off and discard the tough, dark green leafy tops, which resemble the tops of leeks. You will use only the white and pale green part of the stalks. Cut the trimmed stalk in half lengthwise, then slice thinly crosswise. Put the sliced garlic in a large pot of cold water and swish well to dislodge any dirt. Lift the garlic into a sieve or colander with your hands or with a wire-mesh skimmer. Let drain.

3. Melt 2 tablespoons of the butter in a large skillet over moderately low heat. Add the green garlic and season with salt and pepper. Stir to coat with the butter, then cover with a round of parchment paper and the lid, reduce the heat to low, and cook until the green garlic is meltingly tender, about 20 minutes, uncovering to stir occasionally.

4. While the green garlic cooks, melt the remaining 4 tablespoons butter in a small saucepan over moderately low heat. Whisk in the flour. Cook, whisking, for about 1 minute, then add the milk gradually, whisking constantly. Add the thyme sprigs. Adjust the heat to maintain a gentle bubble and cook, whisking often, for about 5 minutes to allow the béchamel to thicken. Stir in the nutmeg. Remove from the heat and let cool for 10 minutes.

5. Whisk the egg yolks, one at a time, into the béchamel. Whisk in the ¼ cup cheese; season with salt and pepper. Remove the thyme sprigs, and stir the cooked green garlic into the béchamel base.

6. With an electric mixer or by hand, beat the egg whites to firm but not stiff peaks. Fold the whites, one-third at a time, into the base. Transfer the soufflé mixture to the prepared baking dish, spreading it evenly. Top with the remaining 2 tablespoons cheese.

7. Bake until the soufflé is well puffed, firm to the touch, and golden brown, 17 to 18 minutes. Serve immediately.

The key to the extraordinary flavor of this gazpacho is letting the tomatoes and their juices stand at room temperature with the other ingredients for an hour before pureeing. The extra time is definitely worth it.

YELLOW TOMATO GAZPACHO

SERVES 6

- ½ pound dense, day-old French or Italian country bread, crust removed, cut into 1-inch cubes
- ¼ cup Champagne vinegar or white wine vinegar
- 2½ pounds yellow or gold tomatoes, peeled, cored, and diced, with juices
- 1 small cucumber, about ½ pound, peeled and cut into 1-inch cubes
- ½ large yellow or gold bell pepper, seeded and cut into 1-inch cubes
- ½ small red onion, sliced
- 1 large clove garlic, minced
- ½ teaspoon cumin seed, toasted
- 2 teaspoons kosher or sea salt
- ¼ cup extra-virgin olive oil, plus more for garnish
- 1 tablespoon sherry vinegar (optional)
- 2 hard-cooked eggs
- 1 small red tomato, sliced into ½-inch wedges
- Pimentón de la Vera (smoked Spanish paprika), mild, medium, or hot, or other paprika

With ripe tomatoes harvested in so many riveting hues these days, gazpacho no longer has to be red. Surprise guests with this golden version, a puree of all the classic gazpacho vegetables—tomatoes, cucumbers, onions, sweet peppers (yellow, of course)—thickened with bread, heightened with vinegar, and scented with cumin. Float a slice of hard-cooked egg and a drizzle of green olive oil on each serving to make a chilled soup with eye appeal. For the tomatoes, look for super-tasty slicing varieties like Lemon Boy, Taxi, Pineapple, Persimmon, or Gold Medal.

1. Put the bread in a large bowl and sprinkle with the Champagne vinegar. Toss to coat the bread with the vinegar. Add the tomatoes, cucumber, bell pepper, onion, garlic, cumin, salt, and olive oil. Toss well. Let stand at room temperature for 1 hour to draw the juices out of the tomatoes.

2. Puree the mixture thoroughly in a blender, in batches. Strain through a medium-mesh sieve to remove the tomato seeds and pepper skins, pressing on the solids. Taste for salt and stir in the sherry vinegar. If the soup seems too thick, thin with cold water. Cover and chill thoroughly.

3. Slice the eggs and set aside 6 pretty slices that include both white and yolk.

4. Divide the soup evenly among bowls. Top each portion with an egg slice and tomato wedge, drizzle with olive oil, and sprinkle with *pimentón*. Serve immediately.

This recipe forgoes pan-searing scallops in favor of grilling. The result: sweet scallops with a subtle char, served here on warm, buttery spinach.

GRILLED SCALLOPS
with wilted spinach & lemon-caper butter

SERVES 4

LEMON-CAPER BUTTER

- ½ cup unsalted butter (1 stick), softened
- 2 tablespoons capers, preferably salt packed, rinsed and finely minced
- 2 teaspoons grated lemon zest
- 2 tablespoons minced fresh Italian parsley

Kosher or sea salt

- 1 pound sea scallops

Kosher or sea salt and freshly ground black pepper

- 1 tablespoon unsalted butter, melted
- 3 bunches (12 to 14 ounces each) spinach, thick stems removed
- 4 lemon wedges

EDITOR'S WINE CHOICE
Light, crisp white Burgundy
(see page 264)

In just a few moments on the stove, a potful of rough fresh spinach leaves wilts down into a silky bed for grilled scallops. A composed butter enlivened with capers and lemon zest creates a simple sauce as it melts on the hot greens and shellfish. Be sure to warm the dinner plates for a few minutes in a low oven to keep the food hot. Both the spinach and the scallops cool off quickly otherwise.

1. Prepare a moderate charcoal fire or preheat a gas grill to medium (375°F). To make the lemon-caper butter, put the butter, capers, lemon zest, and parsley in a bowl and stir with a wooden spoon until smooth. Season to taste with salt.

2. Remove the "foot" or small muscle on the side of each scallop. Halve the scallops horizontally, or slice them in thirds if they are jumbo scallops, so the slices are no more than ½ inch thick. Season all over with salt and pepper and brush with the melted butter.

3. Put the spinach in a large pot with just the washing water clinging to the leaves. Cover and cook over moderate heat, stirring with tongs once or twice, until the spinach is barely wilted, about 3 minutes. Drain in a sieve or colander. Do not press on the leaves or squeeze them to extract more liquid; you want to leave them fairly moist. Return them to the same pot and add half of the lemon-caper butter. Toss with tongs over low heat so that the butter melts and coats the spinach. Taste for salt. Keep the spinach warm while you grill the scallops.

4. Grill the scallops directly over the coals or gas flame, turning once, until they are nicely marked by the grill and no longer translucent, about 5 minutes total.

5. Divide the spinach among warmed dinner plates. Arrange the scallops on top, and immediately slather the scallops with the remaining butter. The butter will melt from the heat of the shellfish. Garnish each serving with a lemon wedge and serve immediately.

In this ingenious recipe, Fletcher cuts thick slabs of cauliflower and grills them like steak. They're phenomenal smothered with the nutty tahini sauce.

GRILLED CAULIFLOWER STEAKS
with tahini sauce

SERVES 4

TAHINI SAUCE

- ¼ cup tahini, stirred well to blend
- ¼ cup water
- 2 to 3 tablespoons fresh lemon juice
- 1 large clove garlic, minced
- 1 tablespoon minced fresh cilantro
- Kosher or sea salt

- 2 medium cauliflowers
- Extra-virgin olive oil
- Kosher or sea salt and freshly ground black pepper
- Chopped fresh cilantro, for garnish

EDITOR'S WINE CHOICE
Full-bodied, rich Pinot Gris (see page 266)

From each head of cauliflower, you can cut two thick "steaks," slicing from top to bottom near the center to yield a pair of slices each held together by the core. The resulting "steaks," seared on the grill, make a head-turning presentation with a creamy tahini sauce. Use any leftover sauce on grilled vegetables, fish, or roasted beets.

1. Prepare a moderate charcoal fire for indirect grilling or preheat a gas grill to medium (375°F), leaving one burner unlit.

2. To make the tahini sauce, in a small bowl, whisk together the tahini, ¼ cup water, and 2 tablespoons lemon juice until smooth. Whisk in the garlic, cilantro, and salt to taste. Taste and adjust with more lemon juice, if desired.

3. Trim each cauliflower, removing any leaves and cutting the stem flush with the base. Set a cauliflower, cut side down, on a cutting board. With a chef's knife, cut 2 "steaks," each about ¾ inch thick, from the center of the cauliflower, so that the core holds each slice together. Repeat with the second cauliflower. Reserve the remaining cauliflower for another use.

4. Put the 4 cauliflower steaks on a tray and brush one side with the olive oil. Season with salt and pepper. Turn the steaks over, brush the second side, and season with salt and pepper.

5. Place the steaks over indirect heat, cover the grill, and cook, turning once, until tender when pierced, about 15 minutes total. For the final minute or so of cooking, uncover the grill and move the cauliflower directly over the coals or flame to char it slightly.

6. Transfer the steaks to a platter and drizzle with the tahini sauce; you may not need it all. Garnish with cilantro and serve hot or warm.

JANET FLETCHER ONLINE
janetfletcher.com

Hominy for slow-cooked carne adovada, page 216

HEART OF THE ARTICHOKE & OTHER KITCHEN JOURNEYS

→ 21

David Tanis

As co-chef at Berkeley's Chez Panisse for over 25 years, David Tanis helped create the unfussy, market-driven style that's influenced a generation of American chefs. Here, in his second cookbook, Tanis presents recipes that have a similar elegant simplicity, with minimal ingredients and bold flavors, inspired by destinations ranging from Vietnam to Morocco. The book begins with Kitchen Rituals, quirky snacks and meals, some as simple as ham on a buttered baguette. Next are Seasonal Menus, with playful titles like "Dead-of-Winter Dinner from the Supermarket" and "Ripeness of Red Chiles," which includes his *carne adovada*. Lastly, there are Simple Feasts for a Long Table, ideas for celebrations like a New Year's Day "Auspicious and Delicious" meal anchored by a pot of black-eyed peas with ham hocks. "It may be a big table," he writes, "but it doesn't have to be a big deal." *Published by Artisan, $35*

Carne adovada is a traditional New Mexican dish of meat marinated in a puree of the state's famous dried red chiles. The meat is baked for two hours, till it falls apart, producing what Tanis calls "the pork of your dreams."

SLOW-COOKED CARNE ADOVADA
with hominy

SERVES 4 TO 6

- 6 ounces dried New Mexico red chiles
- 2 tablespoons lard or vegetable oil
- 1 large onion, finely diced
- Salt and pepper
- 6 garlic cloves, roughly chopped
- 1 teaspoon coriander seeds, toasted and ground
- 1 teaspoon cumin seeds, toasted and ground
- 1 bay leaf
- 3 pounds boneless pork shoulder left whole or cut into large chunks
- Hominy (recipe follows)

EDITOR'S WINE CHOICE
Juicy, spicy Grenache
(see page 268)

The New Mexican way with pork is a celebration of dried red chiles. Basically, you soften the long, leathery chile peppers by simmering them in a little water, puree them into an intense paste, and smother the meat in this marinade. Then the meat, the picante *marinade, and the slow, slow cooking result in the best pulled pork you've ever had.*

Rinse and dry the chiles, then toast them in a dry cast-iron pan over medium heat until they puff a bit and become fragrant, 2 to 3 minutes. Cut the chiles lengthwise in half and remove the stems and seeds. Put the chiles in a small pot of water and bring to a boil. Simmer for about 5 minutes. Let the chiles cool in the liquid. Puree the chiles with a cup of their cooking liquid in a blender until smooth.

Heat the lard or oil in a large skillet over medium heat. Add the onion, season with salt and pepper, and cook for about 5 minutes. No color, no browning. Add the garlic, coriander, cumin, and bay leaf, then add the chile puree and a little salt and simmer for another 5 minutes. Cool the mixture. (You can do this well ahead if you wish.)

Preheat the oven to 350°F. Put the pork in a low roasting pan or a heavy-bottomed ovenproof pot and season generously with salt and pepper. Pour the chile sauce over the pork and mix well to coat. Cover tightly with a lid or foil. Bake the pork for 1½ to 2 hours, until the meat is quite tender and falling apart. (This dish can be made a day or many hours ahead and reheated.) Serve the carne adovada in shallow soup bowls with a big spoonful of the steaming-hot hominy.

HOMINY

- 1 pound dried hominy, soaked overnight in water to cover
- 4 quarts water
- 1 teaspoon salt, or to taste
- 1 small onion, halved and stuck with a clove
- 6 garlic cloves
- 2 carrots, peeled and chunked

Drain the hominy, rinse, and put in a soup pot. Cover with the water, add the salt, onion, garlic, and carrots, and bring to a boil. Reduce the heat and simmer for 1½ to 2 hours, until the kernels have swelled and softened. Discard the aromatics. Taste for salt, and add a bit more if needed. Serve immediately, or reheat when ready.

Tanis sticks to classic roasted chicken flavorings (rosemary, lemon and garlic) but butterflies the bird to help the skin get golden and crispy.

FLAT-ROASTED CHICKEN
with rosemary

- 1 organic chicken, about 3 pounds
- Salt and pepper
- ¼ cup rosemary leaves
- 6 large garlic cloves, sliced
- 2 teaspoons red pepper flakes
- Olive oil
- 1 lemon, sliced

EDITOR'S WINE CHOICE
Creamy, supple Pinot Blanc
(see page 266)

This cooking method yields the most succulent bird, with lots of crisp, caramelized skin and the intense, satisfying flavor of garlic and rosemary. It's easy to do in a hot oven in a low roasting pan or a very large cast-iron pan. It goes without saying, the quality of the chicken matters above all.

This method also works well with game hens.

Wash the bird and pat it dry. Remove the backbone with a pair of poultry shears or with a sharp knife. Push down on the breastbone to open the bird like a book.

Put the chicken in a roasting pan and season generously on both sides with salt and pepper. Sprinkle with the rosemary, garlic, and red pepper flakes. Drizzle with about 2 tablespoons of olive oil. Now, with your hands, gently smear the seasonings all over the bird.

Turn the chicken breast side up in the roasting pan, top with the lemon slices, cover, and refrigerate a couple of hours.

Bring the chicken to room temperature. Preheat the oven to 400°F. Roast the chicken for about an hour, or until it is beautifully browned and the juices run clear from the leg when pierced. Remove from the oven and let rest for 15 minutes.

Put the bird on a cutting board and cut into 6 portions with a heavy knife or a cleaver.

Tanis suggests making these for a winter party—the ingredients are available year-round, and the crab and crème fraîche give the eggs a luxurious edge.

CRAB-STUFFED DEVILED EGGS

1 dozen large organic eggs
1 tablespoon Dijon mustard
¼ cup sour cream or crème fraîche
Generous pinch of cayenne
1 tablespoon snipped chives
½ pound crabmeat, picked over for shells and cartilage
Juice of ½ lemon
Salt and pepper

I really love deviled eggs—especially these. You can quote me.

Bring a large saucepan of water to a boil. Carefully put the eggs into the water and cook for 10 minutes. Remove the eggs to a bowl of ice water, and when they're cool enough, crack them gently and return to the ice water, so they'll be easier to peel.

Peel the eggs. Cut them in half, scoop out the yolks, and put them in a bowl (reserve the egg white halves). Mash the egg yolks with a fork, and fold in the mustard, sour cream or crème fraîche, cayenne, and half the chives. Gently fold in the crabmeat and lemon juice, and season lightly with salt and pepper. Taste and adjust the seasoning, and spoon the mixture into the waiting egg white halves.

Put the eggs on a platter or two, cover, and refrigerate. Just before serving, sprinkle the eggs with the rest of the chopped chives.

The key to a great pho is the broth, so be sure to simmer the meats, vegetables and aromatic spices long enough to allow the flavors to intensify.

PHO (VIETNAMESE BEEF SOUP)

FOR THE SOUP

- 1½ pounds short ribs
- 1½ pounds oxtails or beef shank
- 1 large onion, halved
- One 3-inch piece unpeeled ginger, thickly sliced
- 6 quarts water
- 1 star anise
- 1 small piece cinnamon stick
- ½ teaspoon coriander seeds
- ½ teaspoon fennel seeds
- ¼ teaspoon whole cloves
- 6 cardamom pods
- 2 tablespoons soy sauce
- 1 tablespoon fish sauce
- 2 teaspoons sugar
- Salt and pepper
- 1 pound dried rice noodles
- ½ pound fresh bean sprouts
- 1 sweet red onion, thinly sliced

FOR THE GARNISH

- Mint sprigs
- Cilantro sprigs
- Basil sprigs
- 6 scallions, slivered
- 2 serrano or 6 small Asian chiles, finely slivered
- Lime wedges

In Vietnam, pho is street food, basic, hearty, and filling, sold from a cart with a few little stools in front. Here, you can get pho at little bare-bones sit-down restaurants, where you crowd in for a quick lunch. Platters of mint and basil leaves are stacked up and ready, because they are constantly needed. At such places, there is a rich and long menu of variations, pho with meatballs or tripe, for example. Pho fanatics customize their bowls with all kinds of extras and peculiarities. So you'll want to develop your own house pho.

Classically the soup is finished with thinly sliced raw beef that cooks quickly in the soup, but your pho can be any combination that pleases you.

The broth is the essence of the soup, so it's important to take great care with it. It's not difficult, but it makes all the difference between a pho that sings and one that just sits there.

Bring a large pot of water to a boil. Put in the short ribs and oxtails and boil for 10 minutes, then drain and discard the water. This preliminary boiling makes a cleaner-tasting broth.

Set a heavy-bottomed soup pot over medium-high heat, add the onion, cut side down, and ginger, and lightly char for about 10 minutes, until the halves are charred but not quite burnt. Add the short ribs, oxtails, and the 6 quarts of water and bring to a hard boil, then turn down to a simmer. Add the star anise, cinnamon stick, coriander and fennel seeds, cloves, and cardamom. Then add the soy sauce, fish sauce, sugar, and salt and pepper and let simmer, uncovered. From time to time, skim off rising foam, fat, and debris.

After an hour or so, check the tenderness of the meat. It will probably take an hour and a half for the meat to get really fork-tender.

continued on page 223

pho continued

When the meat is done, remove it from the pot, take the meat off the bones, and reserve. Put the bones back in the pot to simmer in the broth for about another hour and a half.

When the broth is done, taste it for salt and add more if necessary. Strain it through a fine-mesh strainer. Chop the cooked meat and add it to the broth. Cool and refrigerate. (The broth can be made a day ahead.)

When you're ready to serve the pho, put the rice noodles in a large bowl and pour boiling water over them. Let them sit for about 15 minutes to soften, then drain.

Heat the soup to piping hot. Prepare a large platter of the garnishes: a big pile of mint, cilantro, and basil sprigs, slivered scallions and chiles, and lime wedges.

Line up the soup bowls (I love the deep, giant Chinatown-style bowls). Put a handful of noodles in each soup bowl and scatter some bean sprouts on top. Add a few raw onion slices. Ladle the broth and a bit of boiled meat into each bowl. Pass the platter of garnishes and let everyone add herbs, scallions, and chiles and a squeeze of lime.

Pork kimchee with noodles, page 232

SIMPLY MING ONE-POT MEALS

→ 22

Ming Tsai & Arthur Boehm

Chef and cooking show host Ming Tsai has been creating East-West fusion for so long that it's gone from trendy to passé to trendy again. His fourth cookbook doesn't retreat from his signature style, but focuses on simplicity (one cooking vessel in most cases) and thrift (roughly $20 worth of ingredients per dish). Even with such narrow guidelines, Tsai is supercreative: Highlights include a silky, aromatic chicken braised with star anise and ginger and a pungent pork kimchee stir-fry with mung bean noodles. The recipes are divided into chapters by technique (such as braise, wok, sauté, roast) and manage to bring novel ideas to traditional dishes, like his risotto made with sushi rice, shrimp and Thai basil. *Published by Kyle Books, $29.95*

This distinctive way to make whole chicken has the added benefit of creating a soothing broth infused with star anise and other aromatics.

STAR ANISE–GINGER "BRAISED" WHOLE CHICKEN

SERVES 4

- 4 celery stalks, cut into ½-inch pieces
- 2 large carrots, peeled and roll-cut into ½-inch pieces (see Roll-Cutting), or cut conventionally
- 2 large onions, cut into ½-inch dice
- 1 teaspoon black peppercorns
- 2 bay leaves
- 2 sprigs fresh thyme
- ¼ bunch fresh flat-leaf parsley
- 2 star anise
- 2 tablespoons minced ginger
- ½ cup naturally brewed soy sauce or wheat-free tamari sauce
- 2 quarts fresh chicken stock, or low-sodium canned chicken broth, plus extra, if needed
- Kosher salt and freshly ground black pepper
- One 5- to 6-pound whole chicken, wing tips folded over the back

AUTHOR'S WINE CHOICE
A crisp New World Sauvignon Blanc, like Craggy Range "Te Muna Road" from New Zealand

I often wonder why people cook chicken by any other method than this traditional Chinese one, technically a poach-braise. It delivers beautifully tender, silky meat—and it couldn't be easier. All you do is put a chicken in a pot with stock and flavorings, simmer it until it's partially cooked, then remove it from the heat. The bird finishes cooking in the hot liquid, and emerges perfectly done. The chicken's almost fat-free, having left most of its fat in the stock. Serve with crusty bread.

1. In a stockpot or other tall, wide pot or large Dutch oven, combine the celery, carrots, onions, peppercorns, bay leaves, thyme, parsley, star anise, ginger, and soy sauce. Add the stock and season with salt and pepper.

2. Season the chicken inside and out with salt and pepper. Add the chicken to the pot breast side up. It should be completely covered with stock, but if not, add more.

3. Cover and bring just to a simmer over medium-high heat. Reduce the heat to low and barely simmer for 45 minutes. Turn off the heat and let the pot stand, covered, 30 minutes to 1 hour (the chicken won't cook any further after 30 minutes). Remove the chicken and strain the broth, reserving the vegetables. Carve the chicken and serve with the vegetables and bowls of the broth.

ROLL-CUTTING
A traditional Chinese technique that ensures maximum exposed surface area so that cylindrical vegetables like carrots or asparagus cook quickly when stir-fried. Roll-cut vegetables also look pretty. To roll-cut, first slice away the stem end on an angle. Roll the vegetable about a quarter turn away from you and slice again at the same angle, about 1½ inches further down or to the length your recipe directs. Continue rolling and slicing until the vegetable has been entirely cut.

This might be the simplest, most intensely flavorful chicken you've ever tried. Crusty bread would be perfect for soaking up the tasty juices here.

GINGER CHICKEN THIGHS
with parsnips

SERVES 4

- 2 pounds chicken thighs
- Kosher salt and freshly ground black pepper
- 3 tablespoons grapeseed or canola oil
- 2 large onions, cut into 1-inch dice
- 2 tablespoons minced ginger
- 3 large parsnips, peeled and roll-cut into 1-inch lengths (see Roll-Cutting on page 226), or cut conventionally
- 4 celery stalks, roll-cut into 1-inch lengths, or cut conventionally
- 5 sprigs fresh thyme

AUTHOR'S WINE CHOICE
A Shiraz or Syrah, like Radio-Coteau Timbervine from California

Chicken thighs are my favorite part of the bird. They've got just the right meat-to-skin ratios and they really shine in this quick, gingery bake that's great for post-work cooking. This dish also features parsnips, which I think of as white carrots. They're as sweet as carrots but have more character.

1. Preheat the oven to 450°F.

2. Season the thighs with the salt and pepper. Heat a large heavy roasting pan or heavy skillet over medium-high heat. Add 2 tablespoons of the oil and swirl to coat the bottom. When the oil is hot, add the thighs skin side down. Brown, turning once, about 10 minutes. Transfer the thighs to a platter and set aside.

3. Add the remaining oil to the pan, swirl, and heat. When the oil is hot, add the onions, ginger, parsnips, celery, and thyme. Season with salt and pepper and sauté the vegetables, stirring, until softened, about 6 minutes. Top with the thighs, skin side up, and bake uncovered until the chicken and vegetables are done, 30 to 40 minutes. Transfer to a platter or four individual serving plates and serve.

This Asian riff on risotto is just as satisfying as the Italian original. The addition of lime juice and fragrant Thai basil is what makes it so good.

THAI BASIL SHRIMP RISOTTO

SERVES 4

- 2 tablespoons grapeseed or canola oil
- 1 pound small (51 to 60) shrimp, or rock shrimp, rinsed and dried
- Kosher salt and freshly ground black pepper
- 3 tablespoons unsalted butter
- 2 tablespoons minced garlic
- 1 small onion, cut into ⅛-inch dice
- 2 cups koshihikari or other sushi rice, or Arborio rice
- 1 cup dry white wine
- 5 to 6 cups fresh chicken stock or low-sodium canned chicken broth, hot
- 12 Thai basil leaves, cut into very fine strips
- Juice of 1 lime

AUTHOR'S WINE CHOICE

A French Burgundy, like Louis Latour Santenay

Some people think risotto is tricky to make. It's not. All you have to do is pay attention as you add ladlefuls of broth to the rice, so you can judge when the risotto is properly cooked. My Asian version features koshihikari rice, a premium sushi rice that has a higher absorption threshold than that of other rices. Like its Italian cousin, Arborio, it can be cooked to a creamy firm bite. Shrimp and Thai basil complete the dish.

1. Heat a large saucepan over medium-high heat. Add 1 tablespoon of the oil and swirl to coat the bottom. When the oil is hot, add the shrimp and sauté, stirring, until the shrimp are pink, about 1 minute. Season with salt and pepper. Transfer the shrimp to a plate and set aside.

2. Add the remaining tablespoon oil and 1 tablespoon of the butter. When the mixture is hot, add the garlic and onions and sauté until soft, 1 to 2 minutes. Add the rice and sauté, stirring, until the rice has become opaque, about 2 minutes. Add the wine, deglaze the pan, and simmer until the liquid has been absorbed by the rice, 2 to 3 minutes.

3. Ladle in the stock ½ cup at a time, allowing each addition to be absorbed by the rice before adding the next. Continue until the rice is al dente, about 10 minutes. Return the shrimp to the rice, add the basil, remaining 2 tablespoons butter, and lime juice, and stir. Taste and adjust the seasoning.

4. Transfer the risotto to four individual serving bowls and serve.

The salty, spicy tang of kimchee gives an instant flavor boost to the pork tenderloin and mung bean noodles in this assertive stir-fry.

PORK KIMCHEE WITH NOODLES

SERVES 4

- 2 tablespoons naturally brewed soy sauce
- 1 tablespoon minced garlic
- 2 medium pork tenderloins (about 2 pounds), any silverskin removed, cut into ¼-inch slices
- ½ pound mung bean noodles
- 3 tablespoons grapeseed or canola oil
- Kosher salt and freshly ground black pepper
- 1 medium red onion, halved lengthwise and sliced thin
- 2 cups cabbage kimchee
- 1 small zucchini, sliced as thin as possible
- 1 cup fresh chicken stock or low-sodium canned chicken broth
- ½ teaspoon Korean chile pepper flakes or ancho chile powder

AUTHOR'S WINE CHOICE
Trimbach Riesling

AUTHOR'S NOTE
A mandoline makes the job of slicing the zucchini, among other cutting chores, a snap. If you don't own one, I suggest a ceramic model like the one Kyocera makes, which does the job quickly and is also inexpensive.

Stir-fried pork with kimchee is a beloved Korean dish. Kimchee, made usually from fermented cabbage, is wonderfully pungent—though I don't recommend playing spin-the-bottle after eating it. In addition to these ingredients, I've included satisfying mung bean noodles and zucchini. This is a terrific dish—real excitement on the plate.

1. In a medium bowl, combine the soy sauce and garlic. Add the pork, toss, and marinate, refrigerated, for 30 minutes.

2. Meanwhile, place the noodles in a wok and fill with hot water to cover. When the noodles have softened, after about 10 minutes, drain and transfer to a bowl.

3. Dry the wok and heat it over high heat. Add 2 tablespoons of the oil and swirl to coat the pan. When the oil is hot, add the pork, season with salt and pepper, and stir-fry until just cooked through, 6 to 8 minutes. Transfer the pork to a plate, add the remaining tablespoon oil to the wok, and swirl to coat the pan. When the oil is hot, add the onion and stir-fry until soft, about 2 minutes. Add the kimchee and zucchini and season with salt and pepper. Add the pork, stock, and the noodles, mix, and heat through, 1 to 2 minutes.

4. Transfer to four individual serving bowls, garnish with the chile pepper flakes, and serve.

BEST OF THE BEST EXCLUSIVE

Tsai enhances fresh or dried noodles here with tamari, a darker, slightly thicker variety of soy sauce. Its deeper flavor works particularly well with the garlic, chiles and ginger in this substantial vegetarian main course.

STIR-FRIED NOODLES

with spinach, shiitake & ginger

SERVES 4

- ½ pound fresh or dried chow mein or Shanghai noodles
- 3 tablespoons canola oil, plus more for tossing
- 10 ounces shiitake mushrooms, stems discarded, caps sliced ¼ inch thick
- Kosher salt and freshly ground pepper
- 2 tablespoons minced fresh ginger
- 2 large garlic cloves, minced
- 1 to 2 serrano chiles, seeded and minced
- 1 cup thinly sliced scallions, white and green parts separated (about 6 scallions)
- 1 red bell pepper, halved lengthwise and thinly sliced crosswise
- ½ cup vegetable stock
- 2 tablespoons tamari
- 1 tablespoon fresh lemon juice
- 3 cups packed baby spinach

EDITOR'S WINE CHOICE

Ripe, juicy Pinot Noir (see page 269)

1. In a large pot of boiling salted water, cook the noodles until al dente. Drain the noodles and rinse under cold running water until cool. Drain well and toss with oil to prevent clumping.

2. In a very large, deep skillet or wok, heat 2 tablespoons of the oil until shimmering. Add the shiitake and cook over moderately high heat, undisturbed, until browned on the bottom, about 4 minutes. Season with salt and pepper. Using a slotted spoon, transfer the mushrooms to a paper-towel-lined plate.

3. Add the remaining 1 tablespoon of oil to the skillet. Add the ginger, garlic and chiles and stir-fry until fragrant, about 1 minute. Add the scallion whites and the bell pepper and stir-fry until just tender, about 2 minutes. Add the noodles, vegetable stock and tamari and cook, tossing, until the noodles are heated through and most of the liquid is absorbed, about 3 minutes. Add the shiitake, lemon juice and spinach and toss until the spinach just starts to wilt. Season with salt and pepper. Transfer the noodles to a platter, top with the scallion greens and serve.

MING TSAI ONLINE

ming.com

BlueGingerRestaurant

@chefmingtsai

Bart van Olphen (left) and Tom Kime

FISH TALES

→ 23

Bart van Olphen & Tom Kime

Equal parts cookbook, travelogue and eco-crusade, *Fish Tales* is a guide to cooking sustainable seafood. Written by British author-chef Tom Kime and Bart van Olphen, founder of the first sustainable fishmonger in continental Europe, the book is organized around visits to nine sustainable fisheries around the world; the pair get to know the fishermen as they work, harvesting clams by hand in Vietnam and pole-fishing for albacore tuna in California. "Sustainability is not a new buzzword," says Kime. "Communities that live by the sea . . . have fished in this manner for millennia." The recipes are inspired by the culture of the destination: Danish mussels are cooked in a bracing broth of aquavit and caraway seeds; Alaskan salmon is mashed with potatoes into rustic fishcakes. *Fish Tales* is essential reading for any home cook who cares about the future of the oceans. *Published by Kyle Books, $29.95*

Mussels and french fries are a classic combination. It's worth making your own fries for this dish: They're absolutely delicious dipped into the dill mayonnaise.

DANISH MUSSELS
with dill & aquavit

SERVES 2 TO 4

- 1 tablespoon oil
- 2 fresh bay leaves
- ¼ teaspoon crushed hot red pepper
- 1 teaspoon caraway seeds
- 1 onion, finely chopped
- Bunch of fresh dill, coarsely chopped
- 4 sprigs of fresh flat-leaf parsley, coarsely chopped
- ⅓ cup dry white wine
- Salt and freshly ground black pepper
- 5 tablespoons aquavit
- 3½ pounds mussels, cleaned and debearded

FOR THE DILL MAYONNAISE

- 2 egg yolks
- 1 teaspoon Dijon mustard
- 1 teaspoon red wine vinegar
- 1 cup extra-virgin olive oil
- Juice of ½ lemon
- Handful of fresh dill, chopped

AUTHORS' WINE CHOICE
On the boat in the Limfjord we had these sweet mussels with an ice cold Riesling that we had chilled in the harbor. The characteristic acidity of the chilled wine cuts through the richness of the shellfish.

Aquavit is a clear Danish spirit that is often enjoyed with seafood dishes. It is flavored with caraway seeds and has a similar strong taste to the French pastis or Greek ouzo. Either of these two spirits could be substituted for the aquavit. The fresh dill and caraway seeds cut through the richness of the mussels, and you can add a little extra flavoring if you serve these mussels with some fresh dill mayonnaise.

Heat the oil in a large saucepan over medium to high heat. Add the bay leaves, crushed hot red pepper, and caraway seeds. Cook for 1 minute until fragrant and aromatic. Add the onion, reduce the heat, and cook for 5 minutes without letting it color.

Add half the dill, half the parsley, and all the wine and bring to a boil.

When you are ready to cook the mussels, add a pinch of salt, some pepper, and the aquavit to the broth. Add the cleaned mussels, cover, and cook over medium to high heat until the shells have opened, about 4 to 5 minutes.

Meanwhile, make the dill mayonnaise. Drop the egg yolks into a bowl with the mustard, a little salt, and the vinegar. Stir to combine. Gradually pour in the oil, drop by drop and stirring all the time. Continue stirring until all the oil is used up and you have a thick emulsion. Stir in the lemon juice and the chopped dill. Season to taste with salt and pepper.

Remove the mussels from the heat and discard any shells that remain closed. Garnish the dish with the remaining dill and parsley and serve the mussels in large bowls with the dill mayonnaise and lots of fresh bread, or a bowl of hot fries. Once you have tried them, you will see that mussels and fries are a great combination; they are also a good way of soaking up all the lovely liquid in the bottom of the dish.

The bright, tangy salsa verde is perfect with the salmon and lentils, but it's so versatile that it would also be great with other meaty fish, chicken or steak.

GRILLED SALMON
with herb lentils & salsa verde

SERVES 4

FOR THE HERB LENTILS

- 7 ounces Puy lentils
- 4 fresh sage leaves
- 3 fresh flat-leaf parsley stems
- 1 celery rib
- Salt and freshly ground black pepper
- 4 tablespoons olive oil
- 1 tablespoon red wine vinegar
- Grated zest and juice of 1 lemon
- 2 sprigs of fresh dill, chopped
- 3 sprigs of fresh flat-leaf parsley, chopped
- 3 sprigs of fresh basil, chopped

FOR THE SALSA VERDE

- 1 garlic clove
- 2 tablespoons capers, rinsed
- 1 teaspoon Dijon mustard
- 3 sprigs of fresh basil
- 3 sprigs of fresh mint
- Leaves from 3 sprigs of fresh flat-leaf parsley (stems reserved for the herb lentils)
- Juice of ½ lemon
- 1 tablespoon red wine vinegar
- 3 tablespoons olive oil

- Oil, for grilling
- Salmon fillets, 1 portion-sized piece per person, skin on

AUTHORS' WINE CHOICE

The richness of the salmon can be complemented by a crisp white wine with a good balance of fruit and acidity. I would suggest a good-quality dry rosé.

This is a wonderful combination in a very simple recipe. The contrast of textures and the interplay of the colors are as important to the finished dish as the flavors. Everything works together to form a three-dimensional image of delicious food.

First make the herb lentils. In a pan, cover the lentils with cold water and bring to a simmer over medium heat. Add the sage leaves, parsley stems, and celery. Simmer until the lentils are *al dente*, and then remove from the heat and drain. Discard the celery and herbs.

Season the lentils while hot with salt and black pepper, and add the oil, vinegar, and the lemon juice and zest, so they will better absorb all the flavors. When the lentils have cooled, add the chopped herbs.

For the salsa verde, place the garlic and capers in a food processor or in a pestle and mortar and blend or crush until smooth. Add the Dijon mustard and all the herbs, then puree until you have a smooth green paste. Add the lemon juice and red wine vinegar, and then stir in the olive oil. Check the seasoning and add more salt, pepper, and lemon juice, if necessary.

Place a lightly oiled, heavy-bottomed griddle pan over medium to high heat. Season the salmon fillets with salt and black pepper and place in the pan, skin-side down. Grill the salmon for 4 minutes until crisp. Roll the fish over and cook for 2 minutes on each of the other sides. When cooking salmon you want the flesh to be medium-rare in the center; the residual heat will continue cooking the fish after it has been removed from the heat.

Serve the grilled fish with the herb lentils and the salsa verde, perhaps alongside some other vegetables or a mixed peppery leaf salad.

This is a clever take on a now-clichéd dish—Asian-style seared tuna. The turmeric root in the marinade adds Indian flavor, while the julienned snow peas are served raw, bringing a fresh crispness to the dish.

SEARED TUNA
with fresh turmeric, scallion & chile

SERVES 4 TO 6

- ½ small bunch of cilantro, stems and roots reserved
- 2 garlic cloves, peeled
- 1½-inch piece of ginger, peeled and finely sliced
- Salt and freshly ground black pepper
- 2 medium-hot red chiles, seeded and finely chopped
- 1½-inch piece of turmeric root, peeled, or 1 teaspoon ground turmeric (see Authors' Note)
- 2 tablespoons hot water
- 1¾ to 2½ pounds albacore tuna (if you can, buy the tuna in one piece, then cut it into slices weighing about 6 to 8 ounces, allowing 1 steak per person)
- Juice of 2 limes
- 2 tablespoons soy sauce
- Olive oil, for cooking
- 4 scallions, green parts cut into 1¼-inch lengths, cut in half lengthwise and cut into thin strands
- 20 snow peas, ends trimmed and cut into thin strands

EDITOR'S WINE CHOICE
Lush, fragrant Viognier
(see page 267)

AUTHORS' NOTE
Fresh turmeric is available from most Asian grocers and Chinese and Thai specialty stores. Its fresh vivid orange color looks amazing when it is shaved into thin slivers.

Marinating the tuna in turmeric, garlic, and chile means the fish takes on lots of color and flavor to create a very striking dish.

Finely chop the cilantro roots and stems with the garlic and ginger. Place in a pestle and mortar with a pinch of salt. Pound the mixture into a coarse paste. Add the chiles and continue to work into a paste. Peel the flesh of the turmeric into thin slivers (note that fresh turmeric is a very strong dye; if you do not want to dye your hands and everything that you touch bright orange, use it carefully and wear rubber gloves). Place the slivers in a shallow metal bowl. Add the hot water and the spice paste: this will form the marinade.

Season the tuna steaks with black pepper (no salt at this stage as the fish needs to marinate). Place the tuna in the shallow bowl with the marinade, cover, and set aside for 30 minutes. Turn the steaks and baste with the marinade a number of times throughout the time.

Heat a large heavy-bottomed frying pan over medium to high heat. Remove the fish from the marinade and gently shake off the excess. Pat the fillets dry with paper towels. Add the lime juice and soy sauce to the marinade. Season the tuna steaks with a little salt. Do not overseason the fish, because soy sauce is salty.

Do not overload the pan with cold fish or the temperature will drop and the fish will boil rather than be seared; instead cook it in two or three batches. Add a little oil to the pan and sear the tuna for 1 minute, then gently turn it over and cook for another minute for rare; if you prefer medium-rare, allow about another 20 seconds on each side. When removed from the pan, the fish will continue cooking from the residual heat and the salty, acidic marinade.

Remove the tuna from the pan and return it to the shallow bowl with the soy, turmeric, and lime juice dressing. Spoon the dressing over the fish and add the shredded scallions, snow peas, and half the cilantro leaves.

Serve the tuna and shredded vegetables on individual plates or on a central platter for the table. Garnish with the remaining cilantro leaves.

The salmon here is poached in milk to make it even more silky and rich-tasting, while the cayenne pepper in the potatoes gives the fishcakes a bit of heat.

SALMON FISHCAKES
made with herb-crushed potatoes

SERVES 4 TO 6

- 10½ ounces salmon fillets
- 1½ cups milk
- 2 sprigs of fresh flat-leaf parsley, stems reserved
- 10 black peppercorns
- 2 bay leaves
- 1 pound potatoes, peeled and chopped into even-sized pieces
- 4 scallions, finely chopped
- Grated zest of 1 lemon
- Handful of arugula, coarsely chopped
- 2 sprigs of fresh dill
- Salt and freshly ground black pepper
- ¼ teaspoon cayenne pepper
- Olive oil, for frying
- Flour, for dusting

EDITOR'S WINE CHOICE
Dry, crisp rosé (see page 267)

Everyone loves fishcakes, and these are no exception. In this recipe the large, juicy flakes make a lovely contrast to potatoes that are crushed rather than mashed with chopped fresh herbs, arugula, and cayenne pepper—which give the fishcakes a little kick. They are simple to make and economical, too, as they can be made using leftover fish or potatoes. Serve with a little freshly made mayonnaise.

Preheat the oven to 350°F. Place the salmon fillets skin-side down in a roasting pan. Cover with milk, add the parsley stems, black peppercorns, and bay leaves, and cover tightly with tin foil. Poach in the oven for 20 minutes until cooked.

Bring the potatoes to a boil in a pot of salted water. When they are soft, drain and coarsely crush them. You are not making a smooth paste here; you want some texture.

When the potatoes are cool, add the scallions, lemon zest, and arugula. Chop the parsley leaves and the dill together. Add the chopped herbs to the potatoes with salt, pepper, and the cayenne pepper. Mix together, continuing to break up the potatoes without creating a smooth consistency.

When the salmon is cooked, remove from the milk and allow to drain. Flake the salmon and discard any bones or skin. Add the fish to the potato and herb mixture. When mixing together, keep the fish in as large pieces as possible.

Fry a little of the mixture to taste the fishcakes before you roll them all. Adjust the seasoning with salt and black pepper, if desired. Roll the remaining mixture into balls that fit into the palm of your hand or just smaller than a tennis ball. Lightly dust the balls with flour, pat, and then flatten into fishcakes. If the mixture is too wet, add a little extra flour to soak up some of the moisture and hold the fishcakes together.

continued on page 244

salmon fishcakes continued

Heat a pan over medium to high heat. Add a little olive oil and fry the fishcakes until golden brown, about 3 minutes. Using a spatula, gently turn the fishcakes over and brown on the other side. Make sure the oil is hot before you start to cook the fishcakes, and do not overload the pan, as it will cause the temperature in the pan to drop. Drain on paper towels and keep them warm in the oven while you cook the remaining fishcakes. Serve with Roast Garlic and Herb Mayonnaise.

ROAST GARLIC & HERB MAYONNAISE

This mayonnaise is quick and simple to make and is well worth the effort, providing a decadent finishing touch for the salmon fishcakes.

SERVES 6

3 garlic cloves, unpeeled
1 cup extra-virgin olive oil
2 egg yolks
1 teaspoon Dijon mustard
Pinch of salt
1 teaspoon red wine vinegar
Freshly ground black pepper
Juice of ½ lemon
Sprig of fresh flat-leaf parsley, chopped
Sprig of fresh dill, chopped

Place the garlic in a small pan with a little of the oil and cook over medium heat or in the oven at 350°F until golden brown and softened, about 8 to 9 minutes. Set aside to cool. Squeeze the garlic cloves from their skins and crush with the back of a knife. Place the garlic in a bowl and add the egg yolks, mustard, salt, and vinegar. Stir to combine using a wooden spoon.

Gradually pour in the rest of the oil, drip by drip, stirring all the time, to make a mayonnaise. Continue stirring until all the oil is used up and you have a thick emulsion. Add black pepper, the lemon juice, and the chopped herbs and stir to combine. Taste and adjust the seasoning if necessary.

BEST OF THE BEST EXCLUSIVE

Oily fish such as these fresh sardines are at their best served with a vibrant dressing like the one here, made with plenty of herbs, lemon and chiles.

GRILLED FRESH SARDINES

with oregano, garlic & chile

SERVES 4

- ¼ cup extra-virgin olive oil, plus more for brushing
- 2 garlic cloves, thinly sliced
- 2 teaspoons minced fresh red chile with seeds
- 1 teaspoon finely grated lemon zest
- 2 tablespoons fresh lemon juice
- 3 tablespoons finely chopped oregano

Kosher salt and freshly ground pepper

- ¾ teaspoon crushed red pepper
- 12 fresh sardines, cleaned

EDITOR'S WINE CHOICE
Lively, tart Sauvignon Blanc
(see page 266)

1. In a small saucepan, heat 1 tablespoon of the olive oil. Add the garlic and cook over moderately low heat until golden brown, about 3 minutes. Remove from the heat. With a slotted spoon, transfer the garlic to a paper-towel-lined plate. Add 2 tablespoons of olive oil to the saucepan and stir in the red chile, lemon zest, lemon juice and 1½ tablespoons of the oregano. Season the dressing with salt and pepper.

2. In a small bowl, combine the crushed red pepper with the remaining 1 tablespoon of olive oil and 1½ tablespoons of oregano. Season with salt and pepper. Rub the mixture inside each sardine.

3. Light a grill or preheat a grill pan. Brush the sardines with olive oil and season with salt and pepper. Grill over moderately high heat, turning once, until cooked through, about 3 minutes per side. Transfer the sardines to a platter and drizzle with the dressing. Garnish with the fried garlic slices and let stand for 10 minutes before serving.

BART VAN OLPHEN ONLINE

bartvanolphen.com

Bart van Olphen

@FishesMarket

IN THE GREEN KITCHEN

→ 24

Alice Waters

In her latest cookbook, Alice Waters, the godmother of farm-to-table eating, has a paradoxical goal: She wants you to forget recipes, not learn more of them. *In the Green Kitchen* aims to teach "techniques that free cooks from an overdependence on recipes and a fear of improvisation." Here, Waters explains the fundamentals, such as braising, and applies them to her own dishes as well as recipes from star chefs like Thomas Keller and Dan Barber. Waters's Shell Bean and Vegetable Soup comes with two adaptations (one for winter, one for summer), and her method of breading and pan-frying fish fillets could also work with chicken breasts. The book is an excellent resource for anyone who wants to learn how to improvise a dinner; after a few reads, Waters hopes, you'll be "comfortably and confidently without recipes, inspired by the ingredients you have." *Published by Clarkson Potter, $28*

Try experimenting with other herbs, like parsley or thyme, in the seasoning. To ensure tender meat, bring the pork to room temperature before roasting.

PORK RIB ROAST
with rosemary & sage

4 TO 6 SERVINGS

1 bone-in 4- or 5-rib pork loin
3 garlic cloves, peeled and chopped
Salt and fresh-ground black pepper
1 tablespoon chopped rosemary
1 tablespoon chopped sage leaves

EDITOR'S WINE CHOICE
Round, deep-flavored Syrah
(see page 269)

A bone-in pork rib roast has everything: lean and moist meat, a crusty fatty exterior, and rib bones. When you buy the roast, ask the butcher to remove the spinal chine bone and to separate the thin layer of meat on the ribs, stopping about an inch from the end of the bones. This allows you to season the interior of the meat next to the bones. Season the meat 1 or 2 days before cooking; it makes a big difference in the flavor of the roast.

Open the flap of meat next to the rib bones and rub the garlic onto the meat and bones down to the loin meat. Sprinkle liberally with salt, ground pepper, and half the rosemary and sage. Rub the seasonings into the meat. Reassemble the roast and use kitchen string to tie the meat and bones together. Season the outside of the roast, again liberally, with salt, pepper, and the remaining herbs, and rub into the meat. The chopped garlic goes on the inside of the roast; if rubbed onto the outside, it will burn in the oven. Wrap up the roast in the butcher paper, or lightly cover, and refrigerate.

Remove the roast from the refrigerator an hour or so before cooking to let it come to room temperature. Put it in a roasting pan, bone side down; the bones make a sort of natural roasting rack. Preheat the oven to 400°F. Cook the roast for 30 minutes or so, then turn it over in the roasting pan, bone side up, and cook for another 20 minutes. Turn the roast again, bone side down, and cook another 20 minutes or so, until the internal temperature registers 130°F. When the roast is done, let it rest for 15 to 20 minutes before carving.

Skim off some of the fat from the roasting pan, add some water or stock, and scrape up all the browned bits on the bottom of the pan. Pour the juices into a small saucepan and keep warm. When ready to serve, remove the strings from the roast, and cut the meat into thick chops with the bones, or cut the rack of rib bones away from the meat, and slice between the bones to separate them. Return them to the oven for a few minutes if you like them crustier. To the juices in the saucepan, add the juices released from the roast after resting and carving. Slice the meat and serve with the warm juices and the rib bones.

This recipe illustrates the guiding principle of Waters's cookbook. It's a blueprint for a soup that's adaptable to whatever beans and vegetables are in season.

SHELL BEAN & VEGETABLE SOUP

4 TO 6 SERVINGS

3 tablespoons olive oil
1 onion, peeled and diced
1 large carrot, peeled and diced
1 celery stalk, diced
2 garlic cloves, peeled and chopped
2 thyme sprigs
2 bay leaves
Salt
3 cups liquid (bean broth, water, or chicken stock, or any combination of the three)
2 small summer squash, diced
8 ounces green beans, trimmed and cut into 1-inch pieces
½ bunch chard leaves, coarsely chopped
3 cups cooked cannellini, cranberry, or other beans
1 large tomato, peeled, seeded, and chopped
Garlic croutons (optional)
Parmesan cheese

I make this soup year-round with fresh shell beans in the summer and fall, and with dried beans in the winter. The other vegetables in the soup vary with the season. It can be put together quickly if the beans are already cooked.

Heat the olive oil in a large heavy pot over medium heat and add the onion, carrot, and celery. Cook the vegetables gently for 5 to 10 minutes until soft and translucent. Add the garlic and herbs, season with salt, and cook another few minutes. Add the liquid and bring to a simmer. Add the squash, green beans, and chard (or other vegetables in season, such as leeks, fennel, winter squash, kale, cabbage, and potatoes). Simmer until the vegetables are tender, 10 to 15 minutes. Add the cooked shell beans and the tomato and cook for another 5 minutes. Taste and add salt and more liquid, if needed. Serve the soup with a drizzle of olive oil and, if you like, a plate of crusty garlic croutons to dip into the broth. Pass Parmesan at the table.

> **A CLASSIC MINESTRONE** includes pasta in the soup (add 1 to 2 cups cooked pasta, such as orzo or orecchiette, to the soup at the end) and is garnished at the table with a generous spoonful of pesto added to each bowl. The pesto gives a pungent garlicky kick to the soup, in which case you won't need the olive oil and cheese of the original recipe as a garnish.

> **FOR A WINTER VERSION OF THE SOUP,** substitute cubes of winter squash (butternut, Hubbard, pumpkin) for the summer squash and green beans, and use kale in place of the chard. Use canned or preserved tomatoes in place of the fresh tomatoes, or leave them out.

Pickled vegetables to eat with fried fish, page 252

Waters calls for clarified butter, which has a high smoke point, to pan-fry the fish. This allows the fillets to develop a crispy crust without burning.

FRIED FISH
with pickled vegetables

4 SERVINGS

- 4 fish fillets (sole, halibut, or other firm white-fleshed fish; about 5 ounces each)
- Salt and fresh-ground black pepper
- ½ cup all-purpose flour
- 1 egg
- 2 cups fresh breadcrumbs
- 6 tablespoons (¾ stick) unsalted clarified butter
- Pickled vegetables

EDITOR'S WINE CHOICE
Zesty, fresh Vinho Verde
(see page 264)

Tangy and crunchy fresh vegetable pickles are a perfect foil to fried fish. They cut the richness of the buttery breadcrumbs and make a beautiful and colorful plate. This method of breading and cooking the fish is also excellent for chicken breasts.

Season the fish fillets with salt and pepper. Put the following separately into 3 shallow bowls: the flour, the egg beaten with a tablespoon of water, and the breadcrumbs. One fillet at a time, dredge the fish in the flour and shake off the excess, dip in the beaten egg, and finally roll or pat in the breadcrumbs. Refrigerate the fillets for at least 30 minutes to dry the breadcrumb coating.

Heat a cast-iron skillet or other heavy pan over medium heat and add the butter. (To quickly clarify butter, melt it in a small saucepan and skim off the milk solids that float to the top; the milk solids will burn at frying temperatures.) When the butter is bubbling, add the fillets and cook until the bottoms are browned and crisp, 3 to 4 minutes. Turn and cook on the other side until nicely browned and crisp. Remove from the pan and drain briefly on a clean dish towel; serve with a variety of fresh pickles.

BEST OF THE BEST EXCLUSIVE

With just two ingredients—peaches and sweet sparkling Italian wine—this is practically a non-recipe. But the combination is wonderful and refreshing.

PEACHES IN MOSCATO D'ASTI

6 SERVINGS

6 peaches (about 3 pounds), peeled and sliced into wedges
One 375-ml bottle Moscato d'Asti

AUTHOR'S NOTE
If the peaches are hard to peel, dunk them briefly in boiling water, then quickly transfer to ice water to cool before peeling.

In a large, shallow dish, combine the peaches with the wine and toss to coat. Cover and refrigerate until well chilled, about 3 hours. Transfer the peaches and wine to a bowl and serve.

SERVE WITH Crisp butter cookies.

ALICE WATERS ONLINE

chezpanisse.com

 Alice Waters

 @AliceWaters

Cashew chicken, page 256

STIR-FRYING TO THE SKY'S EDGE

→ 25

Grace Young

To food writer Grace Young, stir-frying is more than just a cooking technique. As she says, "The stir-fry brings food to life." In her third cookbook, she adapts classic dishes, like Cashew Chicken and Barbecued Pork Lo Mein, for home cooks unfamiliar with traditional Chinese stir-frying techniques. For example, in her Hunan-style Cumin-Scented Beef with Vegetables, she takes strips of flank steak and blanches them in hot oil before stir-frying (a technique called *jau yau*, or "passing through oil") so the meat becomes remarkably tender. There are sidebars on the various types of stir-frying (dry, moist, clear, simple) and sections on how to choose, care for and use a wok, stock a stir-fry-ready pantry and select Chinese vegetables (or acceptable Western substitutions). All give the home cook the necessary tools to speak the "language of stir-frying." *Published by Simon & Schuster, $35*

Young adds plenty of vegetables and fresh ginger to this traditional Chinese dish, making it lighter and brighter than the saucy take-out staple.

CASHEW CHICKEN

SERVES 2 TO 3 AS A MAIN COURSE WITH RICE OR 4 AS PART OF A MULTICOURSE MEAL

- 1 pound skinless, boneless chicken thigh, cut into ½-inch cubes
- 1 tablespoon minced garlic
- 2 teaspoons soy sauce
- 1½ teaspoons cornstarch
- 1 teaspoon plus 2 tablespoons Shao Hsing rice wine or dry sherry
- ¾ teaspoon salt
- ⅛ teaspoon sugar
- ¼ cup chicken broth
- 2 tablespoons peanut or vegetable oil
- 2 tablespoons minced ginger
- ½ cup sugar snap peas, strings removed
- ½ cup thinly sliced carrots
- ½ cup thinly sliced celery
- ½ cup unsalted roasted cashews

EDITOR'S WINE CHOICE
Fresh, fruity rosé (see page 267)

In America, cashew chicken is one of the most beloved dishes served in Chinese restaurants. Sadly it is often "Westernized," with deep-fried pieces of chicken in a heavy gravy. A true Cantonese cashew chicken should be seasoned with ginger, stir-fried with fresh sugar snaps, carrots, and celery, all in a light sauce that barely clings to the chicken. Look for fresh cashews of the best quality. I often buy unroasted cashews and stir-fry them in a dry skillet or wok over medium heat a few minutes, shaking the pan frequently until they are just light golden. For a richer tasting sauce use dark soy sauce in place of regular soy sauce with the broth. The virtues of a "simple" stir-fry are demonstrated in this easy-to-make recipe.

1. In a medium bowl combine the chicken, garlic, 1 teaspoon of the soy sauce, 1 teaspoon of the cornstarch, 1 teaspoon of the rice wine, ½ teaspoon of the salt, and sugar. Stir to combine. In a small bowl combine the broth, the remaining 1 teaspoon soy sauce, 2 tablespoons rice wine, and ½ teaspoon cornstarch.

2. Heat a 14-inch flat-bottomed wok or 12-inch skillet over high heat until a bead of water vaporizes within 1 to 2 seconds of contact. Swirl in 1 tablespoon of the oil, add the ginger, then, using a metal spatula, stir-fry 10 seconds or until the ginger is fragrant. Push the ginger to the sides of the wok, carefully add the chicken, and spread it evenly in one layer in the wok. Cook undisturbed 1 minute, letting the chicken begin to sear. Stir-fry 1 minute, or until the chicken is lightly browned but not cooked through.

3. Swirl the remaining 1 tablespoon oil into the wok, add the sugar snaps, carrots, celery, and cashews, and sprinkle on the remaining ¼ teaspoon salt. Stir-fry 1 minute or until the sugar snaps are bright green. Restir the broth mixture, swirl it into the wok, and stir-fry 1 minute or until the chicken is just cooked through.

Cooking this stir-fry at home is perhaps the only way for most people to try a terrific Hunan dish rarely seen on Chinese restaurant menus.

VINEGAR-GLAZED CHICKEN

SERVES 2 AS A MAIN COURSE WITH RICE OR 4 AS PART OF A MULTICOURSE MEAL

- 1 pound boneless, skinless chicken thigh, cut into ¼-inch-thick bite-sized slices
- 4 teaspoons dark soy sauce
- 2 teaspoons soy sauce
- 2 teaspoons Shao Hsing rice wine or dry sherry
- 1 teaspoon sugar
- 1 teaspoon cornstarch
- ¼ teaspoon roasted and ground Sichuan peppercorns
- ½ teaspoon salt
- 2 teaspoons sesame oil
- 2 tablespoons peanut or vegetable oil
- 6 scallions, halved lengthwise and cut into 2-inch pieces
- 1 tablespoon minced ginger
- 1 tablespoon minced garlic
- ¼ teaspoon red pepper flakes
- 2 tablespoons Chinkiang or balsamic vinegar

EDITOR'S WINE CHOICE
Ripe, juicy Pinot Noir
(see page 269)

This is a typical Hunan family-style stir-fry. Traditionally the dish is made with dried red chiles, but this recipe has been simplified with the use of red pepper flakes. The Chinkiang vinegar has great depth of flavor and contributes to the sauce's mellow, rich taste; balsamic vinegar is an excellent substitute. If you are cooking in a new wok, after the stir-fry is finished transfer it immediately to a platter—acidic ingredients like vinegar will destroy a wok's new patina.

1. In a medium bowl combine the chicken, 2 teaspoons of the dark soy sauce, 1 teaspoon of the soy sauce, 1 teaspoon of the rice wine, sugar, cornstarch, ground Sichuan peppercorns, and salt. Stir to combine. In a small bowl combine the sesame oil and the remaining 2 teaspoons dark soy sauce, 1 teaspoon soy sauce, and 1 teaspoon rice wine.

2. Heat a 14-inch flat-bottomed wok or 12-inch skillet over high heat until a bead of water vaporizes within 1 to 2 seconds of contact. Swirl in the peanut oil, add the scallions, ginger, garlic, and red pepper flakes, then, using a metal spatula, stir-fry 10 seconds or until the aromatics are fragrant. Push the aromatics to the sides of the wok, carefully add the chicken, and spread it evenly in one layer in the wok. Cook undisturbed 1 minute, letting the chicken begin to sear. Then stir-fry 1 minute or until the chicken is lightly browned but not cooked through. Swirl the soy sauce mixture into the wok and stir-fry 1 minute, or until the chicken is well glazed with the soy sauce. Swirl in the vinegar and stir-fry 30 seconds or until the chicken is just cooked through.

Cucumbers, usually just a salad ingredient for Western cooks, are an integral part of this dish. Cooked crisp-tender, they take on the juice of the tender pork.

STIR-FRIED CUCUMBER & PORK
with golden garlic

SERVES 2 TO 3 AS A MAIN DISH WITH RICE OR 4 AS PART OF A MULTICOURSE MEAL

- ½ cup peanut or vegetable oil
- 3 tablespoons chopped garlic
- 12 ounces lean pork shoulder or butt, cut into ¼-inch-thick bite-sized slices
- 1½ teaspoons cornstarch
- 3 teaspoons soy sauce
- ¼ teaspoon sugar
- ¾ teaspoon salt
- 8 slices ginger, smashed
- 1 large English cucumber, ends trimmed, halved lengthwise, and cut on the diagonal into ¼-inch-thick slices (about 3 cups)

EDITOR'S WINE CHOICE
Full-bodied, minerally Riesling (see page 266)

Garlic mellowed by frying is the main seasoning here. To fry the garlic, you will need to tilt the saucepan or wok slightly while securely holding the handle in order to check the temperature of the oil on a deep-frying thermometer. Make sure the tip of the thermometer does not touch the pan. The oil used to cook the garlic is used again in the stir-fry to give additional flavor; normally I do not recommend reusing oil after deep-fat frying, but this oil is only heated to 280°F and is removed from the heat within 1 minute. The remaining cooled oil can be stored in a jar. If you use the wok to fry the garlic, it must be washed and dried before using it to stir-fry the pork.

1. In a 1-quart saucepan or a 14-inch flat-bottomed wok heat the oil over high heat until the oil registers 280°F on a deep-frying thermometer. Carefully add the garlic. Cook, stirring 30 seconds to 1 minute or until the garlic is light golden. Remove the saucepan from the heat. Remove the garlic with a metal skimmer and put on a plate lined with paper towels. Carefully remove the oil from the wok and reserve. Wash the wok and dry it thoroughly.

2. In a shallow bowl combine the pork, cornstarch, 1½ teaspoons of the soy sauce, sugar, and ¼ teaspoon of the salt. In a small bowl combine the remaining 1½ teaspoons soy sauce and 1 tablespoon cold water.

3. Heat a 14-inch flat-bottomed wok or 12-inch skillet over high heat until a bead of water vaporizes within 1 to 2 seconds of contact. Swirl in 2 tablespoons of the reserved garlic oil, add the ginger slices, then, using a metal spatula, stir-fry 30 seconds or until the ginger is fragrant. Push the ginger to the sides of the wok, carefully add the pork, and spread it evenly in one layer in the wok. Cook undisturbed 1 minute, letting the pork begin to sear. Then stir-fry 1 minute or until the pork is lightly browned but not cooked through. Add the cucumber and stir-fry 30 seconds or until well combined. Sprinkle on the remaining ½ teaspoon salt, swirl the reserved soy sauce mixture into the wok, and stir-fry 1 minute or until the pork is just cooked and the cucumber begins to wilt. Stir in the reserved garlic.

The jau yau *process (described below) is worth the extra step; it makes the lean slices of beef extra-tender. Cumin is typically associated with Indian food but is also very common in Hunan-style meat dishes like this.*

STIR-FRIED CUMIN-SCENTED BEEF
with vegetables

SERVES 2 TO 3 AS A MAIN DISH WITH RICE OR 4 AS PART OF A MULTICOURSE MEAL

- 12 ounces lean flank steak
- 1 tablespoon cornstarch
- 1 tablespoon soy sauce
- 2 teaspoons Shao Hsing rice wine or dry sherry
- 1 tablespoon plus 1½ cups peanut or vegetable oil
- 1 tablespoon minced garlic
- ½ teaspoon red pepper flakes
- 1 cup bite-sized cauliflower florets
- ½ cup thinly sliced carrots
- ½ cup grape or cherry tomatoes, halved
- ¾ teaspoon salt
- 1 teaspoon ground cumin
- ½ cup thinly sliced scallions

EDITOR'S WINE CHOICE
Rustic, peppery Malbec
(see page 268)

Here's a signature Hunan-style robust stir-fry of beef with cauliflower, carrots, and tomatoes, seasoned with cumin, garlic, and red pepper flakes. It is also an example of one of the more advanced stir-frying techniques. Chefs typically practice a technique called jau yau*, or "passing through oil," when bite-sized pieces of meat, poultry, fish, or shellfish are blanched in oil before stir-frying; this process ensures that the ingredients will be more succulent and flavorful. Unfortunately, most restaurants do this badly, which explains why many stir-fries are often sitting in a pool of oil when served. In this case, the beef is blanched in hot oil for 15 seconds and the result is meat that is exceedingly moist and tender. A note of caution: whenever working with hot oil, exercise extra care.*

This is a recipe where I prefer using a wok because it is so well suited for shallow-frying and stir-frying. I have tried shallow-frying in a high-sided 3-quart saucepan, but because of the larger surface area it requires about a cup more oil and the beef sticks to the bottom and sides of the pot. In contrast, the beef never sticks in a carbon-steel or cast-iron wok and the oil only enhances the wok's patina. Make sure the cauliflower florets are bite-sized so they cook in time. I halve or cut larger florets into quarters.

1. Cut the beef with the grain into 2-inch-wide strips. Cut each strip across the grain into ¼-inch-thick slices. In a medium bowl combine the beef, cornstarch, soy sauce, and rice wine. Stir to combine. Stir in 1 tablespoon of the oil.

2. Heat the remaining 1½ cups oil in a 14-inch flat-bottomed wok over high heat until the oil registers 280°F on a deep-frying thermometer. Carefully add the beef and spread it evenly in one layer in the wok. Cook 15 seconds or until the beef is opaque but is not cooked through. Turn off the heat. Remove the beef with a metal skimmer and put it on a plate lined with paper towels. Carefully remove the oil from the wok and reserve. Wash the wok and dry it thoroughly.

continued on page 262

Stir-fried beef continued

3. Heat the wok over high heat until a bead of water vaporizes within 1 to 2 seconds of contact. Swirl in 1 tablespoon of the reserved oil, add the garlic and red pepper flakes, then, using a metal spatula, stir-fry 20 seconds or until the aromatics are fragrant. Add the cauliflower, carrots, and tomatoes and sprinkle on ¼ teaspoon of the salt. Reduce the heat to medium and stir-fry 2 minutes or until the vegetables are crisp-tender. Add the cumin and stir-fry 5 seconds. Return the beef to the wok, add the scallions, and sprinkle on the remaining ½ teaspoon salt. Increase the heat to high and stir-fry 30 seconds to 1 minute or until the beef is just cooked through.

BEST OF THE BEST EXCLUSIVE

Cooking the rice in chicken stock is the key to the deep flavor in this dish. The other trick, says Young, is letting the rice cool fully (preferably overnight) before stir-frying it so the grains don't stick together.

GINGER FRIED RICE

with scallions, eggs & pine nuts

SERVES 4 TO 6 AS A SIDE DISH

- 1⅔ cups chicken stock or low-sodium broth
- 1⅓ cups long-grain white rice
- Salt
- ½ cup pine nuts
- 3 tablespoons vegetable oil
- 4 large eggs, beaten
- Freshly ground white pepper
- 2 tablespoons minced peeled fresh ginger
- 1 cup chopped scallions

EDITOR'S WINE CHOICE
Peppery, refreshing Grüner Veltliner (see page 265)

1. In a medium saucepan, combine the chicken stock, rice and a generous pinch of salt and bring to a boil. Cover and cook over low heat until the stock is absorbed, about 15 minutes. Remove from the heat and let stand, covered, for 10 minutes. Fluff the rice with a fork and transfer to a plate; let cool completely.

2. Meanwhile, in a small skillet, toast the pine nuts over moderate heat until lightly golden all over, about 4 minutes.

3. In a large nonstick skillet or wok, heat 1 tablespoon of the oil over moderately high heat. Season the eggs with salt and white pepper. Add the eggs to the skillet and tilt so they form a pancake. Cook until lightly browned on the bottom, about 1 minute. Using a spatula, flip the egg pancake and cook until just set on the second side, about 10 seconds. Transfer the egg to a cutting board and chop into ½-inch pieces.

4. In the same large skillet, heat the remaining 2 tablespoons of oil over moderately high heat. Add the ginger and cook until fragrant, about 15 seconds. Add the cooled rice, scallions and pine nuts and stir-fry until hot, about 4 minutes. Stir in the egg, season with salt and white pepper and serve.

MAKE AHEAD The cooked rice can be refrigerated for up to 3 days.

GRACE YOUNG ONLINE

graceyoung.com

@stirfrygrace

WINE GLOSSARY

F&W's executive wine editor, **RAY ISLE,** *has created the ultimate user-friendly guide to pairing wine and food. The glossary here—with descriptions of key wine varieties, pairing advice and recommendations for specific bottles to accompany the recipes—is both flexible and focused.*

CHAMPAGNE & SPARKLING WINES

Champagne, which is produced only in the Champagne region of France, is the greatest sparkling wine in the world—it's effervescent and lively, at the same time offering complexity and finesse. Champagnes are usually a blend of grapes, typically Pinot Noir and Chardonnay, often with a touch of Pinot Meunier. They range from dry (brut) to mildly sweet (demi-sec) to very sweet (doux). Different producers, or "houses," have different styles, too, ranging from light and delicate to rich and full-flavored. Many other countries also make sparkling wines. Those from North America tend to be more fruit-forward than most Champagnes. Cava, an inexpensive sparkler from Spain, often has an earthy character. Italy's Prosecco is also affordable, and popular for its engaging foaminess and hint of sweetness. Sparkling wines make great aperitifs, but they're also good throughout the meal, especially with shellfish and salty or spicy dishes.

DRY, LIGHT CHAMPAGNE

Pierre Peters Blanc de Blancs Brut (France)
Pommery Brut Royal (France)
Taittinger Brut La Française (France)

DRY, RICH CHAMPAGNE

Bollinger Brut Special Cuvée (France)
Henriot Brut Souverain (France)
Vilmart et Cie Grand Cellier (France)

DRY, FRUITY SPARKLING WINE

Domaine Chandon Blanc de Noirs (California)
Mionetto Prosecco Brut (Italy)
Roederer Estate Brut (California)

DRY, EARTHY SPARKLING WINE

Gramona Gran Cuvee (Spain)
Jaume Serra Cristalino Brut NV (Spain)
Segura Viudas Brut Reserva (Spain)

DRY, FRUITY SPARKLING ROSÉ

Lucien Albrecht Crémant d'Alsace Brut Rosé (France)
Llopart Brut Rosé Reserva Cava (Spain)
Riondo Pink Argento Raboso Prosecco (Italy)

DRY, RICH SPARKLING ROSÉ

Billecart-Salmon Brut Rosé Champagne (France)
Gruet Rosé Brut (New Mexico)
Jansz Premium Rosé (Australia)

WHITES

albariño & vinho verde

The Albariño grape produces Spain's best white wines, fresh, lively bottlings that pair especially well with seafood—no surprise, as Albariño is grown in Galicia, where the fishing industry drives the economy. Mostly made in stainless steel tanks without oak, Albariño has crisp flavors that suggest grapefruit and other citrus fruits, with a light mineral edge. Vinho Verde, or "green wine," from northern Portugal, often blends the Albariño grape (called Alvarinho there) with local varieties Loureiro and Trajadura. Bottled so young that it often has a lightly spritzy quality, Vinho Verde has a razor-sharp acidity and ocean freshness; it is an ideal match for raw shellfish.

ZESTY, FRESH ALBARIÑO/VINHO VERDE

Broadbent Vinho Verde (Portugal)
Pazo de Señoráns Albariño (Spain)
Salneval Albariño (Spain)

white burgundy & chardonnay

Chardonnay is grown in almost every wine-producing country in the world, and it's used to create wines in a wide range of styles. It is originally from France's Burgundy region, where the best white Burgundies are powerful and rich, with complex fruit flavors and notes of earth and minerals. More affordable Chardonnays from Burgundy—for instance, those simply labeled Bourgogne Blanc—are crisp and lively, with apple and lemon flavors. Chardonnays from America, Australia and Chile tend to be ripe and full-bodied, even buttery, with higher alcohol levels and vanilla notes from oak aging. Recently, however, more and more wine regions have been experimenting with fruity, fresh Chardonnays produced with very little or even no oak aging. Pair Chardonnays in the leaner Burgundian style with roasted chicken or seafood; the more voluptuous New World Chardonnays pair well with pasta dishes made with cream or cheese, with lobster or other rich seafood and with Asian dishes with coconut milk.

LIGHT, CRISP WHITE BURGUNDY

Christian Moreau Chablis (France)
Domaine Roulot Bourgogne Blanc (France)
Louis Latour Mâcon-Lugny (France)

RICH, COMPLEX WHITE BURGUNDY

Domaine Bouchard Père & Fils Beaune du Château Premier Cru (France)
Joseph Drouhin Beaune Clos des Mouches Blanc Premier Cru (France)

FRUITY, LOW-OAK CHARDONNAY

Babich Hawkes Bay Unoaked (New Zealand)
Chehalem INOX (Oregon)
Domaine Chandon Unoaked (California)

RIPE, LUXURIOUS CHARDONNAY

Beringer Napa Valley (California)
Landmark Overlook (California)
Rosemount Estate Show Reserve Hunter Valley (Australia)

chenin blanc

Chenin Blanc is the star of France's Loire region, where it's used for complex Vouvrays and Savennières. Chenin has also proved to be at home in parts of California (particularly the little-known Clarksburg region), in Washington State and in South Africa, which produces some of the best-value white wines around—tart, medium-bodied whites with flavors of apple and peach. The more affordable South African, Californian and Washington Chenin Blancs are good with light fish and simple poultry dishes.

FRUITY, SOFT CHENIN BLANC

Hogue (Washington State)
Indaba (South Africa)
Mulderbosch (South Africa)

COMPLEX, AROMATIC CHENIN BLANC

Champalou Vouvray (France)
Domaine des Baumard Clos du Papillon (France)
Pichot Domaine Le Peu de la Moriette (France)

gewürztraminer

One of the most easily identifiable grapes—the flamboyant aroma recalls roses, lychees and spices such as clove and allspice—Gewürztraminer reaches its peak in France's Alsace region, producing full-bodied wines ranging from dry to quite sweet, with flavors of apricot, apple and baking spices. These wines pair well with Alsatian cuisine—tarte flambée made with ham and Gruyère, for instance. Gewürztraminers from the United States tend to be less dense and unctuous, though they typically have a touch of sweetness and a delicate spiciness. Pair them with Asian food of all kinds.

RICH ALSACE GEWÜRZTRAMINER

Helfrich (France)
Josmeyer Les Folastries (France)
Trimbach (France)

SPICY AMERICAN GEWÜRZTRAMINER

Gundlach Bundschu (California)
Handley Cellars (California)
Navarro Vineyards (California)

grüner veltliner

Grüner Veltliner, from Austria, has become a darling of American sommeliers after decades of near obscurity in the United States. A refreshing, medium-bodied, peppery white wine with stone fruit flavors, it goes with everything from green salads to cold poached salmon to roasted chicken.

PEPPERY, REFRESHING GRÜNER VELTLINER

Berger (Austria)
Nikolaihof (Austria)
Sepp (Austria)

marsanne & roussanne

These two grapes, originally from France's Rhône Valley, have become popular with winemakers in California's Central Coast. The flavor of Marsanne typically suggests peaches and citrus fruits; Roussanne tends to be more subtle, with a mineral backbone. In the bottle, the grapes are often together as part of a blend—for instance, in white wines from the northern Rhône, or in many bottlings from the Santa Barbara area. Either separately or together, Marsanne and Roussanne are a great match for chicken dishes, particularly exotically spiced ones, as well as for fish in complex sauces.

MINERALLY MARSANNE OR ROUSSANNE

M. Chapoutier Crozes-Hermitage Les Meysonniers (France)
Qupé (California)
Tablas Creek Esprit de Beaucastel Blanc (California)

pinot bianco & pinot blanc

These are two names for the same grape; the first is Italian and the second French. The French versions of Pinot Blanc, from Alsace, tend to be rich, musky and creamy, while Pinot Biancos from Italy, mostly from northern regions, are known for zippier acidity, with pear or soft citrus flavors. American Pinot Blancs, from cooler regions in California as well as Oregon, are usually made in the French style. Pour Pinot Blancs with roasted chicken and creamy or cheese-based

WINE GLOSSARY

dishes; Pinot Biancos go nicely with lighter foods, such as green salads with citrusy dressings and flaky white fish.

ZIPPY, FRESH PINOT BIANCO

Abbazia di Novacella (Italy)
Alois Lageder (Italy)
Tramin (Italy)

CREAMY, SUPPLE PINOT BLANC

Domaine Albert Boxler (France)
Elk Cove Vineyards (Oregon)
Hugel & Fils (France)

pinot grigio & pinot gris

Pinot Grigio (from Italy) and Pinot Gris (from France's Alsace) are the same grape variety. Italian Pinots (and others modeled on them) tend to be light, simple wines with suggestions of peach and melon. These crisp, fresh whites are ideal as an aperitif or with light seafood or chicken breast dishes. Bottlings from Alsace are richer, with notes of almonds, spice and sometimes honey. American versions, mainly from Oregon, often tend more toward the Alsace style, and thus are mostly labeled Pinot Gris. They go well with creamy pastas and smoked foods.

LIGHT, FRESH PINOT GRIGIO

Palmina (California)
Terlan (Italy)
Tiefenbrunner (Italy)

FULL-BODIED, RICH PINOT GRIS

Domaines Schlumberger Les Princes Abbés (France)
Domaine Weinbach (France)
MacMurray Ranch (California)

riesling

Riesling is one of the great white grape varieties, and is grown the world over. The style of the wines it produces varies dramatically by region. German Rieslings balance impressive acidity with apple and citrus fruit flavors, and range from dry and refreshing to sweet and unctuous. Alsace and Austrian Rieslings are usually higher in alcohol, which makes them more full-bodied, but they are quite dry, full of mineral notes. Australia's Rieslings (the best are made in the Clare Valley) are zippy and full of lime and other citrus flavors. Those from Washington State tend to split the difference in style, offering juicy, appley fruit and lively acidity, with a hint of sweetness. Rieslings are extraordinarily versatile with food and are a favorite of sommeliers as a result. As a general rule, pair lighter, crisper Rieslings with delicate (or raw) fish; more substantial Rieslings are good with Asian food, chicken, and meaty fish like salmon and tuna.

TART, CITRUSY RIESLING

Fireblock Watervale (Australia)
Mt. Difficulty (New Zealand)
Penfolds Eden Valley Reserve (Australia)

VIVID, LIGHTLY SWEET RIESLING

Charles Smith Kung Fu Girl (Washington State)
Columbia Winery Cellarmaster's (Washington State)
Weingut Selbach-Oster Estate (Germany)

FULL-BODIED, MINERALLY RIESLING

Domaine Marc Kreydenweiss Andlau (France)
Dr. Konstantin Frank (New York State)
Hiedler Heiligenstein (Austria)

sauvignon blanc

Sauvignon's herbal scent and tart, citrus-driven flavors make it instantly identifiable in the glass. Sauvignon Blanc is found around the world, but the best regions for the grape are the Loire Valley in France, where it takes on a firm, minerally depth; New Zealand, where it recalls the tartness of gooseberries and, sometimes, an almost green, jalapeño or bell pepper note; California, where it pairs crisp grassiness and tropical or melon-like flavors; and South Africa, particularly the Stellenbosch region, where it combines the minerality of France with the rounder fruit of California. No matter where it's from, Sauvignon Blanc is a good match for light fish, shellfish, salads and green vegetables. It's a perfect aperitif, too.

LIVELY, TART SAUVIGNON BLANC

Geyser Peak Winery (California)
Honig (California)
Star Lane Vineyard (California)

MINERALLY, COMPLEX SAUVIGNON BLANC

Craggy Range Winery (New Zealand)
Domaine Vacheron Sancerre (France)
Santa Rita Floresta Leyda (Chile)

sémillon

Although Sémillon is best known for the incredible (and quite expensive) sweet wines it produces in Bordeaux's Sauternes region, the grape is used in dry wines, too.
On its own, Sémillon is fairly neutral, with a distinct waxy texture, so it's often blended with Sauvignon Blanc and Muscadelle to add weight and richness to the wine. Sémillon is widely planted in France but is also found in other countries, such as Australia and the United States. Minerally, dry bottlings often have a melon flavor and go well with rich seafood dishes, while the sweet styles are fantastic with cheese courses and fruit or custard-based desserts.

DRY, MINERALLY SÉMILLON

Buty Sémillon, Sauvignon & Muscadelle (Washington State)
Torbreck (Australia)
Vieux Château Lamothe Bordeaux Blanc (France)

SWEET, LUSCIOUS SÉMILLON

Château Coutet à Barsac (France)
Château Doisy Daëne Barsac (France)
Château Grillon Sauternes (France)

soave, verdicchio & gavi

These three light-bodied, usually inexpensive wines from Italy all match well with a wide range of foods. Soave, mostly made from the Garganega grape in the Veneto region, is a fruity white that often has a raw almond note. Verdicchio, from the Marche region, is made from the grape of the same name and has a lemony zestiness that makes it fantastic with seafood. And Gavi, a Piedmont wine made from a grape called Cortese, is typically tart, with an aroma that suggests fresh limes. All three wines pair well with herbal pasta sauces like pesto, with white fish and with fresh vegetable dishes.

FRESH, LIVELY SOAVE OR SIMILAR ITALIAN WHITE

Banfi Principessa Gavi (Italy)
Prà Soave Classico (Italy)
Sartarelli Verdicchio dei Castelli di Jesi (Italy)

vermentino

An up-and-coming white grape from the coastal regions of Italy, Vermentino marries vivacious acidity with stony minerality. The best Vermentinos come from very different parts of Italy—from Liguria in the north and from the island of Sardinia, off the central west coast. Drink Vermentino with simple green salads and seafood dishes of all kinds.

FRESH, MINERALLY VERMENTINO

Argiolas Costamolino (Italy)
Bisson (Italy)
Sella & Mosca La Cala (Italy)

viognier

Viognier produces seductive white wines, lush with peach and honeysuckle aromas, a round, mouth-filling texture and little acidity. The Condrieu region in France's Rhône Valley makes some of the the world's greatest Viogniers, and for this reason they are often quite expensive. California and occasionally Australia have also had success with this grape. Full-bodied Viognier pairs well with grilled seafood or chicken; it's also a good match for most herb-scented foods and those served with fruit salsas.

LUSH, FRAGRANT VIOGNIER

Cambria Tepusquet Vineyard (California)
Cave Yves Cuilleron Condrieu (France)
Clos LaChance Dry (California)

ROSÉS

Rosé—that is, dry rosé—may be the world's most underrated wine. Combining the light, lively freshness of white wines with the fruit and depth of reds, good rosés pair well with a remarkable range of foods, from delicate fish like sole to meats such as pork and veal. This balance of acidity and body also enables rosés to complement a range of ethnic cuisines, such as Chinese, Thai, Mexican and Greek. The best rosés, from Provence in southern France, are typically blends of Rhône grape varieties such as Syrah, Grenache, Cinsaut and Mourvèdre. Italy, Greece and Spain also produce terrific, refreshing rosés. American and Australian rosés, while still dry, tend to be fruitier and heavier, and can also be very good, especially with substantial grilled chicken or fish and with recipes that include fresh tomatoes.

DRY, CRISP ROSÉ

Commanderie de la Bargemone (France)
Domaine Houchart (France)
Tenuta delle Terre Nere (Italy)

FRESH, FRUITY ROSÉ

Edmunds St. John Bone-Jolly (California)
Muga (Spain)
Torre dei Beati (Italy)

REDS

barbera

Barbera, grown primarily in Italy's northwestern Piedmont region, mostly produces medium-bodied wines with firm acidity and flavors suggesting red cherries with a touch of spice. (Barrel-aged versions tend to be more full-bodied, and more expensive.) A great wine for pastas with meat- or tomato-based sauces, Barbera is also good with game and hard cheeses.

BRIGHT, TART BARBERA

Brandini Barbera d'Alba (Italy)
La Spinetta Cà di Pian Barbera d'Asti (Italy)
Michele Chiarlo Barbera d'Asti (Italy)

beaujolais & gamay

Gamay, the grape of France's Beaujolais region, makes wines that embody everything that region is known for: light, fruity, easy-to-drink reds, ideal for a party or a picnic. Typically they are not aged in oak barrels and are released early (Beaujolais Nouveau, which appears on shelves little more than a month after the grapes are harvested, is the extreme example). A small amount of Gamay is grown outside of Beaujolais, but what has been planted pairs well with the same foods as Beaujolais: light chicken dishes, salads, cheeses and charcuterie.

FRUITY, LIGHT-BODIED BEAUJOLAIS/GAMAY

Château Thivin Côte de Brouilly (France)
Georges Duboeuf Beaujolais-Villages (France)
Marcel Lapierre Morgon (France)

cabernet sauvignon

Arguably the most significant red wine grape, Cabernet Sauvignon has traveled far beyond its origins in France's Bordeaux—it's now

WINE GLOSSARY

widely planted in almost every wine-producing country. Depending on climate, Cabernet can make either firm, tannic wines that recall red currants with a touch of tobacco or green bell pepper (colder climates) or softer wines that recall ripe black currants or black cherries (warmer climates). It almost always has substantial tannins, which help great Cabernets age for many years. The classic pairing with Cabernet is lamb, but it goes well with almost any meat—beef, pork, venison, even rabbit.

FIRM, COMPLEX CABERNET SAUVIGNON

Château de Pez (France)
Ladera Howell Mountain (California)
Wynns Coonawarra (Australia)

RICH, RIPE CABERNET SAUVIGNON

Penley Estate Reserve (Australia)
Trinchero Chicken Ranch Vineyard (California)
Twenty Bench (California)

carmenère

Carmenère has emerged as a star grape in Chile, now that its old vines are no longer mistaken for Merlot. Carmenère's origins are the same as Merlot's—France's Bordeaux region—which may account for the confusion. Carmenère tends to have more savory flavors than Merlot, though—ripe plums and berries with notes of coffee and dark spice. This deep, dense wine is terrific with grilled meats, spicy stews and hard cheeses.

SAVORY, SPICY CARMENÈRE

Concha y Toro Casillero del Diablo (Chile)
Santa Rita 120 (Chile)
Apaltagua (Chile)

dolcetto

Though Dolcetto means "little sweet one," wines from this Italian grape are dry, grapey, tart, simple reds distinguished by their vibrant purple color and ebullient berry juiciness. Dolcettos are light-bodied and should be drunk young, with antipasti, pastas with meat sauces or roasted poultry of any kind.

JUICY, FRESH DOLCETTO

Renato Ratti Colombè Dolcetto d'Alba (Italy)
Roagna (Italy)
Vietti Tre Vigne Dolcetto d'Alba (Italy)

grenache

When made well, Grenache produces full-bodied, high-alcohol red wines that tend to be low in acidity and full of black cherry and raspberry flavors. Grenache is often blended with other grapes to make dark, powerful reds in regions such as France's Châteauneuf-du-Pape or Spain's Rioja and Priorato. On its own in Australia and the United States, it can produce deeply fruity, juicy wines that go perfectly with cheeseburgers, grilled meats, sausages and highly spiced dishes.

JUICY, SPICY GRENACHE

Beckmen Vineyards Estate (California)
Borsao Tres Picos (Spain)
Yalumba Bush Vine (Australia)

malbec

Originally used as a blending grape in the Bordeaux region of France (it still is, though minimally), Malbec has found its true home in the Mendoza region of Argentina. There, this imported grape produces darkly fruity wines with hints of black pepper and leather—like a traditional rustic country red, but with riper, fuller fruit. Malbecs are often very affordable, too, and go wonderfully with substantial cuts of meat typical of Argentina, such as grilled steaks and slow-roasted meats, hearty stews and spicy sausages.

RUSTIC, PEPPERY MALBEC

Catena Zapata (Argentina)
Trapiche Oak Cask (Argentina)
Yellow + Blue (Argentina)

merlot

The most widely planted grape in France's Bordeaux region isn't Cabernet Sauvignon; it's Merlot. That's because Merlot blends so well with other grapes, and also because Merlot's gentle succulence and plummy flavors have gained favor as worldwide tastes have shifted toward fruitier, easier-drinking wines. Good Merlots are made in France, Italy, Chile, the U.S. and Australia, and all of them tend to share supple, velvety tannins and round black cherry or plum flavors. The smoothness of Merlot helps it pair beautifully with many foods—try it with pâtés or other charcuterie, pork or veal roasts, rich, cheesy gratins and even hamburgers.

LIVELY, FRUITY MERLOT

Columbia Crest H3 (Washington State)
Estancia Central Coast (California)
Hardys Stamp of Australia (Australia)

DEEP, VELVETY MERLOT

Marco Felluga Varneri (Italy)
Pepper Bridge (Washington State)
Shafer Napa Valley (California)

nebbiolo, barolo & barbaresco

Nebbiolo is the greatest grape of Italy's Piedmont region. And if you ask a farmer, it is unquestionably one of the most difficult to grow. Certainly it is formidable, with fierce tannins and acidity, but it is also gloriously scented—"tar and roses" is the classic description—and has a supple, evocative flavor that lingers on the tongue. Those flavors are more substantial and emphatic in Barolos and more delicate and filigreed in Barbarescos, the two primary wines made from Nebbiolo. Pour good Nebbiolo with foods such as braised short ribs, beef roasts, bollito misto and anything that involves truffles—a classic Piedmont pairing.

COMPLEX, AROMATIC NEBBIOLO
Borgogno Barolo (Italy)
Pio Cesare Barolo (Italy)
Produttori del Barbaresco Barbaresco (Italy)

pinot noir & red burgundy

Pinot Noir probably inspires more rhapsodies—and disappointments—among wine lovers than any other grape. When it's good, it's ethereally aromatic, with flavors ranging from ripe red berries to sweet black cherries, and tannins that are firm but never obtrusive. (When bad, unfortunately, the wine is acidic, raspy and bland.) The greatest Pinot Noirs come from France's Burgundy region, age-worthy wines that are usually quite expensive. More affordable and typically more fruit-forward Pinots can be found from California and Oregon as well as New Zealand, Chile and Australia. Pinot Noir pairs well with a wide range of foods—fruitier versions make a great match with salmon or other fatty fish, roasted chicken or pasta dishes; bigger, more tannic Pinot Noirs are ideal with duck and other game birds, casseroles and stews such as beef bourguignon.

RIPE, JUICY PINOT NOIR
A to Z (Oregon)
Etude Estate (California)
Stoller Estate JV (Oregon)

COMPLEX, ELEGANT PINOT NOIR
Faiveley Nuits-St-Georges (France)
Peregrine (New Zealand)
Scherrer (California)

rioja & tempranillo

Tempranillo, the most widely grown red grape of Spain, is best known as the main component in red Rioja, where it contributes earthy cherry flavors and firm structure. It is also used in wines from almost every other region of Spain and generally produces medium-bodied, firm reds suitable for substantial vegetarian dishes, especially those that include eggplant, and meat dishes of all kinds, particularly lamb.

EARTHY, MEDIUM-BODIED TEMPRANILLO
Bodegas Montecillo Reserva (Spain)
Finca Allende (Spain)
Marqués de Cáceres Crianza (Spain)

sangiovese

Sangiovese is primarily known for the principal role it plays in wines from Tuscany, such as Chianti, Brunello and Carmignano, though these days it is also being grown in the United States and Australia. Italian Sangioveses have vibrant acidity and substantial tannins, along with fresh cherry fruit and herbal scents. New World versions tend toward softer acidity and fleshier fruit. Sangioveses are quite versatile and pair well with rare steaks, game birds (or wild boar), hearty chicken or mushroom dishes and anything with tomato sauce.

CHERRY-INFLECTED, EARTHY SANGIOVESE
Altesino Rosso di Altesino (Italy)
Di Majo Norante (Italy)
Le Macchiole Bolgheri Rosso (Italy)

syrah & shiraz

Probably no other grape scores higher on the intensity meter than Syrah, and it can have very different flavors from one region to the next. It's the marquee grape of France's Rhône Valley, where it makes full-bodied, smoky, powerful reds with hints of black pepper. It has also become the signature grape of Australia, where it's known as Shiraz, and typically produces fruitier, less tannic wines marked by sweet blackberry flavors and occasionally fresh espresso notes. American Syrahs lean more toward the fruitier Australian version, thanks to California's similarly moderate weather; there are a few very good, earthy Syrahs coming from South Africa, too, particularly from the Stellenbosch subregion. Barbecued foods with a smoky char pair nicely with Syrah, as do lamb, venison and game birds.

INTENSE, SPICY SYRAH OR SHIRAZ
Dunham Cellars (Washington State)
Jean-Luc Colombo La Violette (France)
M. Chapoutier La Sizeranne Hermitage (France)

ROUND, DEEP-FLAVORED SYRAH OR SHIRAZ
d'Arenberg The Footbolt (Australia)
Qupé Central Coast (California)
Torbreck Woodcutters (Australia)

FRUITY, LUSCIOUS SYRAH OR SHIRAZ
Rustenberg Brampton (South Africa)
Spring Seed Wine Co. Scarlet Runner (Australia)
Wishing Tree (Australia)

zinfandel

Though Zinfandel is descended from the Croatian grape Crljenak, the wine it produces is entirely Californian in character. The California wine country's easygoing, warm weather gives Zinfandel a jammy, juicy fruitiness (except when it's made into dull, lightly sweet white Zinfandel). Typically high in both alcohol (sometimes too much so) and flavor—boysenberries with a touch of brambly spiciness—Zinfandel is the perfect summer cookout wine, great with grilled burgers, sausages and chicken, pulled pork and even chips and dip.

INTENSE, FRUITY ZINFANDEL
Bogle Vineyards Old Vine (California)
Outpost Howell Mountain (California)
Seghesio Family Vineyards Sonoma (California)

INDEX

Page numbers in **bold** indicate photographs.

INDEX

INDEX

INDEX

CREDITS

FIESTA AT RICK'S
Fabulous Food for Great Times with Friends

Photographs by Paul Elledge. Copyright © 2010 by Paul Elledge. "Roasted Vegetable Enchiladas with Creamy Tomatillo Sauce & Melted Cheese," "Tuna in Jalapeño Escabeche," "Wild Mushroom Queso Fundido," "Chipotle-Glazed Baby Back Ribs" from *Fiesta at Rick's: Fabulous Food for Great Times with Friends* by Rick Bayless with Deann Groen Bayless. Copyright © 2010 by Rick Bayless and Deann Groen Bayless. Used by permission of W. W. Norton & Company, Inc.

GOOD TO THE GRAIN
Baking with Whole-Grain Flours

Recipes reproduced from *Good to the Grain* by Kim Boyce with Amy Scattergood; published with permission by Stewart, Tabori & Chang; copyright © 2010. Photographs by Quentin Bacon.

BROMBERG BROS. BLUE RIBBON COOKBOOK
Better Home Cooking

From *Bromberg Bros. Blue Ribbon Cookbook: Better Home Cooking* by Bruce Bromberg and Eric Bromberg and Melissa Clark, copyright © 2010 by Eric Bromberg and Bruce Bromberg. Photographs copyright © 2010 by Quentin Bacon. Used by permission of Clarkson Potter/Publishers, an imprint of the Crown Publishing Group, a division of Random House, Inc.

COOK ITALY

Excerpted from *Cook Italy* by Katie Caldesi. Published in 2010 by Kyle Books. Text © 2009 by Katie Caldesi. Photography © 2009 by Lisa Linder. Map of Italy on page 44 copyright © 2009 by Marian Hill.

FLOUR
Spectacular Recipes from Boston's Flour Bakery + Cafe

From *Flour* by Joanne Chang with Christie Matheson. Text copyright © 2010 by Joanne Chang; images by Keller + Keller. Used with permission of Chronicle Books LLC, San Francisco. Visit ChronicleBooks.com.

GIADA AT HOME
Family Recipes from Italy and California

From *Giada at Home: Family Recipes from Italy and California* by Giada De Laurentiis. Photographs by Jonelle Weaver, copyright © 2010 by Giada De Laurentiis. Used by permission of Clarkson Potter/Publishers, an imprint of the Crown Publishing Group, a division of Random House, Inc.

THE FRANKIES SPUNTINO KITCHEN COMPANION & COOKING MANUAL

Excerpted from *The Frankies Spuntino: Kitchen Companion & Cooking Manual*. Copyright © 2010 by Frank Falcinelli, Frank Castronovo & Peter Meehan. Photograph on page 84 by Travis Lee Kauffman. Used by permission of Artisan, a division of Workman Publishing Co., Inc., New York. All rights reserved.

A BIRD IN THE OVEN & THEN SOME

Excerpted from *A Bird in the Oven and Then Some* by Mindy Fox. Published in 2010 by Kyle Books. Text © 2010 Mindy Fox. Photography © 2010 Ellen Silverman.

AROUND MY FRENCH TABLE
More Than 300 Recipes from My Home to Yours

Recipes from *Around My French Table: More than 300 Recipes from My Home to Yours* by Dorie Greenspan. Copyright © 2010 by Dorie Greenspan. Reprinted by permission of Houghton Mifflin Harcourt Publishing Company. All rights reserved. Photographs by Alan Richardson.

PLENTY
Good Uncomplicated Food for the Sustainable Kitchen

Reprinted with permission from *Plenty* by Diana Henry, Mitchell Beazley 2010, photographs by Jonathan Lovekin.

THE ESSENTIAL NEW YORK TIMES COOKBOOK
Classic Recipes for a New Century

"Brisket in Sweet-and-Sour Sauce," "Chocolate Dump-It Cake," "Shrimp in Green Sauce," "Spicy, Lemony Clams with Pasta" from *The Essential New York Times Cookbook: Classic Recipes for a New Century* by Amanda Hesser. Copyright © 2010 by The New York Times Company. Copyright © 2010 by Amanda Hesser. Used by permission of W. W. Norton & Company, Inc.

FARM TO FORK
Cooking Local, Cooking Fresh

Four recipes, three interior photos, book cover from *Farm to Fork: Cooking Local, Cooking Fresh* by Emeril Lagasse. Copyright © 2010 by Emeril/MSLO Acquisition Sub, LLC. Reprinted by permission of HarperCollins Publishers. Photography by Steven Freeman.

BAKED EXPLORATIONS

Classic American Desserts Reinvented

Recipes reproduced from *Baked Explorations* by Matt Lewis and Renato Poliafito; published with permission by Stewart, Tabori & Chang; copyright © 2010. Photographs by Tina Rupp.

CHEWY GOOEY CRISPY CRUNCHY MELT-IN-YOUR-MOUTH COOKIES

Excerpted from *Chewy Gooey Crispy Crunchy Melt-in-Your-Mouth Cookies*. Copyright © 2010 by Alice Medrich. Used by permission of Artisan, a division of Workman Publishing Co., Inc., New York. All rights reserved. Photographs copyright © 2010 by Deborah Jones.

SUSTAINABLY DELICIOUS

Making the World a Better Place, One Recipe at a Time

Reprinted from *Sustainably Delicious* by Michel Nischan with Mary Goodbody. Copyright © 2010 Michel Nischan. Photographs © 2010 by Andre Baranowski. Permission granted by Rodale, Inc., Emmaus, PA 18098. Available wherever books are sold.

JAMIE'S AMERICA

From the book *Jamie's America* by Jamie Oliver. Photographs by David Loftus. Copyright © Jamie Oliver, 2009, 2010. Photographs copyright © David Loftus, 2009, 2010. Published by Hyperion. Available wherever books are sold. All rights reserved.

MEAT

A Kitchen Education

From *Meat: A Kitchen Education* by James Peterson, copyright © 2010 by James Peterson. Used by permission of Ten Speed Press, an imprint of the Crown Publishing Group, a division of Random House, Inc. Illustrations by Alex Kaluzshner.

AVEC ERIC

A Culinary Journey with Eric Ripert

From *Avec Eric: A Culinary Journey with Eric Ripert* by Eric Ripert with Angie Mosier and Soa Davies; Wiley 2010; reprinted with permission from the publisher. Photography by Angie Mosier.

ETHAN STOWELL'S NEW ITALIAN KITCHEN

From *Ethan Stowell's New Italian Kitchen* by Ethan Stowell and Leslie Miller, copyright © 2010 by Ethan Stowell and Leslie Miller. Photographs by Geoffrey Smith, copyright © 2010 by Geoffrey Smith. Used by permission of Ten Speed Press, an imprint of the Crown Publishing Group, a division of Random House, Inc.

EATING LOCAL

The Cookbook Inspired by America's Farmers

From *Eating Local: The Cookbook Inspired by America's Farmers* by Sur La Table with Janet Fletcher. Text © 2010 Sur La Table, Inc; photography © 2010 Sara Remington. Published by Andrews McMeel Publishing.

HEART OF THE ARTICHOKE & OTHER KITCHEN JOURNEYS

Excerpted from *Heart of the Artichoke and Other Kitchen Journeys*. Copyright © 2010 by David Tanis. Used by permission of Artisan, a division of Workman Publishing Co., Inc., New York. All rights reserved. Photographs copyright © 2010 by Christopher Hirsheimer.

SIMPLY MING ONE-POT MEALS

Excerpted from *Simply Ming One-Pot Meals* by Ming Tsai and Arthur Boehm. Published in 2010 by Kyle Books. Text © 2010 Ming Tsai. Photography © 2010 Antonis Achilleos.

FISH TALES

Stories & Recipes from Sustainable Fisheries Around the World

Excerpted from *Fish Tales* by Bart van Olphen and Tom Kime. Published in 2010 by Kyle Books. Text copyright © 2009 by Bart van Olphen and Tom Kime. Food photographs © 2009 by Simon Wheeler (except where noted in book's photography credits). Photograph of mussels on page 237 © 2009 by Leonard Fäustle.

IN THE GREEN KITCHEN

Techniques to Learn by Heart

From *In the Green Kitchen: Techniques to Learn by Heart* by Alice Waters, copyright © 2010 by Alice Waters. Photographs by Hirsheimer and Hamilton, copyright © 2010 by Christopher Hirsheimer. Used by permission of Clarkson Potter/Publishers, an imprint of the Crown Publishing Group, a division of Random House, Inc.

STIR-FRYING TO THE SKY'S EDGE

The Ultimate Guide to Mastery, with Authentic Recipes & Stories

Reprinted with the permission of Simon & Schuster, Inc., from *Stir-Frying to the Sky's Edge* by Grace Young. Food photographs by Steven Mark Needham. Copyright © 2010 Grace Young. Food photography copyright © 2010 Steven Mark Needham. Jacket photograph copyright © Steven Mark Needham.